Bi
in N

Bird Finding
in
New England

RICHARD K. WALTON

David R. Godine, Publisher, Inc.

BOSTON

First published in 1988 by
David R. Godine, Publisher, Inc.
Horticultural Hall
300 Massachusetts Avenue
Boston, Massachusetts 02115

LIBRARY OF CONGRESS CATALOGING-IN-PUBLICATION DATA
Walton, Richard K.
  Bird finding in New England.
  Bibliography: p.
  1. Bird watching—New England—Guide-books.
I. Title.
QL683.N67W35 1988   598'.07'23474   87-46283
ISBN 0-87923-726-0

First edition
PRINTED IN THE UNITED STATES OF AMERICA

For Kendall and Charlie

CONTENTS

LIST OF MAPS

KEY
TO MAP SYMBOLS

 lighthouse

– – – – unpaved road

 trail / path

 water

 route numbers

 continuing roads

 boat launch

 observation tower

 marsh

 railroad tracks

 bridge

 parking

 breakwater

 dam

 hill

 mt. summit

—.—. boundary

campground

FOREWORD

STANDING NEAR THE OLD PLUM ISLAND COAST
Guard Station and looking south, one sees the long
beach stretching off through a haze of surf toward the
low promontory of Cape Ann. Inland across the Merrimac River estuary stand the distant white spires and
red brick waterfront of Newburyport. To the north the
shorelines of Massachusetts, New Hampshire, and Maine
fuse imperceptibly and bend seaward again to vanish
under the distinctive silhouette of Mount Agamenticus.
In the ocean to the east, or seemingly suspended over
it, are the Isles of Shoals. New England is on a scale of
its own: all six states would fit within the boundaries
of several larger ones. By North American standards
New England is also impressive for the antiquity of its
settlement; Newbury, from which Newburyport was
formed, was incorporated over 350 years ago. New England's cultural heritage is rich: from Plum Island are
visible localities familiar to Hawthorne, Whittier, and
Longfellow. Not surprisingly its ornithology as well is
a record going back many years: from Plum Island one
can all but see the type locality of "Ipswich" Sparrow,

the site of the first Common Black-headed Gull known for North America, and the island where Great Black-backed Gulls were first found nesting in the United States.

If I speak of Newburyport it's because it's very close to home for me and can serve as an example of the richness awaiting the traveler in New England. High Street is a magnificent architectural expression of the prosperous days of whaling and the West Indian trade, while the meticulously restored downtown area reflects that modern source of prosperity, tourism. The town is worth a visit for many reasons, and so too are the towns upriver, each of them having its own charm and character, its own old mills and boathouses, church-yards and Revolutionary or Civil War monuments, its own back roads with their often imponderable branch-ings and meanderings and stone walls leading off through the woods. All of New England might be described in about these terms.

For those lucky enough to be interested in birds, Richard Walton's book provides precise directions and a clear idea of what species to look for at nearly forty of New England's best known bird watching localities. For anyone, bird watcher or not, it leads to very beau-tiful places. These, like Newburyport, can be the focal point of wider exploration along other lines. They can be visited at any time of the year, too: New England's seasons are so different as to impose, each of them, a certain frame of mind, and their succession is forever revealing a new way of viewing the same thing. It has been a pleasure to revisit some of my favorite places in these pages and I am sure that other readers will find the same delight as I in knowing them.

DAVIS W. FINCH
East Kingston, New Hampshire

INTRODUCTION

MOST BIRD WATCHERS HAVE ONE OR TWO FA-vored places, often close to home, which annually provide hours of enjoyment. In some ways, these backyards, neighborhood parks, and local weedfields are unexcelled. The delight of seeing a new bird on such familiar ground, or simply sighting an old acquaintance, is a continuing source of amusement. On our home grounds we are seldom disappointed; expectation and reality reflect each other.

When we travel farther afield anticipation builds. We expect to be rewarded for our efforts, in new vistas, new memories, even new birds for our life lists. New England's varied topography, changing seasons, and diverse bird populations offer some exciting possibilities. Whether you are a native New Englander or a visitor, there are always new grounds to explore.

Included in the present volume are sites which are representative of New England habitats and accessible to the general public. For each state, the major site descriptions are followed by a supplemental list, suggesting additional birding locales. Because most of the sites are more productive at some seasons than at others, best times of year have been indicated at the beginning of each description and should be taken into consideration when planning your trips. Birders who have to make choices about areas to visit first should go to those indicated by **boldface** type; these indicate the more productive stops on each itinerary.

While the magic of birding often involves highly personal discovery, intimate and unplanned moments in some unexpected place, or the chemistry of friendship and the sharing of a bird, I hope this guide will lead you to areas where the circumstances of time and place will combine to provide a few such special experiences.

RICHARD K. WALTON
Concord, Massachusetts

New England's Landscape

ONE WAY TO DEFINE THE NATURAL FEATURES of New England is by looking at the region's bird life. The settings brought to mind by such species as Greater Shearwater, Piping Plover, Scarlet Tanager, Upland Sandpiper, and Gray-cheeked Thrush reflect a variety of seascapes and landscapes. While one popular image of birds includes the notion that these winged creatures are free to roam the skies at will, setting down whenever and wherever they wish, in reality the success of each species is determined by its ability to fulfill fairly strict habitat requirements. That New England can boast a relatively great diversity of bird species reflects, in the main, the presence of differing habitats capable of supporting various migrant and resident bird populations. An understanding of the landforms and plant communities that underlie these habitats should increase the bird watcher's success while developing at the same time a greater appreciation of the New England region.

Lying along New England's western border in Vermont, western Massachusetts, and the northwest corner of Connecticut are the oldest of the New England mountains. The Green Mountains, the Berkshire Hills, and the Taconic Mountains are all part of the Appalachian chain and share its ancient lineage. In the northern section of the Green Mountains several peaks, including Mt. Killington and Mt. Mansfield, reach above 4,000 feet. In contrast to these peaks, the southern Green Mountains and the Berkshire Hills are characterized by a high plateau. West of the plateau, on the New York–New England border, are the rugged Taconic Mountains. Mt. Riga in Connecticut, Mt. Greylock in Massachusetts, and Mt. Equinox in Vermont are part of this range.

The other great mountains of New England are the White Mountains. Largely granitic formations, these mountains comprise a scattered range from northern New Hampshire to central Maine. The dominant peaks of the White Mountains include Mt. Washington (6,288 feet) in New Hampshire's Presidential Range and Mt. Katahdin (5,267 feet) in Maine.

Between the mountains and south to the coastal lowlands of New England lies a gently rolling landscape punctuated by hills and valleys. Occasionally, a larger hilltop, even a small mountain, rises above the surrounding uplands. The archetype for this landform is Mt. Monadnock in southern New Hampshire.

Another significant feature of New England is the Connecticut River Valley. The Connecticut River travels some 400 miles from the Connecticut Lakes in northern New Hampshire to Old Lyme and Old Saybrook on the Connecticut coast. A relatively fast moving, narrow stream in its upper reaches, the river widens in parts of Massachusetts and Connecticut to form the Connecticut Valley Lowland. Closely associated with these lowlands are a series of basalt (hardened lava) ridges. Mt. Tom in western Massachusetts and West Rock in New Haven, Connecticut, are classic examples of such ridges.

The peaks of the Green and the White mountains, the rolling upland with its scattered monadnocks, the Connecticut Valley Lowlands, and the basalt ridges were all created millions of years before the glaciers. Yet it is often the relatively recent era of glaciation that is credited with creating the New England landscape. Certainly the great ice sheets had significant effects on the region, but the basic framework had existed for eons.

During the glacial era a series of ice sheets spread out over large sections of North America, including all of present-day New England. A major effect of the glacial movement was the layer of till (unsorted rocks, clays, and sands) which the ice sheet dragged along and deposited over much of the region. In addition to leaving behind their legacy of poor, rocky soils, the glaciers removed an estimated 10 to 15 feet of bedrock in many areas.

At the same time the glacier was carving out valleys and headwalls in one place, it was redepositing materials in another. Glacial erratics, bedrock boulders of various sizes, are scattered throughout New England. In southeastern New England the glacier created numerous drumlins, gently rounded hills composed mainly of clay. As the last glacier was halted by a warming climate, the ice sheet left other reminders of its presence. At the southern limit of the glacier's range, the ice front disgorged massive amounts of till creating sizable ridges known as terminal moraines. At these same junctures, as well as at innumerable other locales where the ice front paused, the rushing meltwater sorted gravel and sand across extensive outwash plains. Block Island, Martha's Vineyard, Nantucket, and Cape Cod are the products of this era.

During its final stages the glacier abandoned large blocks of ice in numerous spots. These slow-melting chunks gave rise to the many kettle holes and ponds so characteristic of the region today. The final remains of the ice itself formed vast lakes of meltwater throughout New England. Glacial Lake Vermont, Lake Hitchcock, Lake Merrimack, and others eventually drained, leaving broad lowlands and river valleys. By the end of the glacial era, the immense quantities of water that for millennia had formed the ice sheets were released. The resulting rise in the sea level pushed the coastline inland as it reflooded areas of the continental shelf which had long been exposed.

Together with a range of climates, these various New England landforms establish conditions for several different biomes, or life zones. While it is possible to give generalized descriptions of New England's typical biomes, the realities of transitional zones, areas of overlap, and diversity of habitat within each zone create a complex rather than a simple map.

The Atlantic Ocean forms New England's southern and eastern perimeter. Offshore, a series of banks, from Cox's Ledge off Rhode Island to Brown's Bank in the Gulf of Maine, create an important pelagic zone. The relatively shallow, nutrient-rich waters flowing across these banks attract numerous marine organisms including concentrations of seabirds. Along the Atlantic shore and Long Island Sound, a coastal zone consisting of a series of islands, bays, inlets, sand beaches, marshes, and tidal flats form an ever-changing front between the land and the sea. As one moves east along Maine's shoreline, coastal marshes are gradually replaced by rocky headlands, and the number of offshore islands increases. Important nesting and staging areas for a variety of shorebirds, herons, gulls, and terns occur all along this coast.

Five generalized types of forest communities can be described in New England. Because of a number of factors, including natural succession and the activities of man, each zone includes a range of habitats which support various bird populations at different times of the year. The southernmost forests of New England are within the oak–hickory zone. Most of Connecticut, southern Rhode Island, and south-central Massachusetts lie within this area. The southeastern corner of New England and its attendant islands is dominated by the oak–pitch pine zone. Disjunct portions of this community are also found along the Maine coast, and inland in areas often termed "barrens." In Maine, New Hampshire, and Vermont the northern hardwood zone is predominant. Besides the birch, beech, and maple that are typical of these forests, the tree composition often includes hemlock and white pine.

Between this northern forest and the oak–hickory forest to the south lies the transitional zone. A patchwork of both northern hardwoods and oak–hickory forests covers large portions of central Massachusetts as well as smaller areas in Connecticut, New Hampshire, and Maine. Often slight differences in local geography determine the forest composition.

The fifth forest type, the spruce–fir zone, occurs in relatively small sections of New England's northern forest. The cool, moist conditions typical of portions of the Maine coast, the northern boglands, and the high mountainsides are conducive to the growth of balsam fir and one or more of the spruces. A variety of birds, including many of the northern warblers and boreal species, inhabit this zone.

Finally, limited areas of the arctic–alpine zone are

found above treeline on the tallest New England mountains. Because of the attendant harsh climate, only low-growing herbs and shrubs survive the desiccation and short growing season of the highest elevations. Even here, however, a few species of birds find suitable nesting habitat in summer.

Within each of these generalized zones, varying local conditions result in different habitats. From offshore upwellings, coastal thickets, and slash areas in the oak–pine community to vernal ponds, open meadows, northern bogs, and mountain cirque, a rich variety of habitats provide the diversity necessary for the resident and migrant bird populations. Like the great mountains of the Paleozoic Era, each dune, pond, and field is constantly changing. An appreciation of the landscape within this context of change offers a useful perspective to the naturalist.

P A R T   O N E

States & Sites

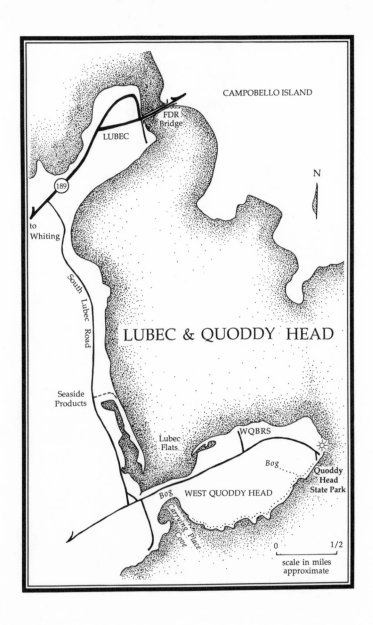

M A I N E

Lubec, West Quoddy Head, and Campobello

SUMMER / FALL

WASHINGTON COUNTY, MAINE, CALLS ITSELF "The Sunrise County." And the residents of Lubec, the most easterly community along the Maine coast, see the sun first—at least on those mornings when fog is absent. A majority of travelers, heading "down east" to Lubec, start out from the Bar Harbor area. As one drives eastward from Ellsworth along Route 1, shopping-mall– fast-food commercialism is largely left behind, and the realities of rural Maine become apparent. While the scene includes postcard villages and harbors, poverty and the effects of a long winter are also part of the picture. For the bird watcher, Lubec and several nearby locales offer the possibility of seeing large concentrations of shorebirds, a variety of nesting warblers, and a selection of boreal species. Visiting this region in early summer will increase your chances with the warblers and boreal residents. Shorebird numbers will be low at this time, however. The southward migration of the arctic-nesting shorebirds begins in July, peaks in August, and continues through early fall. A visit in mid-August will assure the bird finder an opportunity to enjoy the height of the shorebird movement as well as providing a reasonable chance to find a variety of warblers and perhaps one or two of the boreal specialties. If you decide to make the trip in June or July be prepared for blackflies, and be sure to take along plenty of repellent.

Most of the present generation of birders have grown up with only the legends of flocks of birds so numerous they obscured the sun. Many of these stories involved the now-extinct Passenger Pigeon, although nineteenth-century market gunners also recorded immense flocks of shorebirds. Edward Howe Forbush, in his *History of the Game Birds, Wild-Fowl and Shore Birds of Massachusetts and Adjacent States* (1912), relates numerous accounts such as Dunlin ". . . in such flocks as to seem at a distance like a moving cloud," and Eskimo Curlew ". . . in millions that darkened the sky." While it is true that nowadays fog is more likely than shorebirds to obscure the sun in Maine, Lubec offers the opportunity to see concentrations of shorebirds that number not in the hundreds, but in the thousands.

Two items that should increase your success with the abundant shorebirds are a spotting scope and a tide chart. The 20- to 28-foot tides in this area dictate the optimal times for shorebird viewing. Birding is best during the period from three hours before to three hours after the high tide. When the tide is farther out, the birds disperse, and observation becomes difficult at best. An excellent vantage point for seeing shorebirds is on the extensive **Lubec Flats**. To reach this area take Route 189 east from Whiting for about 9 miles. At the intersection of Route 189 and South Lubec Road go south (right) following the signs for Quoddy Head State Park. About 2 miles after this intersection you will see Seaside Forest Products on your right. On the left, next to utility pole Number 68, a dirt road leads down to a peninsula that borders the flats. Here, a mixed sand and black-pebble beach forms the shoreline of South Lubec and Quoddy Head. The flats stretch eastward from this beach. In August, Semipalmated Sandpipers will likely be the prevalent species. At times over ten thousand of these sandpipers will be feeding here. Other common species include Semipalmated Plover, Least Sandpiper, Black-bellied Plover, and Sanderling. If you are birding this area on a rising tide and are tempted to wander out onto the flats, take caution: the tide comes up extremely fast, and the water is frigid.

Farther south (toward Quoddy Head) on the South Lubec Road you will find a pull-off that is adjacent to the shoreline. As the tide approaches the high-water mark this is a good spot from which to observe the roosting flocks. Although it seems unlikely that hundreds of shorebirds could be inconspicuous, you will have to look carefully to pick out the well-camouflaged flocks on the beach. Sitting quietly on the shore will often put the observer in the middle of a spectacular shorebird show. As beach space becomes limited numerous small flocks fly past, often within feet of the bird watcher, as the birds search for a place to roost. Be on the lookout for Greater and Lesser yellowlegs, Ruddy Turnstone, and Red Knot, as well as the species mentioned above. During the latter part of August, White-rumped Sandpiper can be quite numerous; later still, during the latter part of September and throughout October, Dunlin numbers peak. Continue along the South Lubec Road until you come to the Quoddy Head road (2.6 miles after the Route 189/South Lubec Road intersection). Go left here and look for a small parking space located a little over .5 mile on your left. This spot provides access to the flats, and from here you can work the Quoddy Head shore. Other species regularly recorded on the flats include Solitary Sandpiper, Short-billed Dowitcher, Western Sandpiper, Whimbrel, Willet, and Lesser Golden-Plover. Rarely, a Baird's Sandpiper or a Marbled Godwit turns up. Given the number of birds passing through this area, it is safe to say that most rarities pass unnoticed. The more time you spend studying the shorebirds here, the greater becomes the possibility that you may add a new species to the Lubec list.

West Quoddy Head has several areas besides the flats that will be of interest to the visiting birder. Approximately .25 mile from the intersection of South Lubec and Quoddy Head roads you will come to **Carrying Place Bog**. This bog is one of only a few raised coastal peatlands in the United States. Typical plants of the bog include pitcher plant and sundews. Because there is no access into the bog, you should confine your investigations to the edges (two other bogs with walking trails are described below). Bank Swallows nest in the peat along the edge of the bog. Just east of the bog a trail crosses a grassy meadow to **Carrying Place Cove**. Vesper and Savannah sparrows can often be found in or on the edges of the meadow. The cove itself may have a few shorebirds or gulls, and rarely, gray seals are seen hauled out on the rocks. This is a good vantage point at which to scan the treelines on the mainland and Quoddy Head where Common Raven, Bald Eagle, and Sharp-shinned Hawk are sometimes seen.

Continue east on the Quoddy Head road until you see a sign for the **West Quoddy Biological Research Station** (WQBRS) on your left. The station is open to the public from the end of June through the end of September. Educational displays on coastal and marine topics as well as pamphlets and books will be of interest to visiting birders. On Saturdays and Sundays during the summer months staff naturalists lead walks which focus on the ecology of West Quoddy Head. The view northward, behind the WQBRS buildings, offers a good panorama of the Lubec Flats. At low tide, with the aid of a scope, you may be able to find harbor seals with their pups (August) hauled out on the Wormell Ledges. Look also for Cliff Swallows hawking above the meadow as well as flotillas of Common Eider and Red-breasted Mergansers in the bay. Several, if not all, of the posts of the fishing weirs will likely be crowned with Double-crested Cormorants.

The woodlands between the WQBRS and the **West Quoddy Head Lighthouse** are a good place to look for passerines. If you drive to the end of the Quoddy Head road you will find a parking lot directly above the lighthouse. Park here and walk the edges of the road back toward the research station. A good variety of warblers are summer residents here, including Yellow, Common Yellowthroat, American Redstart, Black-throated Green, Northern Parula, Black-and-white, and Canada. Look also for Tennessee, Magnolia, Yellow-rumped, Cape May, Bay-breasted, and Blackburnian warblers. In some years, White-winged or Red crossbills can be numerous here. With luck, you may even come across a Spruce Grouse on the edge of the dense woodland.

Be sure to walk down to the Quoddy Head lighthouse, located on the promontory that forms the easternmost tip of the United States. The waters between

West Quoddy Head and Grand Manan Island are an ideal spot to scan for seabirds and marine mammals. Harbor porpoise and minke and finback whales are regularly seen here during the summer months. Gulls to look for include Herring Gull, Great Black-backed Gull, and Bonaparte's Gull. In late summer, Black-legged Kittiwake can often be found on Sail Rock, just offshore. Besides rafts of Common Eider, Black Guillemot, Maine's most common alcid, are often to be found here. Check the rocks for Purple Sandpiper (a few in August), and scope the ocean for Northern Gannet.

A visit to **Quoddy Head State Park** should be a priority for all birders visiting this area. You will see signs and the access road immediately north of the lighthouse area. This road leads to a parking lot, a picnic area, and the trailheads. Take some time to study the display boards on the edge of the parking lot. One informs the visitor that this area experiences 59 days of fog annually. Take heart if you have arrived on one of these days; the birds often remain active during foggy weather. Even without the birds, the combination of ocean, surf, rocky beaches, volcanic cliffs, spruce–fir forest, and bog create an exquisite natural setting. Before starting your explorations, you may want to spread a few breadcrumbs on one of the picnic tables. This may entice the Gray Jays out of the woodlands.

The intertidal area of the rocky beach below the parking lot is an interesting place to begin your investigations of the park. Here hermit crabs and dog whelks, barnacles and periwinkles, sea urchins and sea cucumbers get their living in or around the tidal pools and rock faces. One of the most fascinating creatures of this habitat is the nudibranch, or "sea slug." These small (to 1 inch), pinkish, shell-less snails sport delicate branched gills that wave gently in the water. Birds you may see winging along the shore include those mentioned in the lighthouse section as well as Ring-billed Gull, Arctic and Common terns, and Common Loon.

The main trail in the park skirts the southern headlands of West Quoddy Head and thus offers an excellent view seaward. Sections of this trail pass through dense stands of spruce and fir woodlands, and it is in this habitat that you may find one or more of the boreal species that occur in the region. Boreal Chickadees are permanent residents here, as are Gray Jays, although the presence of the latter species is erratic. Both Spruce Grouse and Black-backed Woodpecker have been recorded in the park. The former is notoriously elusive, however; the latter, downright rare. You should have less trouble finding several of the resident warbler species; also keep a look out for Golden-crowned Kinglet, Winter Wren, and Dark-eyed Junco. If you follow the trail to its end (2 miles) you will be at Carrying Place Cove (mentioned above). From here you can return via the same trail or walk across the meadow and back along the Quoddy Head Road.

Several of the park trails provide access to the interior sections of West Quoddy Head. This is a special world in its own right. The aroma of balsam pervades sections of the dark spruce–fir forest, while the paths are alternately decked in carpets of fern, patches of bunchberry, and stands of twinflower. Occasional clumps of alder and groves of yellow birch provide contrast with the boreal conifers. One trail leads to a bog where there is a boardwalk with interpretive markers. This is a good spot to find nesting Yellow-bellied Flycatcher, Swainson's and Hermit thrushes, and White-throated Sparrow; Lincoln's Sparrow and Palm Warbler are also among the possibilities here. The park staff, and a few fortunate birders, have found Spruce Grouse in the area just before the boardwalk begins.

If possible, visit the park at several different times of

day as well as in the fog and in the sunshine. These various times and conditions each seem to lend a different mood and flavor. Quoddy Head State Park is a place worth returning to; with a little effort, your time here will provide some special memories.

Although the birds you see on **Campobello** can't be added to your New England list, you shouldn't pass up the opportunity to spend some time on this picturesque island. To reach Campobello Island, which is part of the Canadian province of New Brunswick, take Route 189 through Lubec and cross the Franklin Delano Roosevelt Bridge (U.S. citizens do not need a passport). Follow the main road north for a little over a mile to the entrance for the F.D.R. Summer Cottage. Across from the entrance, a gravel road goes right (east) into the Roosevelt Campobello International Park. Take this secondary road for 1.5 miles to the **Eagle Hill Bog**. A boardwalk provides good access into the bog where plants including baked-apple, lambkill (sheep laurel) leather-leaf, Labrador-tea, and sweet gale are well marked. Included among the nesting birds of Eagle Hill Bog are Palm Warbler and Lincoln's Sparrow. On the southern side of the boardwalk a side trail leads out to an observation tower. This is a good spot from which to observe the Osprey nesting in the area. You may want to continue east on the park road to Raccoon Beach and Liberty Point. The road passes through wooded sections as well as providing access to ocean views, and there are numerous places to stop and bird. Return to the main road across from the Roosevelt Cottage.

Turn right and follow the signs to Head Harbour (approximately 9 miles from the F.D.R. residence). The final section of the road to **Head Harbour** and the **East Quoddy Head Light** is secondary road but is easily negotiated. The northern tip of Campobello Island is not

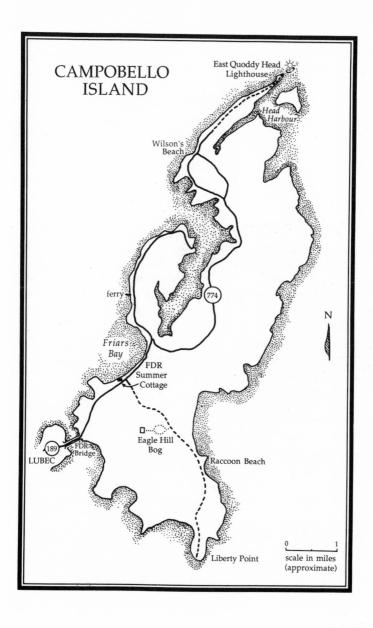

CAMPOBELLO ISLAND

East Quoddy Head
Lighthouse

Head Harbour

Wilson's
Beach

ferry

774

N

*Friars
Bay*

FDR
Summer
Cottage

189
LUBEC
FDR
Bridge

Eagle Hill
Bog

Raccoon Beach

Liberty Point

0   1
scale in miles
(approximate)

only beautiful, it is also a great place to watch birds. Between the latter part of August and mid-September thousands (sometimes millions) of Red-necked Phalaropes gather offshore. Curiously, Red Phalarope is entirely absent at this season here. Large numbers of Bonaparte's Gulls are normally present during the same time period. Although Black-legged Kittiwake numbers peak during the winter, a few can usually be found in late summer. At low tide you can cross over to East Quoddy Head Lighthouse for another view to the ocean (don't get stranded by the incoming tide). After you have seen a few thousand phalaropes you may want to turn your attention to the marine mammals. Harbor porpoise, finback whale, and minke whale are regularly seen off this rugged headland. Humpback whale, northern right whale, and Atlantic white-sided dolphin are much less common but also possible. If you want to tour this area by boat consult Captain Huntley (see Machias Seal Island).

Wilson's Beach is a little over 2 miles south of the Head Harbour point. Stop here and scan the water for phalaropes and gulls. To have an even closer view of the various seabird concentrations you should plan to take the **Deer Island Ferry**. Continue south on Route 774 to the intersection at the north end of Friars Bay. Follow the signs for the Deer Island Ferry (less than 1 mile). This tiny ferry runs from June through September, making the round trip seven times daily. There is no need to take your car. Observing the phalaropes and gulls from the vantage point of the ferry and Deer Island itself makes this excursion well worthwhile. A short walk south from the ferry landing will bring you to the campground at Deer Island Point. From the tip, an enormous collection of Bonaparte's Gulls—and usually a Little Gull, a Common Black-headed Gull, or even something rarer—can be observed. If possible, schedule your visit to the island approximately two hours before high tide. This will put you in place for the phenomenal movement of water and birds through the Head Harbour Passage. An hour and a half on the island will still allow you to catch the next ferry back to Campobello.

Lubec does not have a wide choice in accommodations, and what is available is open seasonally. The Eastland Motel, The Overview Inn, and The Home Port Inn offer rooms. The Sunset Point Trailer Park has trailer and tent sites. There are several general stores and a food market in town. Campobello Island also has inns and a campground. If you are headed to Eastport, Cobscook Bay State Park has shorefront campsites.

An instructive way to visit and bird in this area is by enrolling in one or more of the summer workshops held by the **Institute for Field Ornithology**, part of the University of Maine at Machias. Instructors are nationally recognized experts, and all workshops combine classroom, laboratory, and field sessions. They visit the areas described here as well as Machias Seal Island. Low-cost housing in the university's dormitory is available for attendees. For information contact:

Dr. Charles D. Duncan, Director
Institute for Field Ornithology
University of Maine at Machias
9 O'Brien Avenue
Machias, Maine 04654
207-255-3313 ext. 289

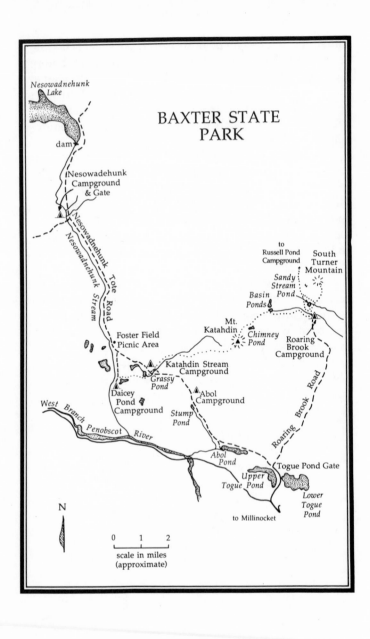

Baxter State Park

LATE SPRING / EARLY SUMMER

THE 200,000-ACRE BAXTER STATE PARK IS
situated in north-central Maine. While the park is dominated by the treeless summits of the Katahdin Range,
the majority of its acreage consists of woodland and
wetland habitats. Percival Baxter's energies and wealth
were largely responsible for the park's creation. It was
Baxter's desire that this land "forever be left in its natural wild state and forever [be] kept as a sanctuary for
wild beasts and birds." Hikers and naturalists have also
benefited from Baxter's gift, as the park preserves an
exquisite portion of Maine's wilderness country.

Pamola, the legendary, eaglelike god of Katahdin, is
said to become enraged with those who climb the
mountain. It seems, therefore, that hikers wishing to

complete the Georgia-to-Maine Appalachian Trail, which ends on Mt. Katahdin, have no choice but to risk incurring the wrath of the gods. Fortunately for birders there is little need to ascend Maine's highest (5,267 feet) peak. Most of the avian attractions can be found along park roads or reached after relatively short hikes. The best time for birding the park is between early June and mid-July.

To reach Baxter drive north on Route 95 and take Exit 56 at Medway for Millinocket. **Park Headquarters** are in Millinocket at the intersection of Central and Sycamore streets next to the McDonalds. It is important that campers stop here to make or confirm reservations for the various campgrounds in the park. Advance reservations (by mail only) are suggested. Contact:

Reservation Clerk
Baxter State Park
64 Balsam Drive
Millinocket, Maine 04462

Maps, bird lists, and books are also available at the headquarters. For first-time visitors, a short slide show on Baxter is also offered. Birders having any inclination to camp should try to make arrangements to stay in the park. The convenience and beauty of the various campsites makes the effort worthwhile. No commercial services are available within the boundaries of Baxter State Park. Various motels and restaurants can be found in the Millinocket area.

From Millinocket take Routes 11 and 157 through town following the signs for Baxter State Park. The distance from park headquarters to the **Togue Pond Gate** is 18 miles. An entrance fee of $5 per car is charged. Upper and Lower Togue ponds, just south of the gate, often have at least one pair of nesting Common Loon.

Also check the general vicinity for Pileated Woodpecker, Tree Swallow, Cliff Swallow, Pine Warbler, and Chipping Sparrow.

One of the most popular birding areas at Baxter is **Sandy Stream Pond**. To reach this area follow Roaring Brook Road 8 miles to the Roaring Brook Campground. The campground is an ideal place to spend the night and has an interesting variety of summer residents. Nesting species include Least Flycatcher, American Robin, Warbling Vireo, American Redstart, and Dark-eyed Junco. Just past the ranger station and across Roaring Brook a trail leads to Sandy Stream Pond. It only takes 10 minutes to reach the pond, but many birders will want to spend several hours here. Along the initial portion of the trail you should hear or see Swainson's Thrush and White-throated Sparrow, two of the premier songsters of the park. Other species to look and listen for are Nashville Warbler, Northern Waterthrush, and Rose-breasted Grosbeak. Take some time to enjoy the bunchberry, common wood sorrel, and clintonia growing along the path. Once you reach Sandy Stream Pond follow the path along the eastern side. The trail passes through stands of northern white cedar, spruce, and balsam fir. Here one can experience the typical sights, sounds, and odors of the boreal forest. Three spur trails lead to view points overlooking Sandy Stream Pond; explore each of these. Besides the panoramas of Katahdin and South Turner Mountain you may well see one or more moose grazing at the pond's edge. Check the pond for Ring-necked Duck or Common Merganser and the edges for American Bittern. Big Rock, one of the view points, provides a fine place at which to look back at the edge of the forest. A little "pishing" is sure to attract several of the nesting birds. Resident warblers include Yellow-rumped, Blackburnian, Black-and-white,

Common Yellowthroat, and Canada. The high-pitched song of the Golden-crowned Kinglet is often heard here, and your squeaking may bring one or two into view. Blue Jays are common, and their rarer cousin the Gray Jay is occasionally seen. In the denser stands of spruce and fir you may even find Yellow-bellied Flycatcher or Boreal Chickadee. There is usually a pair of Winter Wrens at the north end near a stream.

Many birders make the loop around Sandy Stream Pond by following Sandy Stream Pond Trail northwest to Russell Pond Trail and then returning to Roaring Brook Campground on the Russell Pond Trail. This loop is approximately 3 miles, and the terrain is relatively easy; allow a little over three hours for hiking and birding. One advantage of taking the loop is the opportunity to find birds of both boreal and hardwood forests. The aspen, birch, beech, and maple stands are particularly attractive along the northern and western sides of the route. Four species of vireos, Solitary, Warbling, Philadelphia, and Red-eyed, may be found here, so you may want to review their various songs. Also Black-throated Blue and Black-throated Green warblers are likely.

Another local trail worth investigating is the Roaring Brook Nature Trail. Pamphlets for the self-guiding tour are available at the ranger station in the campground. Inveterate hikers may want to take Chimney Pond Trail into the Basin Ponds and then on to Chimney Pond (2,914 feet). This is a relatively long trek (6.6 miles round trip) and should not be attempted by birders out for a stroll. Possible rewards for those making the effort include Black-backed Woodpecker, Ruby-crowned Kinglet, Gray-cheeked Thrush, Bay-breasted and Blackpoll warblers, and perhaps some crossbills. (Nonhikers can try for several of these species in other locations mentioned below.) Chimney Pond is the base camp for many climbers on their way to the summit of Katahdin. Once above timberline the bird life becomes as thin as the air. However, nesting Water Pipits are a specialty of the tundra habitat. Common Ravens are also frequently seen around the higher peaks.

Roaring Brook Road offers many places to pull off and search for birds. Common species in the northern hardwoods and mixed forest include Northern Flicker, Downy and Hairy woodpeckers, Black-capped Chickadee, Wood Thrush, Red-eyed Vireo, and Ovenbird. Even more interesting is the **Nesowadnehunk Tote Road**, which goes up the western side of Baxter. About 3 miles northwest of the main gate is the **Abol Beach and Picnic Area**. The entrance road to the picnic area has second-growth habitat where Chestnut-sided and Mourning warblers can be found. Also look for Hermit Thrush and Magnolia, Yellow-rumped, Black-throated Green, American Redstart, and Northern Parula warblers in this vicinity. Abol Pond may produce a waterbird or two, and the dumpsters here are on the regular route of one of Baxter's numerous (though seldom seen) black bears. Take a few minutes to stroll over to Abol Falls. On hot days you may even be tempted to try the natural water slide.

Two miles past the picnic area you will find Stump Pond, on the left. Pause here to look for moose and listen for the croaking of the Common Ravens that often patrol the area. Eastern Kingbird and Olive-sided Flycatcher are possibilities. On sunny days it's difficult to drive this road without seeing numerous tiger swallowtail and white admiral butterflies. Almost as numerous as the butterflies are the Cedar Waxwings, whose wiry call is often heard overhead.

Three miles northwest of Stump Pond is the **Katahdin**

Stream Campground, another excellent place to camp and bird. The open campgrounds and clear, cold pool offer a refreshing contrast to the surrounding woodlands. Numerous Barn Swallows are often insecting over the pool, while robins and grackles are constantly about the campsites. A short walk northeast along Katahdin Stream (Hunt Trail) will bring you to a world pervaded by the odor of balsam fir. Look for twinflower and speedwell along the path. Also try the short trail that ascends the hillside behind tent site Number 23. Besides affording the chance of a good variety of birds, including Veery, Blackburnian and Magnolia warblers, and White-throated Sparrow, the short climb ends with a magnificent view of the Katahdin Range to the northeast. The sights and sounds are particularly beautiful in the early evening. Another short hike which can be productive for birders is the trail to Grassy Pond. Winter Wren, Black-and-white Warbler, and Northern Waterthrush are regularly seen or heard along the path and boardwalks. With luck you may even come across a Boreal Chickadee or Black-backed Woodpecker. In the evening moose are frequently found at Grassy Pond.

Approximately 2.5 miles from Katahdin Stream Campground a road leads south to Daicey Pond Campground. There are good birding opportunities along the **access road**. Nesting Broad-winged Hawk, Ruby-crowned Kinglet, and Tennessee Warbler can all be found along this stretch. A self-guiding nature trail circles Daicey Pond; interpretive booklets are available in the campground. Farther north along the Nesowadnehunk Tote Road is the **Foster Field Picnic Area**. Walking along the field-forest edge will likely turn up a good variety of birds. As you continue along the road look for Purple Finches and Evening Grosbeaks.

Birders wishing to increase their chances with the

boreal specialties of Baxter will want to continue north to the flatlands between the **Nesowadnehunk Gate and Nesowadnehunk Dam**. The distance from Foster Field Picnic Area to the Nesowadnehunk Dam is approximately 9 miles. Once you pass the entrance to Nesowadnehunk Field Campground pull off at any spot that seems to have interesting habitat. Second-growth slash areas may produce Mourning Warbler. Check spruce–fir stands for Tennessee, Cape May, Bay-breasted, and Blackpoll warblers. The occurrence of these warblers (except Blackpoll) is often tied to outbreaks of spruce budworm, and thus the numbers present vary considerably. Spruce–fir stands with many dead trees should be investigated for three-toed woodpeckers. Black-backed Woodpecker has nested in the area where Nesowadnehunk Stream comes close to the road. A few pairs of Sharp-shinned Hawk also nest here, and if you are fortunate you may see one. As is the case with several of the boreal species, finding a Spruce Grouse is often more a matter of luck than persistence. While this species is fairly common in this area, many a birder has been frustrated in his or her quest for this bird. Consider it a good day if you add this one to your list. Several old logging roads lead off the main road and pass through good birding habitat. If you decide to try one of these make sure you keep your bearings and know the way back.

Birding in Baxter can be a true wilderness experience. Several items will help to assure that your visit is a comfortable and safe outing. Insect repellent will help to discourage the many blackflies that are sure to find you in late spring and early summer. A compass and Baxter topographical trail map will keep you on course. Good maps are available at headquarters in Millinocket. Finally, it is a good idea to carry food and other supplies into the park as none of these items are available within Baxter. For more information contact:

Baxter State Park
Park Headquarters
64 Balsam Drive
Millinocket, Maine 04462
207-723-5140

Machias Seal Island

SPRING / SUMMER

IN MARCH AND APRIL, AS WINTER RELAXES its grip on the Northern Hemisphere, Atlantic Puffins leave their offshore wintering grounds and head for nesting sites on coastal islands between Labrador and Maine. The destination for some of these birds is Machias Seal Island, at the southern limit of the summer puffin colonies. This low-lying 15-acre granite isle is located 10 miles off the coast. Because of the island's interesting summer residents (avian), as well as its convenience to the mainland, Machias Seal has become a traditional stop for birders.

While ownership of the island has been the focus of considerable debate between Canadian and U.S. interests, the various alcids and terns seem to know exactly

whose territory this is, especially during the nesting season. Besides the sizable Atlantic Puffin population, Razorbills, Common Murres (a few non-nesters), Black Guillemot, and Arctic and Common terns are regularly seen here in summer.

Boat trips to Machias Seal are most easily arranged between the end of May and the beginning of September. The optimal time for seeing the nesting species is in June. Captain Barna Norton and his son, Captain John Norton, run trips daily (weather permitting) during the summer months. Norton sails from Jonesport (early in the season) and Cutler. The trip to Machias Seal from Cutler normally takes an hour. For reservations and other details contact:

Barna B. Norton
RR 1–340 Main Street
Jonesport, Maine 04649
207-497-5933

Captain Edwin (Butch) Huntley also travels to Machias Seal Island from Lubec and Cutler. His vessel, the *Seafarer*, offers excellent visibility while underway, and Butch is especially knowledgeable about, and expert at, finding marine mammals. For information contact:

Captain Edwin Huntley
9 High Street
Lubec, Maine 04652
207-733-5584

During the height of the nesting season (until August 1) the Canadian Wildlife Service limits the number of people landing on the island to 30 per day, on a first-come-first-served basis. Thus it may pay to get an early start. Useful items to take on these trips include foul-weather gear, to protect you and your binoculars, a "tern hat," to provide nesting terns a target other than your scalp, and food and drink. Veterans of the trip dress warmly, even in midsummer, when the ocean chill can still be severe. Landing on Machias Seal Island is not always easy. The captains anchor offshore, and if seas are calm, transfer passengers to rowboats and row them to the Canadian Coast Guard rampway. Here, tides and surf often require a nimble scramble over slippery rockweed to the terra firma of the island. Birders normally have up to two to three hours on the island. A series of paths, observation posts, and blinds provide good access to the nesting colonies. If seas are running, it is possible that landings on the island will not be permitted. You should still be able to see a few puffins, however.

En route to the island, Leach's or Wilson's storm-petrels and Pomarine or Parasitic jaegers may be seen. In August, Manx Shearwaters are occasionally found. Harbor Seals and often Gray Seals can be seen on nearby North Rock if the captain is asked to take a quick look.

Mount Desert Island
Acadia National Park

SPRING / SUMMER / FALL

THERE IS NO BETTER SPOT AT WHICH TO ENJOY
the birds of Maine than on Mt. Desert Island. Between
the summit of Mt. Cadillac and the surf of Ship Harbor
lie a variety of habitats which have attracted over 300
species of birds as well as uncounted numbers of bird
watchers. Rocky shore, marsh, meadow, bog, heath,
forest, and mountaintop are all represented here. The
birding opportunities are enhanced by these varied habitats as well as by several other factors. Besides attracting the normal variety of birds found where land meets
sea, Mt. Desert lies at the border of the northern and
temperate life zones. Thus, the birder can count on

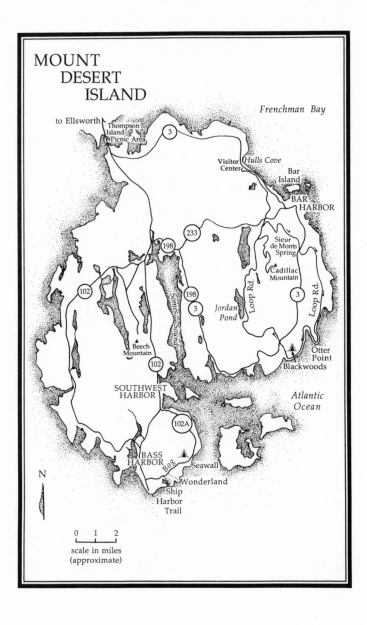

MOUNT
DESERT
ISLAND

Frenchman Bay

to Ellsworth

Thompson
Island
Picnic Area

③

Visitor
Center

Hulls Cove

Bar
Island

BAR
HARBOR

②③③

⑲⑧

Sieur
de Monts
Spring

Cadillac
Mountain

⑩②

Somes Sound

⑲⑧

③

Jordan
Pond

Loop Rd.

Loop Rd.

③

Beech
Mountain

⑩②

Otter
Point
Blackwoods

SOUTHWEST
HARBOR

*Atlantic
Ocean*

⑩②A

BASS
HARBOR

Bog

Seawall

Wonderland

Ship
Harbor
Trail

N

0   1   2

scale in miles
(approximate)

seeing species typical of both of these regions. Add to this easy access, excellent facilities, and the chance to enjoy a fresh lobster dinner in a picturesque cove, and you have the makings of a memorable weekend (or month).

The best time to visit Mt. Desert Island is between early June and late September. While the fall shorebird migration begins in July and peaks during August, the summer passerine residents are most active during June. But don't fret if your plans bring you here any time during the summer months. There will be plenty of birds to search out and enjoy.

Mt. Desert Island is indeed an island, but unlike most of the islands of the Maine coast, it is connected to the mainland by a bridge. This bridge is located approximately 10 miles south of Ellsworth, Maine. To reach Ellsworth take Route 3 east from the Maine Turnpike to Belfast and then Route 1 north to Ellsworth. The island itself is divided into two lobes by Somes Sound.

Close to half of the total land area of Mt. Desert Island is managed by the federal government as Acadia National Park. Your first destination, once inside the park, should be the visitors' center. This is located near Hulls Cove in the northeast corner of the island; directions are well marked. The visitors' center is open from mid-June to mid-October (off-season information at park headquarters west of Bar Harbor on Route 233). The center has a large relief map of the island which will help you to orient yourself and plan your field trips. You will find a good selection of books for sale here, many of them written for the naturalist and birder. You may also want to take in one of the frequent showings of the park's 15-minute introductory film, *Search for Acadia*. Three items that all visiting birders should pick up before leaving the center are a park map, bird list, and weekly schedule of events.

As you will see from your map there are many places to visit during your stay in Acadia. If this is your first visit to Mt. Desert, a good overview will include a leisurely tour along the eastern highlands and **Loop Road**. Pull out frequently to enjoy the spectacular views, and mark your map for return visits. A prime location many birders often head to first is that section of the island south of Southwest Harbor. You can work your way west across the island on Route 233 and then go south on Route 102. A productive birding area is **Ship Harbor Trail**, and if you like warblers this is the place to go. Eighteen species of warblers nest in this area, and you should see or hear many of them, including Tennessee, Northern Parula, Magnolia, Black-throated Green, Bay-breasted, American Redstart, and Ovenbird. The trail is set up as a figure-eight, starting in a dense spruce–fir forest, and continuing along the shoreline, where it eventually reaches a rocky promontory with a view seaward. If you can bring yourself to ignore the warblers for a few minutes you should also be able to find nesting Dark-eyed Junco and perhaps a thrush or two as you walk the trail.

Another "must" trail in this immediate vicinity is **Wonderland**. The trail goes south from Route 102A. This walk takes you out a peninsula through spruce–fir woods, across open areas of granite ledge and pitch pine, to the rocky beach front. Look for Ruby-crowned and Golden-crowned kinglets in this area as you add to your warbler list. This is also a good spot to see and hear Olive-sided Flycatcher and crossbills. Other northern species you may find here are Yellow-bellied Flycatcher and Boreal Chickadee.

Across from the Wonderland parking lot is Big Heath or **Seawall Bog**. The opportunity to stand ankle deep in the sphagnum moss amid orchids and pitcher plants, while being serenaded by the White-throated Sparrow is a true delight. But tread softly and stay on the paths; this is a delicate area, and it is up to the users to protect it. Bog specialties include Palm Warbler and Lincoln's Sparrow.

The entire area from Bass Harbor to the Seawall Campground is worth going over several times. Stop your car at various places to walk the roadside, and you're almost assured of finding interesting birds and plants. Look for Nashville, Yellow, Blackburnian, and Black-and-white warblers. **Bass Harbor Marsh** is another place you will want to explore. Many birders would be content to spend their entire stay in this one section of Mt. Desert Island. With camping facilities at Seawall and ample lodging and food in and around Southwest Harbor, this is certainly a possibility. In case you want a bigger piece of the pie, however, let's look at some other opportunities.

On the southeastern coast of the eastern lobe is a scenic peninsula with **Otter Point** at its tip. Although you won't find any otter here, it is definitely a place worth exploring. A trail leads north from the parking lot, and you won't have to go more than 50 yards before you realize that this is a very special place. Here, among the fir, spruce, and jumble of downed branches and tree trunks, you can sit on a soft bed of moss, reindeer lichen, and small cranberry and listen to the birds. Chances are you will soon have for company a Swainson's Thrush and one or two warbler species. Because the boreal forest is often very dense, a working knowledge of birdsong greatly increases one's awareness of the birds in these areas. If it's the nesting season you should also have many opportunities to see the residents as they come close to scold or inspect you. Black-backed Woodpecker and Gray Jay are two northern specialties to look for here. South of the parking lot you'll find a picturesque headland overlooking the Atlantic Ocean. This is an ideal spot to watch for gulls and cormorants; you should even find Black Guillemot without much trouble.

To find many of the bird species typical of the eastern deciduous forest you should head for **Sieur de Monts Spring**. This area is reached via an access road leading from the northeastern section of the Loop Road. Directly adjacent to the parking lot you will find the Acadia Wild Garden (an excellent opportunity to brush up on your plant identification skills), Nature Center, and the Abbe Museum of Stone Age Antiquities. If you want to bird this area, you'll have to arrive early, as it's normally crowded with tourists. If you don't beat the crowds, however, you can follow the carriage road north from the Spring toward Great Meadow. Incidentally, there are 40 miles of these carriage roads in Acadia, and if you have a bicycle (rentals in Bar Harbor) they provide excellent access to many good birding spots. For the hiker there is a trail network of 120 miles crisscrossing the park.

Late summer and early fall is the season to spend some time enjoying the shorebird migration. There are several prime spots on Mt. Desert Island for seeing shorebirds. One good location is the flat (or bar) between **Bar Harbor and Bar Island**. Try to arrive here two to three hours before high tide. The best access is from Bridge Street. A scope will help you locate such common species as Black-bellied Plover, Ruddy Turnstone, Red Knot, and Semipalmated Sandpiper on the rising tide. The **Thompson Island Picnic Area** on the causeway, and the flats and shoreline between Seawall and Bass Harbor Head, may also be productive.

Although Acadia is one of the most heavily visited

national parks in the United States, its relatively large size (35,000 acres) allows each visitor to find the degree of solitude he or she requires. While Thunder Hole or the Sand Beach may at times be overrun with tourists and bathers, a short walk along any trail will normally lead to a quiet, peaceful spot where the natural wonders of the park can be enjoyed to their fullest. The **Jordan Pond Nature Trail** is a self-guiding walk that will introduce you to many of the common plants of Acadia. Another way to increase one's appreciation of the park is to participate in one or more of the scheduled walks. Park naturalists provide programs on everything from tide pools to stargazing. Visitors can also join regularly scheduled bird walks to various locations in the park. Cruises to the islands in Frenchman Bay and elsewhere are offered by the park service and private boat owners. Another suggestion for the visiting naturalist is a trip to the College of the Atlantic in Bar Harbor. A bookstore and natural-history museum make this an attractive stop for both children and adults. The Oceanarium in Southwest Harbor provides displays and short talks by the staff on marine biology and the fishing industry. Finally the Gilley Museum in Southwest Harbor has a collection of hand-carved birds native to Mt. Desert Island.

If time allows, there are two side trips that are well worth taking. Both are off Mt. Desert Island but are in Acadia National Park. **Isle au Haut** is to the south and is reached via Route 15 to Stonington, where you take the passenger ferry to the island. This area is a good bet for migrants during late May and September. **Schoodic Peninsula** is north of Mt. Desert and can be reached via Route 186 south from West Gouldsboro. The rugged headlands of Schoodic provide a good vantage point to look for seabirds or wintering ducks.

On the less cerebral side, Bar Harbor offers many

opportunities for the dedicated shopper interested in improving the economy of the State of Maine. Also, don't miss a visit to one of the pastry shops in downtown Bar Harbor. The Jordan Pond House, in the park itself, serves meals as well as "high tea." Hotel, motel, and bed-and-breakfast accommodations are plentiful throughout the island. For those planning to spend a week or more, housekeeping cottages are also available. There are two campsites in the park (Seawall and Blackwoods) as well as many private camping facilities. Birders traveling with their children may be interested in certain "incentives" to be found in the area. Miniature golf, various amusements, and fast food can be found on Route 3 north of the park on the road to Ellsworth.

Monhegan Island

SPRING / FALL

SEVERAL ORNITHOLOGISTS HAVE SUGGESTED,
no doubt with tongue in cheek, that if you wait long
enough in one place all the birds will come to you.
While most birders have neither the time nor the patience to adopt this strategy, individuals inclined to
begin such an experiment would do well to move to
Monhegan Island, 10 miles off the midcoast of Maine.
Monhegan has long held the title of "best migrant trap"
in Maine; and given the way the island keeps collecting
records for most of New England's typical birds, as well
as for vagrants, there seems little doubt it will retain
this crown for the foreseeable future.

The best time to bird Monhegan Island is during the
latter half of May and throughout September. Ferry
service to the island is provided by the *Laura B.* out of

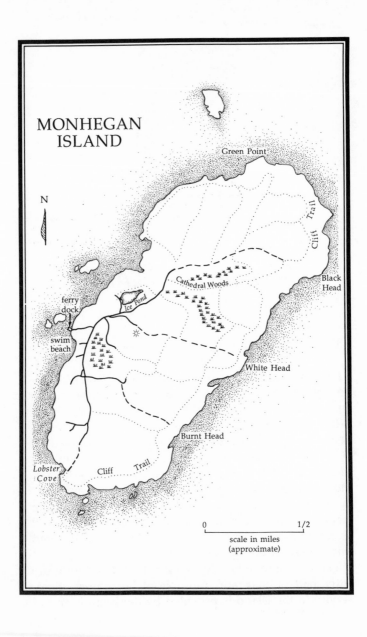

MONHEGAN
ISLAND

N

Green Point

Cliff Trail

Black
Head

Cathedral Woods

ferry
dock

Ice Pond

swim
beach

White Head

Burnt Head

Lobster
Cove

Cliff   Trail

0   1/2
scale in miles
(approximate)

Port Clyde (see details below). To reach Port Clyde take Route 1 northeast from Bath to Thomaston and then go south on Route 131.

In any review of Monhegan's bird life it is tempting to highlight such species as Magnificent Frigatebird, Gyrfalcon, White-winged Dove, Say's Phoebe, and Northern Wheatear. Lesser lights in the annual parade of the unusual include Western Kingbird, Blue Grosbeak, and Dickcissel. Indeed these, as well as many other vagrants, have occurred on the island. For many birders, however, the real stars of the Monhegan show are the more typical New England birds: spring flocks of brightly colored wood-warblers at the Ice Pond, resident seabirds in the waters north of Green Point, and the falcons of fall chasing prey within sight of the village. A comprehensive list of the birds of Monhegan would be similar to a regional check list. Suffice it to say that in both spring and fall birders can count on seeing an excellent representation of New England bird life; any vagrants will be icing on the cake.

You can start your birding on the *Laura B.* The 10-mile trip from Port Clyde to Monhegan Island can be especially productive in the fall. Look for Northern Fulmar, Greater Shearwater, Manx Shearwater, Wilson's Storm-Petrel, Northern Gannet (also in spring), and Red-necked Phalarope. You might even see an Atlantic Puffin from the Eastern Egg Rock or Matinicus Rock colonies.

Once you reach the island you should have little trouble finding the birds. Monhegan's small size (1.5 by .5 miles) and extensive network of trails make it relatively easy to cover. The best areas for migrant passerines are between the **Ice Pond** and **Lobster Cove**. Also check the **wet meadow** on the edge of town. As you walk south to Lobster Cove investigate the numerous thickets along the way. In fall, hawk watching can be excellent along this stretch and also at the cove. From Lobster Cove you can continue around the southeast end of the island on **Cliff Trail** and loop back on **Burnt Head** trail.

Also take time to hike out to **White Head** and **Black Head** on the eastern side of Monhegan. At the northern end of the island check the red spruce forest of **Cathedral Woods** for resident warblers and **Green Point** for seabirds.

Spring and fall migrants include numerous flycatchers, thrushes, vireos, warblers, finches, and blackbirds. A few of the birds seen regularly are Olive-sided and Yellow-bellied flycatchers, Swainson's and Hermit thrushes, Solitary and Philadelphia vireos, Indigo Bunting, Evening Grosbeak, and White-crowned and Lincoln's sparrows. Over 20 species of wood-warblers have been seen on Monhegan in late May. Fall birders can expect a similar variety of warblers (first half of September) as well as a good show of Merlins and Peregrine Falcons (mid-September to mid-October). Fall is also the time when the majority of vagrants are found on Monhegan. Red and White-winged crossbills can show up any time. Summer residents of particular interest are Common Eider, Black Guillemot, and Common Raven. In the coniferous stands of the Cathedral Woods look for nesting Red-breasted Nuthatch, Golden-crowned Kinglet, Winter Wren, Blackburnian and Blackpoll warblers, and White-throated Sparrow.

Monhegan is also well known for what it *doesn't* have: cars, electricity, and shopping malls, for example. In this age of fast this and instant that, this delightful island offers a real change of pace. So enjoy the birds and relax! For another account of Monhegan, including the possibilities in winter, see *A Birder's Guide to the Coast of Maine* (1981) by Elizabeth and Jan Pierson.

Because the better birding months are generally off-season on Monhegan, your choice of accommodations will be somewhat limited. The Trailing Yew offers room and board and is open from mid-May through mid-October. For information write or call: The Trailing Yew, Lobster Cove Road, Monhegan Island, Maine 04852; 207-596-0440. The Shining Sails (open year round) has efficiency apartments with ocean views. Contact The Shining Sails, Box 44, Monhegan Island, Maine 04852; 207-596-0041. Reservations are strongly suggested.

While the Monhegan general store has general supplies, including food, beer, and wine for efficiency-apartment renters, visitors should bring certain items. A flashlight is a "Monhegan necessity"; a down jacket and rain poncho may also come in handy. Birders wishing hard liquor should bring their own, as spirits are not for sale on the island.

Ferry service to Monhegan varies according to the season. Normally there is one trip per day in May and two per day in September. To confirm schedules and make reservations contact: Boat *Laura B.*, Box 238, Port Clyde, Maine 04885; 207-372-8848.

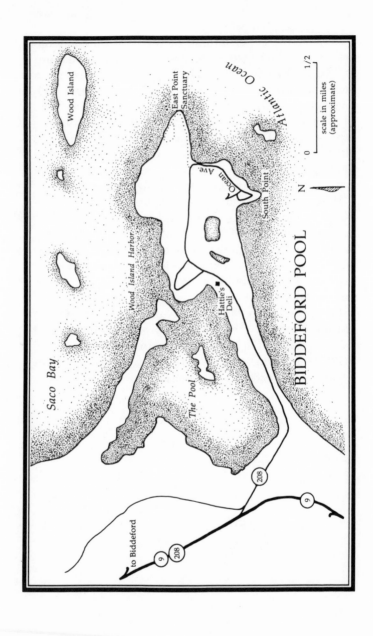

Wood Island

Saco Bay

Wood Island Harbor

East Point Sanctuary

Atlantic Ocean

Ocean Ave.

South Point

The Pool

Hattie's Deli

to Biddeford

9

208

9

208

9

208

N

BIDDEFORD POOL

0   1/2

scale in miles
(approximate)

Biddeford Pool and Scarborough Marsh

SPRING / SUMMER / FALL

SALT MARSHES, TIDAL FLATS, AND COASTAL thickets. Excellent examples of these productive birding habitats can all be found at Biddeford Pool and the Scarborough marshes in southern Maine. In May, and again from late July through October, an impressive variety of herons, waterfowl, shorebirds, gulls, terns, and migrant landbirds are found here. Add to this diversity the spice of Tricolored Heron, Marbled Godwit, Bonaparte's Gull, and Roseate Tern, and the reasons for a visit become clear.

To reach **Biddeford Pool** take Exit 4 off the Maine Turnpike (Route 95). Follow Route 111 east; turn right onto Route 9 and Route 208. Where Routes 9 and 208 split, continue on Route 208 (to the left) which takes you into Biddeford Pool. Look for the pool and Hattie's Deli on your left. Not only is Hattie's a great place to have a meal (homemade chowder and baked goods), but parking here provides the best access to the pool. This is private property, so please ask at the restaurant for permission to park while you bird. Park on the grass strip to the left of the parking lot so that there is plenty of room for Hattie's customers.

As with most tidal areas, timing is an important factor in seeing the birds of Biddeford Pool. If you can schedule your arrival at the pool three to four hours before high tide, you will be able to bird the pool on the rising tide, explore some of the nearby thickets when the tide is full (and the shorebirds are elsewhere), then return to catch the feeding flocks on the falling tide. The pool tends to fill and empty fairly quickly, so timing is important. From the back of Hattie's Deli walk out across the marsh to the edge of the pool. In late summer butterflies can be an attractive feature of the marsh. Look for large wood nymphs, eastern black swallowtails, and buckeyes. Blooming gerardia and sea-lavender also add their color to the landscape. Typical migrants seen on the flats in August include Black-bellied and Semipalmated plovers, Greater and Lesser yellowlegs, Willet, Whimbrel, Ruddy Turnstone, Semipalmated and Least sandpipers, Dunlin (fall), and Short-billed Dowitcher. Other regular, though less common species, are Solitary Sandpiper, Hudsonian Godwit, Red Knot, Western Sandpiper, White-rumped Sandpiper, Pectoral Sandpiper, Stilt Sandpiper, and Long-billed Dowitcher. Rarities that have been recorded at Biddeford Pool include Marbled Godwit and Baird's Sandpiper. Although you will have to negotiate several ditches, walk along the edge of the marsh to get views of the different areas of the flats and inlets.

Snowy Egret, Black-crowned Night-Heron, and Glossy Ibis nest to the north of Biddeford Pool off Prouts Neck (see Scarborough Marsh map). These species and Great Blue Heron, Great Egret, Little Blue Heron, and Green-backed Heron can, at times, be found feeding around Biddeford Pool.

Before you leave Hattie's check the thickets along the beach access road across from the deli. Continue north from Hattie's going right at the fork; in less than a mile you will reach the corner at Ocean Avenue. Park here for the Maine Audubon Society's **East Point Sanctuary**. In springtime, check the church grounds for migrant warblers. A path, beginning at a chain-link fence, skirts a golf course, continues out around the rocky headland, and ends in a loop path through thickets on the north side of the point. From late August through October this can be an excellent area for passerine migrants. As you walk along above the shoreline check for shorebirds resting on the shingle beach and scope the ocean and offshore rocks for flocks of eiders, cormorants, and gulls. You may find one or two Great Cormorants in with the Double-crested Cormorants; also look for Bonaparte's Gulls and Roseate Terns. Once you reach the thickets the birding possibilities increase. Besides the usual cat-birds, chickadees, goldfinches, and waxwings, a good variety of kinglets, vireos, and warblers are possible during migration. Common migrants include Golden-crowned and Ruby-crowned kinglets, Solitary and Red-eyed vireos, and Northern Parula, Yellow-rumped, Palm, Blackpoll, and Black-and-white warblers. Other warblers, as well as a variety of flycatchers, thrushes, and sparrows, can also be expected. While walking around East Point keep an eye out for hawks. Northern Harriers

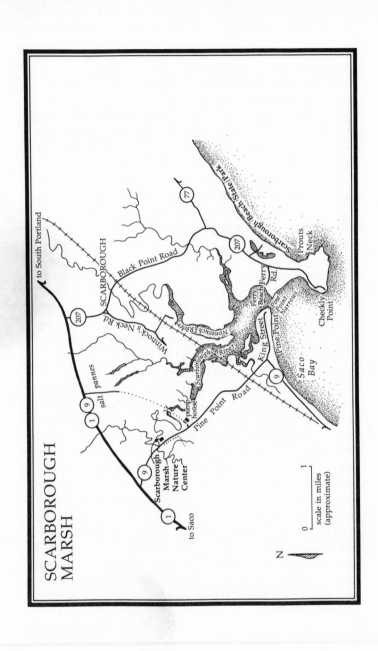

SCARBOROUGH MARSH

to South Portland

SCARBOROUGH

Black Point Road

to Saco

salt pannes

Winnock's Neck Rd

Nonesuch River

Scarborough River

Scarborough Marsh Nature Center

pump house

Pine Point Road

King Street

Pine Point

Ferry Beach

Ferry Rd.

Scarborough Beach State Park

Prouts Neck

Pine Point Narrows

Saco Bay

Checkly Point

N

0   1

scale in miles
(approximate)

are regular migrants; occasionally a Merlin or a Peregrine Falcon is sighted here.

After returning to your car you may want to continue south on Ocean Avenue to South Point. From here you can scan the ocean and Fortunes Rocks Beach for seabirds and shorebirds. Return via Ocean Avenue. Part of the charm of the town of Biddeford Pool is that it has avoided much of the commercialism of nearby Route 1 locales. Its quiet streets, small harbor, and lack of crowds make Biddeford Pool an enjoyable spot in which to spend some time. There are, however, only limited accommodations. Wells, Maine, and the Scarborough area have extensive tourist facilities.

To reach the Scarborough marshes return to Biddeford and take Route 1 north for approximately 6 miles. Turn right onto Pine Point Road (Route 9) and proceed a little less than a mile to the **Scarborough Marsh Nature Center**. The center, open from mid-June through Labor Day (9:30 A.M. to 5:30 P.M.), is run by the Maine Audubon Society in cooperation with the Maine Department of Inland Fisheries and Wildlife. Services offered by the center include educational displays, book sales, scheduled walks, and canoe rentals. Staff members are available to answer questions about the Scarborough marshes.

The Scarborough marshes constitute an extensive (over 3,000 acres) tidal area where five major streams drain into Saco Bay. With each cycle of the tide the living conditions for an extraordinary diversity of plants and animals are defined and redefined. Brackish marsh, salt marsh, mudflats, and sand flats are major components of this rich estuary. The early settlers of Scarborough were well aware of the treasures of the marsh. A town history tells of 14,000 bushels of clams being dug in one winter and of a Scarborough hunter who was said to have killed 42 ducks with only three shots. Fortunately the area has also been appreciated for its beauty. Winslow Homer spent the last 20 years of his life here, and many of the artist's works were inspired by local features of the natural world.

From the bird watcher's point of view, the Scarborough estuary can be divided into the western and eastern sections. Plan to visit both sides of the marsh to get the full picture of the estuary and to explore all the birding spots. The Nature Center provides good access to the points of interest on the western side. Directly across from the center a trail leads along the edge of the marsh, eventually reaching an abandoned road that passes alongside a tidal creek and pools. Check the tidal areas for Greater and Lesser yellowlegs, Least and Semipalmated sandpipers, Short-billed Dowitcher, and Semipalmated Plover. You may also be able to "squeak-up" one or two Sharp-tailed Sparrows from the marsh grasses, and the chances are good that a Belted Kingfisher will be feeding in the area. Check the trees on the south side of the marsh; Snowy Egret, Great Blue Heron, Green-backed Heron, and even Glossy Ibis use these perches.

Another area worth investigating is a short distance along Pine Point Road southeast of the Nature Center. Park next to the pump house and follow the path leading out into the marsh along an abandoned railroad bed. Look for Savannah and Sharp-tailed sparrows in the marsh grasses as well as herons and shorebirds along the banks and flats of the Scarborough River. With luck you may even flush a Least Bittern or an American Bittern. Willet have nested in this section of the marsh, so watch for these flashy shorebirds. Continue across the bridge and follow the path to a point just before it enters the woods. The **salt pannes** east (right) of the path often have an excellent variety of shorebirds; in fall Lesser Golden-Plover, Whimbrel, White-rumped, Pectoral, and Stilt sandpipers, as well as Wilson's Phalarope, are regularly seen here. Also look for Tricolored and Little Blue herons. Although you are liable to see American Black Ducks and Mallards most anytime, the greatest variety of ducks occur in early spring and fall. Maine's fall hunting season (from October through mid-December), however, is not a good time for bird watchers to visit.

Another productive birding area on the western side is **Pine Point Narrows**. The narrows are located 3 miles southeast of the Nature Center. Follow Pine Point Road toward Pine Point and take a left on King Street, which will bring you to a harborside area with parking. The flats of Pine Point Narrows attract a variety of herons, gulls, terns, and shorebirds. Plan to visit this area on a falling or rising tide, not at high tide. During August, Hudsonian Godwits are regular, while Marbled Godwit is occasionally seen. Other shorebird possibilities, besides those mentioned in the Nature Center section, are Black-bellied and Piping plovers, Whimbrel, Sanderling, Dunlin (fall), and White-rumped Sandpiper. Bar-tailed Godwit and American Avocet are two rarities which have occurred at Pine Point Narrows. Least and Common terns can often be seen (through late summer) feeding at the mouth of the harbor.

To reach the eastern section of the Scarborough estuary return to Route 1 and proceed north. In approximately 3 miles turn right on Black Point Road (Route 207). In a little over .5 mile turn right on **Winnock's Neck Road**. Continue on, bearing left at the fork, to a railroad crossing. Check the salt pannes in this area for shorebirds. Besides species already mentioned, Killdeer, Stilt Sandpiper, Solitary Sandpiper, and Pectoral

Sandpiper are to be found here. From here, follow Winnock's Neck Road to its end. This is a tidal area of the Nonesuch River, and the mudflats attract many of the same birds mentioned in the Pine Point Narrows section. Gulls are also a feature of this area. Look for Great Black-backed, Herring, Ring-billed, Bonaparte's, and an occasional Laughing Gull. Return to Black Point Road and continue south; shortly, you will pass through an extensive marsh area. Because it's difficult to see much from the road, you may want to pull off here and look for herons and bitterns.

Continue south on Black Point Road, turning right at the major intersection following Route 207 toward Prouts Neck. Look for Ferry Road on your right. Take Ferry Road to the **Ferry Beach** parking lot (fee in season). This puts you on the eastern side of the Pine Point Narrows at the mouth of the estuary. Go left and walk along the crescent beach, scanning the flats as you go. This is an excellent area for fall shorebirds, with at least one record for Curlew Sandpiper. Bonaparte's Gulls congregate here in good numbers each fall. Throughout the area you will no doubt notice the ongoing development of much of the shorefront. Given the importance of the estuary for innumerable organisms, including resident and migrant bird populations, this type of "progress" may be cause for concern.

Return to Route 207 and continue out Prouts Neck. Although the neck itself is largely residential, with public parking almost nonexistent, a drive out to the road's end at **Checkly Point** can be interesting. The seaward view is best, from a birding point of view, in winter, but is worth checking for terns (Least, Common, Arctic, Roseate, or Forster's) in summer and early fall. If you really want to explore the point, look for a parking spot in the vicinity of the Black Point Inn and hike out. There is even a small bird sanctuary on Prouts Neck. As you head back north on Route 207 look for Scarborough Beach State Park on your right (just past Ferry Road). This is one of Maine's finest sand beaches, and if the weather is warm it may be a good idea to join the crowds rather than fight them. In winter, long after the crowds have departed, specialties such as Harlequin Duck, Barrow's Goldeneye, and King Eider occur here.

Route 1 offers a full range of tourist facilities—from motels and fast food to waterparks and miniature golf. At the height of the tourist season, it is advisable to make reservations. For those wanting to go first class, try the Black Point Inn on Prouts Neck. This venerable establishment proclaims ". . . unpretentious elegance, recognized the world over." For elegance of a different sort, try Bailey's Pine Point Resort in West Scarborough. This is a campground with a difference: swimming pools, saunas, video and game rooms, and more. Actually it's great for the kids and convenient to the Scarborough Marsh Nature Center (just north of Bailey's). For those inclined toward less elegant or less stimulating accommodations, a little exploring should turn up a quiet inn with a comfortable bed.

Moosehorn National Wildlife Refuge (Baring Unit): Calais
nesting woodcock, warblers, waterfowl, boreal species

Machias: Machias
summer-resident passerines and seabirds

Deblois Barrens: Cherryfield
nesting Upland Sandpiper, Whip-poor-will, Vesper Sparrow

Rangeley Lakes Region: Appalachian Trail: Rangeley
summer-resident passerines including boreal specialties

Belgrade and Messalonskee Lakes: Belgrade Lakes
summer-resident waterfowl and passerines

Kennebunk Plains: Route 99 West Kennebunk
summer-resident passerines

SEE:

–*A Birder's Guide to the Coast of Maine.* 1981. Elizabeth and Jan
   Pierson. Down East Books.

–*Enjoying Maine Birds.* 1985. Maine Audubon Society.

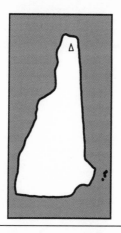

NEW HAMPSHIRE

Pittsburg and the Connecticut Lakes

SUMMER

EVEN TO THOSE WELL TRAVELED IN NEW EN-
gland, the Connecticut Lakes region of New Hampshire
is a surprise. As one proceeds from Colebrook along
Route 3, a sign on the west side of the road marks the
location of the 45th parallel of latitude. From this point
northward, the traveler is closer to the North Pole than
to the Equator, and although visitors to the region will
not encounter glaciers or polar bears, the passage across
the 45th sets the stage for a North Country experience.

This section of New Hampshire is bordered to the
south by the prominent peaks of the White Mountains,
to the west by Vermont, to the east by Maine, and to

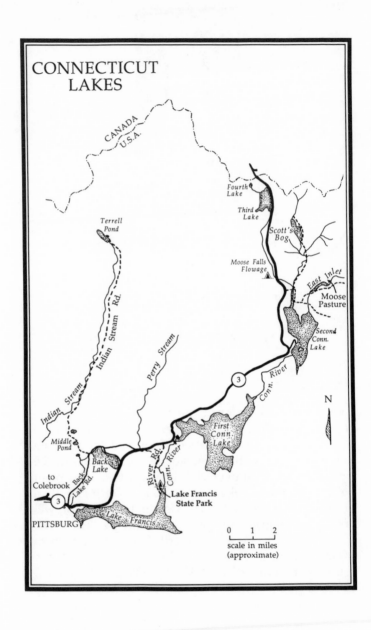

CONNECTICUT LAKES

the north by Quebec. There is no better way to get an overview of the North Country than by driving the 26 miles from the southern edge of the town of Pittsburg to the Canadian frontier. This section of Route 3 passes at first through the relatively flat river bottom with its attendant fields, meadows, and pastures, and then up and down a series of hills and vales. Gradually, as one travels northward, the ups and the downs become more frequent and the broader valley sections decrease. Although it is not particularly noticeable, there is a gradual increase in altitude as you work your way toward Canada. The village of Pittsburg is 1,300 feet above sea level, while the altitude at the border is 1,000 feet higher. One striking change along this route is the decreasing amount of apparent human activity. While Pittsburg has all the familiar sights and sounds of rural New England, variety stores and gas pumps, lodging facilities and boat rentals, trinket stores and bait shops gradually thin out to the north. By the time one passes the upper reaches of First Connecticut Lake, civilization is largely left behind. Here one can begin to develop a feeling for the wilderness of the North Country.

The landscape of the undeveloped areas is dominated by woodlands and water. The two major components of the woodlands are the fir–spruce stands and the northern hardwoods. Because most of this area's timber has been cut at least once, these woodlands are in various stages of succession. The more recently cut "slash" areas contain a mixture of shrubs as well as pioneering species such as aspen and birch. In other cut-over areas conifers have begun a comeback. Mature stands of maple, beech, and birch also occupy sizable areas. While balsam fir, white spruce, and red spruce often constitute the densest forest, recently there has been a significant amount of damage to portions of these woodlands by spruce budworms.

The original course of the Connecticut River through the North Country has been modified by dams and impoundments created to control and utilize the river's water. The major lakes include Lake Francis just east of Pittsburg village and the three Connecticut lakes lying northward to the border. Back Lake, Perry Stream, and Indian Stream, as well as numerous other watercourses, all form part of the local Connecticut River drainage. Willows and alders are common shrubs along the shores of the various streams and ponds, while black spruce and tamarack occur in the bogs. Small stands of arbor vitae occur in some swamps.

This varied landscape provides ideal habitats for many of New England's most interesting bird species. The bird finder will do well to sample various locales. A majority of the habitats are accessible by car and foot, although a canoe will be useful in certain areas.

Like the white admiral and tiger swallowtail butterflies that constantly flutter past, American Robins and Cedar Waxwings seem nearly ubiquitous in the North Country. It is, however, the less-common permanent and summer residents that will be of most interest to the bird seeker. Highlights of the area are Common Loon, Common Merganser, Spruce Grouse, Common Snipe, Northern Saw-whet Owl, Yellow-bellied Sapsucker, Black-backed Woodpecker, Olive-sided Flycatcher, Yellow-bellied Flycatcher, Gray Jay, Common Raven, Boreal Chickadee, Ruby-crowned Kinglet, and Philadelphia Vireo. Warbler species include Tennessee (irregular), Cape May (irregular), Bay-breasted, Blackpoll, Mourning, and Wilson's. Other specialties are Lincoln's Sparrow, Rusty Blackbird, and Red and White-winged crossbills (erratic). The bird watcher should bear in mind that while some of these species are fairly common, others are uncommon, irregular, or rare, and that more than persistence and good luck may be necessary to complete the list. A mid-June visit should improve your chances of seeing or hearing the various summer residents.

Heading east along Route 3 out of the village of Pittsburg one soon comes to the **Lake Francis** boat ramp on the right. Pull in here and scan the lake for loons and other waterbirds. If you haven't already applied a good dose of insect repellent, do it now. The blackfly populations are vigorous through June, and mosquitoes follow in their wake. An even better area from which to look for ducks and loons is at the boat-launch site on **First Connecticut Lake**. Also, the park and picnic area here usually harbor a pair or two of sapsuckers, and you may find a Spotted Sandpiper teetering along the shore. Directly across Route 3 from First Lake dam look for a Cliff Swallow colony under the eaves of a white building. The road between First Connecticut Lake and Second Connecticut Lake provides many opportunities to stop and sample a variety of habitats. The birder will soon become aware that the song of the White-throated Sparrow is the refrain of the North Country. Two members of the thrush family, Swainson's Thrush and Veery, are also frequent singers in the chorus.

A word about birdsong. A familiarity with the songs and the calls of the local birds is particularly helpful in the North Country, a heavily wooded area. You are bound to hear many more birds than you will see, and knowing the vocalizations will help you to track down unusual or uncommon species.

The section between First Connecticut Lake and Second Connecticut Lake should also get you started on your warbler list. Common species in the area include American Redstart, Nashville Warbler, Northern Parula, Yellow-rumped Warbler, and Common Yellowthroat. In areas with conifers look and listen for Black-throated Green, Magnolia, and Blackburnian warblers. Check any slow-moving or stagnant wetlands for Northern Waterthrush. The boat-launch area at Second Lake provides another opportunity to look for waterbirds.

Perhaps the best birding habitat on **Route 3** occurs **between Second Connecticut Lake and Third Connecticut Lake**. This area is less developed than the southern portion and is, on average, at a higher altitude. Check the slash area just south of Moose Falls campgrounds for Least Flycatcher, Mourning Warbler, and Lincoln's Sparrow. A little farther north, the boat launch for the **Moose Falls Flowage** offers a good place to look for waterbirds. Check the conifers around the shore for Blackpoll Warbler and Dark-eyed Junco. The rare Cape May Warbler has also been recorded in this area, but as with the Tennessee Warbler, numbers fluctuate from year to year. You may turn up one or two of the boreal species here, with Gray Jay and Boreal Chickadee both distinct possibilities. As you drive north to the border you will find other roadside areas worth investigating. Pay particular attention to the slash areas and spruce flats.

Although there are many excellent birding opportunities along Route 3, the birder should also explore at least a few of the many side roads in this region. While a majority of these local roads are unpaved, the gravel and dirt surfaces are normally in good condition. Caution should be exercised after periods of heavy rain and during the early-spring mud season. The **East Inlet Road** and the **Moose Pasture** (a bog) are often mentioned by experienced North Country birders as being among the finest areas in the entire region. Three miles north of the Second Connecticut Lake boat ramp an unmarked road leaves Route 3 to the east. This is the road to East Inlet, and it crosses a bridge in .3 mile (distances given are from Route 3). Turn right after crossing the bridge and proceed to the 1.3-mile point, where the road forks. Bear left and continue to the 1.9-mile point, where there is a bridge and dam with the East Inlet pond on the north side of the road. The Moose Pasture can be reached by canoe from this point (at the north side of the pond). In 1951 when conservation officer Fred Scott introduced Tudor Richards to this area, East Inlet and the Moose Pasture held more than one ornithological surprise. Scott and Richards recorded such nesting species as Black-backed Woodpecker (formerly Black-backed Three-toed Woodpecker), Ruby-crowned Kinglet, and Lincoln's Sparrow. Top honors, however, went to the nesting Three-toed Woodpecker (formerly Northern Three-toed Woodpecker). Add to these rarities the regular occurrence of Spruce Grouse, Gray Jay, and Common Raven, and it is easy to see why this area is often frequented by birders. Wood Duck, Hooded Merganser, and Ring-necked Duck also nest in the East Inlet vicinity.

You don't have to reach the dam at East Inlet to begin your quest. A slash area opposite the first bridge (.3-mile point) has nesting Wilson's Warbler, Lincoln's Sparrow, and Rusty Blackbird. Frequent stops between first bridge and East Inlet are recommended. Check the dense conifer stands for Yellow-bellied Flycatcher and Boreal Chickadee and the dead spruces and birches for woodpeckers. You might also want to try the **Scott's Bog Road** (left at the .3-mile bridge). Although less well groomed than the East Inlet fork, the road provides access to some choice habitat.

Another side road worth investigating is **River Road**. This takes you the 2 miles from Route 3 to Lake Francis State Park. Slash areas along the road provide nesting territories for Chestnut-sided Warbler and Field Sparrow. Halfway to the campgrounds you will come to a covered bridge. This riparian habitat, where Perry Stream flows into the Connecticut River, is a favored area for anglers. It is also a good spot to look for flycatchers, including Least, Alder, Eastern Phoebe, and Eastern Kingbird. Also check the conifers for warblers. In and around the campground proper you should find sapsuckers, kinglets, Red-breasted Nuthatch, a good selection of warblers, and a Ruby-throated Hummingbird or two. The view of Lake Francis affords the opportunity to look for Common Loon and Common Merganser as well as a panorama of the sky to look for hawks. Osprey and Broad-winged Hawk are seen from here fairly regularly.

At the northern edge of the village of Pittsburg (across from the Trading Post), **Back Lake Road** leaves Route 3 in a northerly direction. At approximately 2.5 miles an unmarked dirt road leaves Back Lake Road to the left (west). You will notice this road soon after Back Lake comes into view on the right. The initial section of the road passes through a stand of northern hardwoods and is good habitat for Red-eyed Vireo, Rose-breasted Grosbeak, and Ovenbird. In .5 mile a private road to the left leads down through a community of cabins and campsites. The conifers in the mixed-forest areas are good locations for Olive-sided Flycatcher, Solitary Vireo, and various warbler species. After leaving this area turn left, continuing on the main dirt road (.3 mile) to Middle Pond. Check here for nesting ducks. This road continues north and intersects with Indian Stream Road in approximately 1 mile. For the adventuresome, **Indian Stream Road** continues north for some

10 miles toward Terrell Pond and passes through much good habitat along the way. There are, in fact, numerous other side roads to explore. A Roads and Trails map for the Connecticut Lakes Region is available and can be purchased at the Pittsburg general store.

Two nonbirding activities are recommended for the visiting naturalist. Five miles north of River Road on Route 3, between First Connecticut Lake and Second Connecticut Lake, you can join the moose watch. One or more moose are often browsing in this area. This largest member of the deer family is fairly common in the North Country. An ungainly, Dr. Seuss-like character, with a hump on its shoulders and a bell hanging from its throat, the moose is a fascinating animal to watch and appreciate. Besides man, the only predator of the North Country that might take on a moose is a black bear, and a trip to the Pittsburg town dump (Back Lake Road from the Trading Post, on the left before Back Lake) during the evening hours may turn up a black bear or two. Unfortunately, the privilege of seeing these magnificent animals may be ended by the behavior of thoughtless humans. Bears are not circus animals, but rather wild and potentially dangerous mammals. Black bears, and indeed moose, need to be afforded respect and distance.

The North Country is not a fancy place. Most visitors come here to fish or enjoy nature and are satisfied with simple, basic services. There are many lodging and camping facilities in Pittsburg; Northern Trails Motel has comfortable accommodations, and Lake Francis State Park has attractive campsites. The Family Restaurant offers good, basic food; their breakfast and coffee are excellent. For slightly more commodious treatment you might want to try The Glenn on First Connecticut Lake. Reservations are suggested.

Route 145 between Pittsburg and Colebrook is an

attractive alternative to Route 3. The road reaches 2,000 feet, has views of a beautiful waterfall, and passes a few good cedar swamps. For those who can't get enough of the North Country, there is an entire wilderness to explore in the Lake Umbagog region of the Rangeley Lakes. Route 26 east from Colebrook will take you to Errol, a good starting point for your investigations. A canoe and bushwacking experience will be most helpful at Umbagog, where the waterbirds excel those in the Pittsburg area. See also the chapters on Island Pond in Vermont and Baxter State Park in Maine.

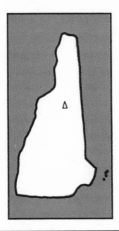

White Mountains and Pinkham Notch

SUMMER

> On the mountains, especially at Tuckerman's Ravine, the notes even of familiar birds sounded strange to me. I hardly knew the wood thrush and veery and ovenbird at first. They sing differently there.
>
> H. D. THOREAU
> JULY 16, 1858

IT IS PERHAPS NOT SURPRISING THAT THO-reau, a native of the Massachusetts flatlands, was confused by the birdsong he heard in the White Mountains. Because of their relatively great height and the attendant variation in climate, the mountains provide a wide

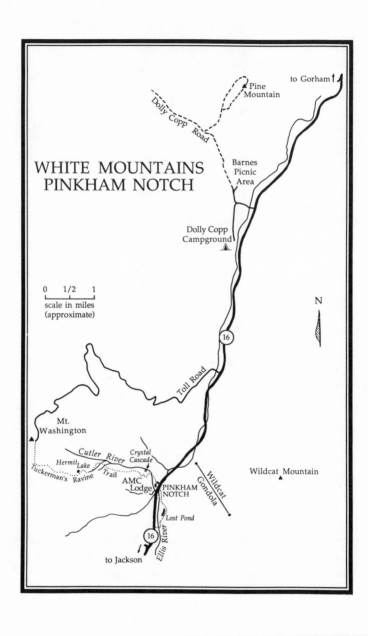

range of habitats. Each of these habitats has a fairly distinct avifauna and thus offers the birder a sometimes confusing diversity of bird life. From the valley floors to the 2,000-foot altitude, a deciduous forest, consisting mainly of the northern hardwoods, dominates the landscape. Between 2,500 and 4,500 feet, coniferous stands of fir and spruce are the predominant plants. Above the 4,000- to 5,000-foot range to the peaks of the summits the arctic-alpine habitat supports only low-growing shrubs and herbaceous plants. In between these three major habitats are two other ecological zones. Between the northern hardwoods and the fir–spruce levels lies a mixed forest composed of yellow birch and conifers. Between the spruce–fir forest and the arctic–alpine tundra lies an area of stunted dwarf conifers referred to as the "Krummholz." Scattered patches of Krummholz are also found in the tundra zone, nearly to the peak of some mountains. Because of variations in exposure (especially north-south orientation), slope, light, and moisture, these five zones occur not in strict altitudinal layers, but rather as a series of broad parallel brush strokes alternatively falling and rising as they spread across the face of the mountains. The summer bird life of the White Mountains can be roughly defined within each of these zones. By looking at selected members of the thrush family we see some representative examples of the relationships between habitat and distribution in the mountains.

In general the Wood Thrush and Veery are residents of the lower deciduous forest; Swainson's Thrush inhabits the mountainside coniferous zone, and Gray-cheeked Thrush nests close to the tree line. In a perfect, though much duller, world we might proceed to a certain altitude and await a specific thrush. In reality several factors, including the mobility of the birds themselves, and the sizable areas of habitat overlap, make our quest for the thrushes somewhat more interesting. An awareness of the habitat affinities of the local bird life will, however, help to sort out the various species. In hindsight the thrushes Thoreau heard in Tuckerman's Ravine, at timberline, sounded different because they were different. His veery and woodthrush were, most probably, Gray-cheeked Thrush and Swainson's Thrush.

There are many birding possibilities in the White Mountains, with dozens of peaks over 4,000 feet. A good way to start, however, is to follow in Thoreau's footsteps with a visit to Mt. Washington, and the Appalachian Mountain Club (AMC) facilities at **Pinkham Notch** provide an ideal home base for the White Mountain bird seeker. The lodge, at 2,000 feet above sea level, is in the area of transition between the deciduous hardwoods and the fir–spruce zone. Here, without having to go very far, the birder will find species from several habitats. Right around the parking lot you will find birds associated with northern hardwoods, including American Crow, Red-eyed Vireo, Black-throated Green Warbler, American Redstart, and Rose-breasted Grosbeak. Also here, besides the Barn Swallows that seem constantly overhead, are summer-resident Ruby-throated Hummingbird, Cedar Waxwing, and American Goldfinch.

A convenient way to begin a more general exploration of the area is to take a leisurely walk along the **Lost Pond Trail**. This trail, actually a short section of the famed Maine-to-Georgia Appalachian Trail, begins directly across Route 16 from the AMC headquarters. The initial section of the trail crosses a wet meadow and the Ellis River. Besides being home to the resident beaver, the area harbors nesting Least Flycatcher, Eastern Kingbird, and Chestnut-sided Warbler. The trail turns south as it enters the woods and soon reaches the junction of the Ellis and Cutler rivers. The 15-minute (.5-mile) walk to Lost Pond takes you along a path lined with trillium, bunchberry, mountain wood sorrel, hobble-bush, striped maple, yellow birch, beech, and balsam fir. The pond itself is rimmed with conifers and massive blocks of granite. Look for Red-breasted Nuthatch, Purple Finch, and Solitary Vireo in the trees bordering Lost Pond. Philadelphia Vireo have also been reported from this area. The easiest way back to the AMC camp is to retrace your steps. The trail continues past the pond, however, and soon joins Wildcat Ridge Trail, which comes out on Route 16 (.1 mile from the juncture). It is then possible to walk back along the highway or make a loop to the lodge using several other trails.

A word about hiking trails in the White Mountains. Although most trails are well marked, hikers should not start out without knowing where they are headed and what route they plan to follow. A trail guide is essential (available at AMC headquarters), and a compass advisable. This is not a place to wander. The AMC's suggestions for proper clothing, food, and provisions (posted at headquarters) should be heeded. The peaks can be dangerous in bad weather, even in summer.

One area of deciduous woodlands that has good access and offers an easy hike is the trail to **Pine Mountain**. To reach this area drive north from the AMC headquarters toward Gorham for approximately 6.5 miles. Enter the road to the Dolly Copp campground (*not* the picnic area). Continue for 1.9 miles to the trailhead, bearing left at the Barnes Picnic Area. You will find a place to leave your car on the left and a trail sign on

the right. The trail to Pine Mountain is a wide dirt road maintained by the Horton Center, a private organization which has a shelter and chapel at the summit. The beginning of the trail is 1,600 feet above sea level, while the altitude at the summit is 2,400 feet. Distance to the summit is 1.6 miles, and the round trip takes approximately two hours (not including time out for birding and a picnic). Pine Mountain Trail passes through a forest of typical northern hardwoods: beech, birch, and maple; and because of clearing operations at various spots the hiker will find both slash areas and mature woodlands. Birds to look for along the trail include Ruffed Grouse, Eastern Wood-Pewee, Black-capped Chickadee, Wood Thrush, Black-throated Blue Warbler, Ovenbird, and Scarlet Tanager. In the slash areas check for Chestnut-sided Warbler, Nashville Warbler, Common Yellowthroat, and Dark-eyed Junco. A northern specialty you may find in the cut-over areas is the Mourning Warbler. The view at the summit offers fine looks along the Androscoggin, Moose, and Peabody rivers. Check the skies here for resident Broad-winged Hawks and perhaps a soaring Common Raven. The Ledge Trail is an alternate route leading back from the summit to the main trail, but contains difficult sections. The easiest way back to your car is to return along the Pine Mountain trail.

Another trail you should consider is the **Tuckerman's Ravine Trail**, which leads to the summit of Mt. Washington (6,288 feet). This trail begins at AMC headquarters and passes through northern hardwoods, fir–spruce habitat, Krummholz, and tundra as it winds its way 4 miles to the highest peak in the Presidential Range. Although one guide book characterizes Tuckerman's Ravine Trail as "the shortest plus the easiest ascent of the mountain," you will need to be in excellent physical shape and knowledgeable about mountain trekking to make the entire 4.5-hour hike. For less-ambitious bird seekers, a hike along the beginning section of the trail is a good option. Whatever portion of Tuckerman's you plan to do, check on weather conditions at AMC head-quarters and follow their advice regarding provisions to take along. A relatively easy hike will take you up to First Bridge which crosses the Cutler River. On your way you pass through mixed deciduous and coniferous forest. Summer-resident birds along this portion of the trail include Downy and Hairy woodpeckers, Winter Wren, American Redstart, Black-throated Green Warbler, Blackburnian Warbler, Pine Siskin, Brown Creeper, and Swainson's Thrush. A few steep yards past the bridge will take you to Crystal Cascade, a picturesque waterfall and an ideal spot to enjoy a picnic lunch. For the inveterate hiker, the trail continues west (and up!) for 2 miles to the Hermit Lake Camping Shelter at the 3,800-foot level. Along this route, and particularly in the Hermit Lake area, are dense stands of conifers. Here the bird seeker has a good chance of finding several species of northern affinity. Possibilities include Yellow-bellied Flycatcher, Olive-sided Flycatcher, Boreal Chickadee, Ruby-crowned Kinglet, Gray-cheeked Thrush, and Rusty Blackbird. Also be on the lookout for Spruce Grouse and Black-backed Woodpecker. From Hermit Lake, Tuckerman's ascends into the ravine itself on the way to the summit. Above timberline the bird life becomes sparse, with only Dark-eyed Junco, White-throated Sparrow, and Common Ravens being regularly recorded in the arctic–alpine zone. The possibilities for unusual plants, however, increase on the tundra. Such delicate alpine species as diapensia, alpine azalea, and Lapland rosebay await the visitor to the summit gardens.

There are alternatives to hiking the Tuckerman's Ravine Trail which also get the bird finder to timberline and above. The 8-mile **Mt. Washington Toll Road** is easier on your legs but harder on your car. The road leaves Route 16 north of AMC headquarters (c. 3 miles). The road surface is good, with alternating sections of pavement and gravel, but has enough steep grades to warrant taking an automobile in good mechanical condition. The road ascends the mountain through all the major habitats and has convenient pull-offs (particularly in the wooded sections). The diversity of mountain bird life that can be seen along this road ranges from the Bobolinks that nest in the meadow at the foot of the toll road to the Common Ravens that frequent the summit. When you arrive above the 2,000-foot level take advantage of all the rest stops. In mixed forest and fir–spruce areas you can begin looking for the species mentioned in the Tuckerman's section. Other possibilities include Winter Wren, Golden-crowned Kinglet, Northern Parula, Bay-breasted, Magnolia, Black-throated Blue, and Blackpoll warblers, and Red and White-winged crossbills (erratic). Rarities of this area are Three-toed Woodpecker and Gray Jay. Still another way to join the ravens is to take the gondola (fee) up Wildcat Mountain (just north of AMC headquarters on Route 16).

Certainly the most convenient lodging for the Mt. Washington area is the AMC facility at Pinkham Notch. Simple, yet comfortable, rooms and hearty family-style meals are available here. More importantly, you will find that an atmosphere of "sympatico" exists between hikers and bird watchers. Evening programs, a resident naturalist, and book sales are all part of the Pinkham AMC program. The "Croo" will even pack a generous trail lunch to keep you going during the day. This is a great place to stay, but call ahead (603-466-2727) to make reservations. The Dolly Copp Campground is a spacious facility with both wooded and meadow sites. It is also convenient to the Pine Mountain Trail. If mountain fever strikes, Gorham and Jackson are close by, ready and waiting to satisfy your more commercial needs. For the kids, the Attatash Water Slide to the south on Route 302 should be attractive.

Other areas in the White Mountains worth exploring for their bird life include Dixville Notch (1,871 feet, on Route 26), Franconia Notch (1,896 feet, on Route 3), Crawford Notch State Park (Route 302), the Kangamagus Highway (to 2,800 feet) between Conway and Lincoln, and Lost River Reservation (Route 112).

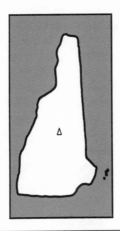

Squam Lake and Vicinity

SPRING / SUMMER / FALL

THE LAKES REGION OF CENTRAL NEW HAMP-
shire, once a sparsely populated farming region, has
seen significant development in the last three decades.
The shores of Lake Winnipesaukee have suffered most
of these "improvements." At present, upscale devel-
opments are replacing rural cottage communities. The
once quiet coves and wooded shoreline along much of
the lake's perimeter are gradually disappearing. Fortunately there are still a few places where the peaceful
solitude is as likely to be interrupted by the cry of a
loon as it is by the sound of human activity. Squam
Lake, northwest of Winnipesaukee, is an ideal place to
enjoy the natural features of the Lakes Region. Besides
nesting loons, a variety of migrant and summer-resident

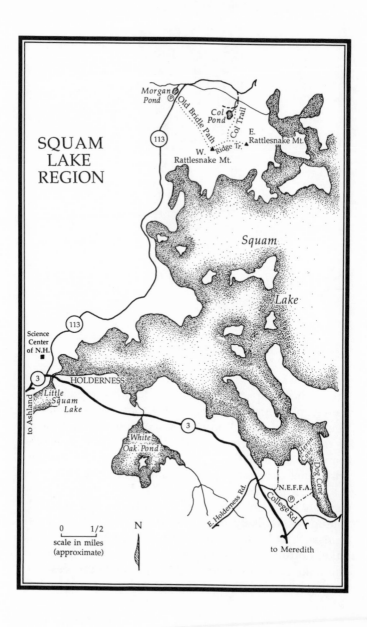

SQUAM
LAKE
REGION

Morgan Pond

Col Pond

Old Bridle Path

Col Trail

E. Rattlesnake Mt.

W. Rattlesnake Mt.

Ridge Tr.

113

Squam

Lake

113

Science Center of N.H.

3

HOLDERNESS

to Ashland

Little Squam Lake

White Oak Pond

3

Heron Cove

Dog Cove

N.E.F.F.A.

E. Holderness Rd.

College Rd.

to Meredith

0   1/2
scale in miles
(approximate)

N

waterfowl, flycatchers, thrushes, and wood-warblers make this region an interesting one for the bird watcher.

The locales in this account are easily reached via Route 93 in New Hampshire. On your way north, a visit to the **Audubon Society of New Hampshire** (ASNH) headquarters in Concord is recommended. To reach the headquarters exit Route 93 onto Route 89; take the first exit (Bow) and go left on South Street toward Concord. In .75 mile go left on Iron Works Road, and follow this 1 mile to the intersection with Clinton Street. Go left on Clinton under Route 89. Take the first right onto Silk Farm Road and look for the Audubon Society of New Hampshire sign. This facility houses an extensive library as well as several displays and a shop with a good selection of books, records, maps, and check lists which visiting naturalists will find useful. You may also want to spend some time investigating the woodlands and Turkey Pond in the immediate vicinity.

Return to Route 93 and proceed north to Exit 24 (Ashland and Holderness). Take Route 3 through Holderness. In 3.9 miles from the intersection of Routes 3 and 113 in Holderness, go left on an unmarked road, and in .4 mile park adjacent to the sign for the Chamberlain–Reynolds Memorial Forest. This **New England Forestry Foundation Area** (N.E.F.F.A.) property is a good place to begin your explorations of the birds of the Lakes Region. A network of trails pass through northern hardwoods, old meadow, red pines, hemlock groves, and alder–willow swamp. Maps and trail signs are posted at various locales about the property. One route which samples the major habitats follows the woodland road (Middle Fire Road) from the parking area to a small, second-growth clearing. From here bear left (north) to Middle Meadow Trail. Follow this (stay left at fork where Swamp Fire Road branches right) to a brook. Before

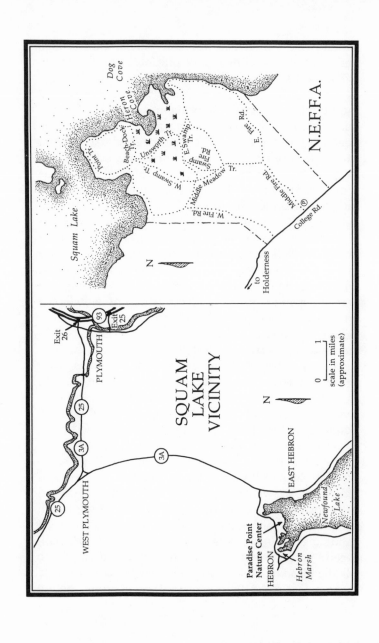

crossing the brook, turn right onto East Swamp Trail. This skirts the southern edge of the swamp and leads to the Unsworth Nature Trail, a boardwalk which crosses the swamp. Beach–Dock Trail and Point Trail go around the point and return to the Unsworth Nature Trail. Return along the boardwalk and take the Swamp Fire Road or Middle Fire Road (see map posted at start of Unsworth Trail) back to the clearing.

The N.E.F.F.A. forest contains fine stands of yellow birch, maple, and mature hemlock. Hobblebush is a typical shrub of the understory, and there is some striped maple. Common woodland residents are Black-capped Chickadee, Red-breasted Nuthatch, Veery, Hermit Thrush, Scarlet Tanager, Ovenbird, and White-throated Sparrow. Other, less-common nesting species include Broad-winged Hawk, Ruffed Grouse, Pileated Woodpecker, and Winter Wren. Red-eyed and Solitary vireos and Black-throated Blue, Yellow-rumped, Black-throated Green, Blackburnian, and Pine warblers can also be seen and/or heard in the hardwoods or hemlocks. Check the woodland perimeters of the swamp for Magnolia and Canada warblers. Once you're on the boardwalk look and listen for Alder and Willow flycatchers, Warbling Vireo, Yellow Warbler, Red-winged Blackbird, and Swamp Sparrow. With luck you may even come across a Virginia Rail, a sporadic summer resident.

Heron Cove, on the northeast side of the N.E.F.F.A. property, often has a pair of summer-resident Common Loons. In 1986 the Heron Cove loons were one of 12 pairs that nested on Squam Lake. The many sheltered coves, islands, and inlets on Squam provide ideal nesting habitat for this magnificent species. In fact, Squam Lake normally has as many nesting pairs of loons as the much larger Lake Winnipesaukee. Other waterbirds you may see on Dog Cove include Great Blue Heron, American Black Duck, Mallard, and Wood Duck.

During migratory periods a variety of flycatchers, warblers, and sparrows pass through the woodlands and marsh. From mid-April through May and again from mid-August through October the procession includes Olive-sided and Yellow-bellied flycatchers, both kinglets, Philadelphia Vireo, Cape May, Bay-breasted, and Blackpoll warblers, Lincoln's and White-crowned sparrows, and Rusty Blackbird.

Return to Holderness and go right (north) on Route 113. Shortly, on your left, you will see the entrance for the **Science Center of New Hampshire**. The center has a variety of live-animal exhibits, including white-tailed deer, bobcat, and black bear as well as a trail system designed to instruct visitors about New Hampshire's natural communities. During the summer (July and August) various talks and workshops for children and adults are scheduled. The SCNH is open daily 9:30 A.M. to 4:30 P.M. from May through October. Weekend hours in the spring and fall are 1:00 to 4:00.

Continue north on Route 113 a little less than 5.5 miles to the parking lot for Mt. Morgan and **West Rattlesnake Mountain**. The trail up West Rattlesnake (1,243 feet) passes through fine deciduous woodlands with a good representation of local breeding birds. Before you start your hike, bird the area around the parking lot and walk to Morgan Pond. Eastern Wood-Pewee, Least Flycatcher, Red-eyed Vireo, and Black-and-white Warbler can be found in the woods bordering the parking area. To reach the pond follow the short path at the back of the parking lot (not the main Mt. Morgan trail) or walk east on Route 113. Morgan Pond is currently inhabited by a family of beavers. White pines and deciduous woodlands encircle this delightful pond where resident American Black Duck, Alder Flycatcher, and Chestnut-sided Warbler occur. You may also see or hear Yellow-throated or Warbling vireos here.

Cross Route 113 to the trailhead for Old Bridle Path which ascends West Rattlesnake Mountain. A leisurely round-trip hike to the summit of West Rattlesnake takes about one hour and provides good birds and excellent scenery. If you wish, you can make a half-day outing of the hike by extending your route along the Ridge Trail and the Col Trail, as described below. Typical woodland residents along Old Bridle Path include Great Crested Flycatcher, Hermit Thrush, and Rose-breasted Grosbeak. Perhaps the most common vocalization you will hear as you ascend the mountain is the song of the Ovenbird. Other warblers to listen and watch for are Black-throated Blue, Northern Parula, Yellow-rumped, and Pine. Plan to take some time at the summit, reached by a short spur trail to the right, to rest on the granite outcroppings and enjoy the view of Squam Lake and the surrounding countryside. If you choose, you can continue along the Ridge Trail toward East Rattlesnake Mountain. Descend on the Col Trail (go left, north) to the Col Pond area and walk out the dirt road to Route 113. Go left (southwest) on 113 to return to the parking lot. Those birders taking the shorter hike and wishing to bird the Col Pond area can drive north on 113 (.9 mile) and go right down a dirt road which soon crosses a stream over a wood-plank bridge. The Col Pond vicinity can be particularly active during the fall migration. Beverly Ridgely, one of Squam Lake's birding authorities, reports resident Northern Goshawk and Barred Owl as well as sightings of porcupine and moose from the Col Pond area. Birders visiting this area would do well to obtain a copy of Ridgely's *Birds of the Squam Lakes Region*. This volume (1987, revised) is an excellent local reference of use not only to birders, but hikers as well (available from Squam Lakes Association, P.O. Box 204, Holderness, New Hampshire 03245).

Return to Route 93 via Holderness and Ashland. Proceed north to Exit 26 and go west on Routes 3A and 25 toward West Plymouth. Turn south (left) on Route 3A. In just under 6 miles go right on the road to Hebron. Look for the entrance to **Paradise Point Nature Center** (PPNC) on the left in 1 mile. This 43-acre Audubon Society of New Hampshire property is on the north shore of Newfound Lake. The nature center (open June 28 to September 1), library, and self-guiding trails are maintained by ASNH for public use.

Paradise Point consists mainly of mature hemlock forest with scattered stands of red spruce and northern hardwoods. Because of the preponderance of forest cover, summer-resident woodland birds are a feature. As might be expected, a variety of woodpeckers can be found here. Yellow-bellied Sapsucker as well as Downy, Hairy, and Pileated woodpeckers are seen regularly. Nesting warblers include Black-throated Blue, Black-throated Green, Blackburnian, Black-and-white, and American Redstart.

Birders looking for species associated with more northerly latitudes may find Winter Wren, Golden-crowned Kinglet, Swainson's Thrush, or Dark-eyed Junco while walking the trails. Even the diminutive Northern Saw-whet Owl has been found at Paradise Point in summer.

Other summer residents to look for are Red-breasted Nuthatch, Brown Creeper, Hermit Thrush, Red-eyed Vireo, Ovenbird, White-throated Sparrow, and Purple Finch. Take time to walk along the shore of Newfound Lake. While Common Loon and Common Merganser have both nested here in the past, their occurrence is now irregular.

If the nature center is open on the day you visit, stop to inquire about recent bird sightings. Booklets for each of the five self-guiding trails are available. Those birders planning an extended stay in the area may want to take advantage of educational programs for adults and/or the day camp for children. Contact:

Paradise Point Nature Center
North Shore Road
East Hebron, New Hampshire 03232
603-744-3516
(May 1–August 31)

Approximately 1 mile west of PPNC is the **Hebron Marsh**, another property of the Audubon Society of New Hampshire. Go left onto a dirt road just before reaching Hebron village and park near the Hebron Marsh sign. A path crosses the field to a trail leading to an observation tower overlooking the marsh. This is a good spot for waterbirds, especially during migration. In summer look for Great Blue Heron, Wood Duck, and Belted Kingfisher.

Birders touring the Squam Lakes Region will find motels, cottages, and camping facilities along Route 3 between Ashland and Holderness.

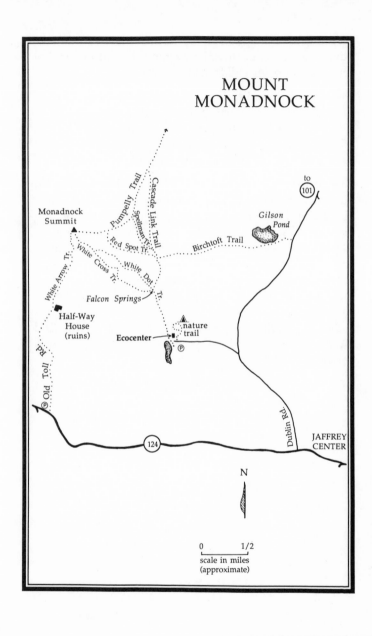

MOUNT MONADNOCK

to 101

Gilson Pond

Monadnock Summit

Pumpelly Trail

Cascade Link Trail

Spellman Tr.

Red Spot Tr.

Birchtoft Trail

White Arrow Tr.

White Cross Tr.

White Dot Tr.

Falcon Springs

Half-Way House (ruins)

nature trail

Ecocenter

Old Toll Rd.

Dublin Rd.

JAFFREY CENTER

124

N

0   1/2
scale in miles
(approximate)

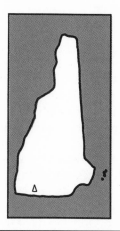

Mount Monadnock

SUMMER

Mт. MONADNOCK, IN SOUTHERN NEW HAMP-
shire, is a New England landmark. The mountain itself
dominates the regional landscape, while the view from
the summit (3,165 feet) encompasses much that is typically New England. For the past century and a half,
Monadnock has been a perennial stop for New England
naturalists. The bird life there has received the special
attention of a succession of individuals from Thomas
Nuttall in the 1820s to Elliot and Kathleen Allison in
the 1980s. While wetlands, meadows, and second-growth
woodlands around the base of the mountain host the
typical mix of summer residents, the northern hardwoods on the lower slopes and the spruce–scrub cover
on the mid- to upper slopes harbor a variety of breeding

birds that are normally uncommon or absent this far south. An early-summer visit to Mt. Monadnock offers the possibility of seeing a good representation of New England's inland bird life.

From Nashua, New Hampshire, go west on routes 101A and 101 to Peterborough and then follow Route 202 south to Jaffrey. From Jaffrey take Route 124 to Jaffrey Center and follow signs to Monadnock State Park (fee). No pets are allowed in the park. Because Monadnock is readily accessible from a number of urban centers, the park and trails are often crowded. It has been estimated that over 100,000 people climb the mountain each year. Only Japan's Mt. Fuji attracts more climbers. The foliage season, from mid-September through October, draws the largest crowds, although any fine weekend from spring through fall may bring out the hikers. Weekdays from mid-June to mid-July may be the best bet for seeing and hearing more birds than people.

Adjacent to the main parking lot is the **Monadnock Ecocenter**. Open from mid-June through October, the center has exhibits and written material dealing with the region's natural history. On Saturdays during the summer months, ecocenter guides lead hikes which focus on a variety of topics including geology, botany, and ornithology. For information call 603-532-8053. A self-guiding nature trail in the vicinity of the Ecocenter offers a good introduction to the ecology of the area (interpretive booklet available at center). A walk along the trail introduces the visitor to many of the common plants encountered on a hike to Monadnock's summit. Familiarity with such species as beech, yellow birch, striped and sugar maple, and red spruce should add to your appreciation of the different life zones on the mountain.

Before starting out for the summit make sure that you have a trail map (available at the entrance gate). The "Information Guide for Climbing" included on the back of the trail map has useful suggestions; read it *before* your hike. Just north of the Monadnock Ecocenter a main feeder trail leads out to the area known as Falcon Springs (good water). From Falcon Springs the climber has several choices of routes to the summit. While the White Cross and White Dot trails offer the most direct routes to the top, a more leisurely (but longer) hike along the **Cascade Link Trail** and the **Pumpelly Trail** is likely to produce more birds. Allow three to four hours for the round-trip hike on the most direct route. A hike combining an ascent on the Cascade Link and Pumpelly trails with a descent on the **White Cross and Spruce Link** trails will provide a good sampling of Monadnock's various habitats. Allow five hours or more if you linger to enjoy the birds.

The lower slopes of Mt. Monadnock (between the ecocenter and the intersection with Birchtoft Trail along Cascade Link Trail) are forested with northern hardwoods, pine, and hemlock. Typical deciduous trees include paper and yellow birch, beech, and sugar maple. Common bird species in this life zone are Eastern Wood-Pewee, Blue Jay, Black-capped Chickadee, Winter Wren, Veery, Hermit Thrush, Wood Thrush, American Robin, Gray Catbird, Cedar Waxwing, Red-eyed Vireo, and Scarlet Tanager. Warblers to be expected in this same area are Chestnut-sided, Black-throated Blue, Black-throated Green, Blackburnian, Black-and-white, American Redstart, Ovenbird, and Common Yellowthroat.

A decrease in the variety of hardwoods and a preponderance of yellow birch and red spruce characterize a transitional zone on the mountain (where the Birchtoft, Red Spot, and Spellman trails intersect with Cascade Link Trail). Here, as well as in the purer stands of red spruce, and in the spruce scrub at the upper limit of vegetation, the bird watcher will encounter the "northern" species of the upper slopes. Birds to be looked for include Red-breasted Nuthatch, Swainson's Thrush, White-throated Sparrow, and Dark-eyed Junco. Warblers nesting on the upper slopes are Nashville, Magnolia, Yellow-rumped, and Canada. Interestingly, yellowthroats and towhees, which are common summer residents at the base of the mountain, make use of similar habitat in the scrub zone near the summit.

An alternative approach to birding Mt. Monadnock can be found on the west slope of the mountain. West of Jaffrey on Route 124 is the **Old Toll Road** access. This trail leads out from a parking area to the **White Arrow Trail** at the Half-Way House, and then on to the summit. When the state park is crowded, this route offers fewer people and most of the same birds.

A variety of birds may be seen from the top of Monadnock. Over the last decade summer-resident Turkey Vultures have become a regular feature of the mountain. Red-tailed and Broad-winged hawks are also fairly common. Although most of the large, black songbirds you see will be American Crows, keep an eye out for Common Raven.

Monadnock's relatively high elevation creates habitats similar to those 250 to 500 miles farther north. As a result a number of additional species with northern affinities have been recorded here. While not regular summer residents, birds such as Northern Saw-whet Owl, Yellow-bellied Sapsucker, Olive-sided and Yellow-bellied flycatchers, Golden-crowned Kinglet, and Solitary Vireo have all been found here in summer. Among the rarer possibilities are Gray-cheeked Thrush, Philadelphia Vireo, Bay-breasted and Blackpoll warblers, Rusty

Blackbird, Red Crossbill, and Pine Siskin. Recently there have been some indications that Evening Grosbeaks are nesting on the mountain.

Although it is tempting to spend all your time searching for the "northern" birds on the upper slopes of Monadnock, there is also an interesting variety of birds to be found at the base of the mountain. A tour of the rural roads skirting Monadnock should produce a number of the common summer residents, including Ruffed Grouse, Eastern Kingbird, Great Crested Flycatcher, Least Flycatcher, House Wren, Northern Oriole, and Rose-breasted Grosbeak.

Hawk-watching enthusiasts should consider a trip to Monadnock in the fall. There is normally a good flight of Broad-winged Hawks in mid-September, and the scenery is exquisite. Local hawk watchers often hike to Bald Rock (off the White Arrow Trail at 2,500-foot level) to catch the show. The fall is also an especially good time to see the ravens.

The campgrounds at Monadnock State Park are conveniently located next to the main trailhead. Because space is limited (32 sites), you may want to call ahead (603-532-8862) to determine the availability of sites; no reservations are accepted. Jaffrey Center has a number of inns, and bread-and-breakfast accommodations. During foliage season, finding a room within 50 miles of Mt. Monadnock may not be possible without reservations.

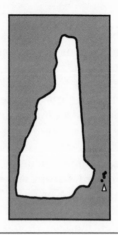

Isles of Shoals

SPRING / FALL

THE ISLES OF SHOALS LIE ASTRIDE THE NEW
Hampshire–Maine border 6 miles off the coast in the
Gulf of Maine. Like the sea which encircles them, the
islands' prosperity has undergone a recurrent ebb and
flow over the last four centuries. Originally based on
maps by Captain John Smith of Jamestown Colony fame,
European knowledge of the island goes back at least to
the early seventeenth century. The ensuing two hundred
years saw primitive fishing outposts developed into
thriving maritime communities on various of the islands. During the latter half of the nineteenth century,
after the fishing industry had largely disappeared, a
resort community flourished on Appledore, the largest
of the Isles of Shoals. The name of Celia Thaxter is

closely associated with this period. Thaxter played host to a steady stream of American writers, artists, and musicians who summered on Appledore and shared in the high culture. Thaxter was also an important voice in one of the earliest bird-protection movements in America. Articles such as her "Woman's Heartlessness" decried the use of bird plumes on fashionable ladies' hats. Organizations including the Massachusetts Audubon Society, then in its formative years, often reprinted Thaxter's writings.

While the era of high culture on the Isle of Shoals faded in the early years of the twentieth century, interest in the natural history of the islands began to build when the University of New Hampshire instituted the Marine Zoological Laboratory on Appledore in 1928. After a period during which the island was abandoned following World War II, Cornell University established the Shoals Marine Laboratory (SML) in 1966. Soon afterwards the University of New Hampshire became a partner in this venture. Research and education in the natural sciences have since played an important part in island history.

Captain John Smith's initial characterization of the islands as "many of barren rock . . . but three or foure . . . [with] Cedars" was probably something of an oversimplification. Today several of these granite islands have extensive areas of low-growing shrubs as well as rocky shore and meadow-community plants. The cover provided by this vegetation is used by both migrant and nesting birds. The Isles of Shoals are inhabited by a variety of summer-resident herons and seabirds. The nesting birds of Appledore include Snowy Egret, Little Blue Heron, Black-crowned Night-Heron, Glossy Ibis, and Common Eider. While the breeding birds are a bonus for visiting bird watchers, most birders come here to see the plentiful spring and fall migrants. An island visit in May or September is sure to provide opportunities to see numerous herons, hawks, shorebirds, flycatchers, vireos, and warblers. On a good weekend in the fall 100 or more species can be expected. During the 1980s, birders with the Audubon Society of New Hampshire have recorded a total of over 150 species on their annual fall trips. A few of the regular migrants are Northern Harrier, Merlin, Dunlin, Yellow-bellied Flycatcher, Blue-gray Gnatcatcher, Solitary Vireo, and Magnolia, Cape May, Blackburnian, Bay-breasted, and Blackpoll warblers. Adding spice to the list are uncommon or rare sightings of Ruff, Caspian Tern, Western Kingbird, Yellow-breasted Chat, Dickcissel, and Lark Sparrow. In general a good representation of New England migrants can be seen here. In addition, the low-growing vegetation and small size of the Isles of Shoals makes finding and observing the birds relatively easy.

Even if you are a member of the yachting set, individual birding ventures to the Isles of Shoals are difficult to arrange. Most of the islands are private and/or have restricted access. The best way to visit is with one of the regularly scheduled birding trips. SML offers a non-credit, four-day course titled "Island Bird Study." Spring and fall sessions include birding, natural-history lectures, and trips to various marine bird colonies. SML dormitories and dining facilities are used by participants. To receive specific information about these courses contact:

Shoals Marine Laboratory
G14 Stimson Hall
Cornell University
Ithaca, New York 14853

Another possibility is to join the Audubon Society of New Hampshire on its Appledore Island weekend. This tour, which includes transportation, food, and lodging, is normally run in the fall (early September). Birding, bird-banding demonstrations, intertidal walks, and evening activities are all part of the program. Contact:

Audubon Society of New Hampshire
3 Silk Farm Road
P.O. Box 528-B
Concord, New Hampshire 03301

The Star Island Corporation organizes natural-history conferences on Star Island each summer. Many of these annual gatherings contain a birding component. Contact:

Star Island Corporation
110 Arlington Street
Boston, Massachusetts 02116

The *M/V Thomas Laighton* provides regularly scheduled boat service (mid-June through Labor Day) twice a day (11:00 A.M. and 2:00 P.M.) from Portsmouth, New Hampshire, to Star Island. Once on board, passengers can usually observe a few birds along the Piscataqua River as far seaward as buoy K2R. While a limited number of passengers on the morning run are allowed to disembark on Star and remain there, returning to Portsmouth with the later tour, the birding opportunities are restricted by these schedules. Contact:

Isles of Shoals Steamship Company
315 Market Street
Portsmouth, New Hampshire 03801
603-431-5505

For a detailed account of the Isles of Shoals see *Ten Miles Out* by Lyman V. Rutledge (1984, Peter E. Randall, Publisher).

NEW HAMPSHIRE
SUPPLEMENTAL LIST

Lake Umbagog: Errol
summer-resident and migrant waterfowl and marshbirds

Pontook Reservoir: Dummer
summer-resident marshbirds

Pondicherry Refuge: Whitefield
summer-resident and migratory waterfowl and northern passerines

Mt. Cardigan: Cardigan State Park: Orange
summer-resident northern passerines

Mt. Sunapee: Mount Sunapee State Park: Newbury
summer-resident northern passerines

Mt. Kearsarge: Rollins State Park: Warner
summer-resident northern passerines

Spofford Lake: Chesterfield / Lake Wantastiquet (Connecticut River Impoundments): Hinsdale
migratory waterfowl, migratory shorebirds (Hinsdale impoundments)

Great Bay: Portsmouth
migrant and wintering waterfowl

Hampton–Seabrook Estuary and Harbor: Hampton and Seabrook
migrant shorebirds and herons, wintering seabirds

SEE:

–*A Checklist of the Birds of New Hampshire*. 1982. Kimball C. Elkins. Audubon Society of New Hampshire, Concord, New Hampshire.

–*Guide to the Preserves of The Audubon Society of New Hampshire and Notes on Good Birding Areas*. Steele Environmental Resource Center, The White Mountain School, Littleton, New

Hampshire, and Audubon Society of New Hampshire, Concord, New Hampshire (see also *Supplement*).

–*Natural Areas of New Hampshire.* Steele Environmental Resource Center, The White Mountain School, Littleton, New Hampshire.

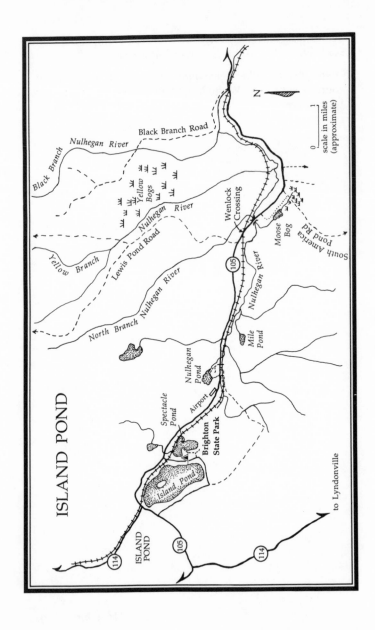

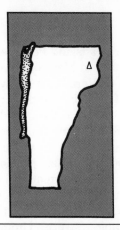

V E R M O N T

Island Pond

SPRING / EARLY SUMMER

MENTION ISLAND POND TO MOST NEW ENglanders and chances are you'll receive a blank stare. Those individuals who do know of Island Pond are likely to be familiar with the prize-winning lake trout or 15-point bucks that sportsmen seek in this region. Others will recall reading something of the uneasy relationship that exists between Island Pond's townfolk and the sizable religious community that has taken up residence among them. A few trivia buffs may even be aware that this is the home of the late Chief Don Eagle, a professional wrestler of some status in the 1950s, and the birthplace of Rudy Vallee. Most likely, however, Island Pond won't ring any bells. Relative obscurity is a way of life in the Northeast Kingdom of Vermont.

Even among birders Island Pond remains largely unknown. On Big Days in May, however, you will likely find one or more of Vermont's knowledgeable birders here, checking off their hundredth species for the day before 10:00 A.M. Island Pond is truly a jewel among New England birding spots. Summer-resident woodpeckers, flycatchers, thrushes, vireos, wood-warblers, blackbirds, finches, and others provide an opportunity to find an excellent representation of New England's inland nesting bird life. Adding spice to the search is the likelihood of discovering one or more of the boreal residents, including Spruce Grouse, Black-backed Woodpecker, Gray Jay, Common Raven, Boreal Chickadee, and/or White-winged Crossbill, but don't count your grouse, woodpecker, or jay until you've seen them. These three, in particular, can be a problem even at Island Pond. With persistence you should find one of the three, with luck two. If you find all three send your contribution directly to the Vermont Department of Fish and Wildlife—one of several organizations helping to preserve this exquisite habitat.

To reach Island Pond take Route 91 in Vermont or Route 93 in New Hampshire north to St. Johnsbury, Vermont. From St. Johnsbury follow Route 91 north about 7 miles to Exit 23 at Lyndonville. Take Route 5 through town to Route 114 (go right at the fork north of town). Follow Route 114 for 23 miles to Island Pond.

Like many areas in northern New England, the Northeast Kingdom is crisscrossed by miles of logging roads. These secondary dirt and gravel roads provide access to many square miles of uninhabited country. Several of these roads are described at the end of this account. For birders less inclined to set off into the wilderness, good examples of hardwood and boreal habitats can be found near Island Pond.

Southeast of Island Pond is **Brighton State Park** on the shores of Spectacle Pond. The park is an excellent place to camp, and the hardwood and mixed forests there have a good variety of nesting birds. From late May through early July, a walk along the roads leading through the campgrounds should produce Broad-winged Hawk, Yellow-bellied Sapsucker, Least Flycatcher, Eastern Wood-Pewee, Veery, Red-eyed Vireo, American Redstart, Ovenbird, Scarlet Tanager, Purple Finch, and Chipping Sparrow. A nature trail (self-guiding booklet available at the center) leads out from a small nature center and passes through mixed deciduous and coniferous woodlands. Birds you may encounter along the trail include Ruffed Grouse, Barred Owl, Hairy Woodpecker, American Robin, and Northern Parula, Black-throated Green, Black-throated Blue, and Canada warblers. Boreal Chickadees are occasionally found here, and even the rare Black-backed Woodpecker is on the park's bird list. While they have not nested here recently, Common Loon can sometimes be found on the pond.

Two miles east of the road to Brighton State Park on Route 105 is the John H. Boylan State Airport. Stop at the southeast end of the runway to check the shrubby growth and wetlands. American Woodcock and Common Snipe are in residence here during the breeding season, and this is a good spot to catch their display flights and songs. Whip-poor-will can also be heard in the vicinity. Just ahead on Route 105 a dirt road goes left into a sandy field (across from the dirt ramp to a bridge crossing the railroad tracks). Take the dirt road (right at the fork) .2 mile to a open area above **Nulhegan Pond**. Sundews and horned bladderwort line the pond's edge. Walk the border of the pond and look and listen for Great Blue Heron, American Bittern, Spotted Sandpiper, Northern Flicker, Alder Flycatcher, Hermit Thrush, Nashville and Wilson's (rare) warblers, Common Yellowthroat, and Lincoln's and Swamp sparrows.

One of the best birding areas in the Island Pond region is the **Wenlock Management Area**. From Nulhegan Pond follow Route 105 east 3.5 miles to a railroad crossing (Wenlock Crossing) and another .4 mile to a bridge over the Nulhegan River. In the next 1.6 miles, four roads (dirt) join Route 105 from the south (right). The second, third, and fourth roads provide access to an excellent variety of habitats, including spruce–fir forest, cedar swamp, and bog. The second road is .4 mile from the bridge. Note this as you continue on to the third road which is 1 mile from the bridge. The third road is **South America Pond Road**. Go right here and in approximately .25 mile you will come to a flooded **Cedar Swamp**. Look for a place to park which will put you at least partially off the road and out of the way of the logging trucks. Incidentally, logging vehicles have right of way along these roads, and you're bound to come up on the short side of any argument with these thundering 16-wheelers.

The Cedar Swamp and the edges of the spruce–fir forest along South America Pond Road are good places to start your investigations of the boreal habitat of the Island Pond region. Summer residents of the swamp and shrubby borders include Chimney Swift, Olive-sided Flycatcher, Winter Wren, Cedar Waxwing, Northern Waterthrush, and Tennessee, Nashville, Magnolia, and Canada warblers. Rusty Blackbird has also nested in the swamp, although numbers seem to be declining of late. White-winged Crossbill is another possibility, especially if there is a good cone crop. Perhaps the "best" bird of the Cedar Swamp is the Black-backed Woodpecker, but don't be surprised if you have some difficulty with this one. Along the edges of the forest look and listen for Yellow-bellied Flycatcher, Boreal Chickadee, Red-breasted Nuthatch, Brown Creeper, Hermit and Swainson's thrushes, Golden-crowned Kinglet, and Solitary Vireo.

A **path** leaves South America Pond Road to the west (right, as you come in) just before the road dips down to the Cedar Swamp. A pile of boulders lies at the beginning of this trail. This path roughly parallels Route 105 for a little over .5 mile, eventually coming out on Route 105 at the second road (described above as being .4 mile from the Nulhegan River bridge). The path cuts through the heart of the spruce–fir forest and provides excellent access into this habitat.

A word of caution about exploring boreal woodlands. Birders tempted to leave the beaten path and strike off into the forest should be aware that because of the density of the vegetation, it is relatively easy to become disoriented. If you decide to bushwack, a compass and topographic map are recommended.

Birds to look for along the path include Gray Jay, Hermit Thrush, Ruby-crowned Kinglet, and Yellow-rumped, Blackburnian, Chestnut-sided, and Bay-breasted (uncommon) warblers. Dark-eyed Juncos and White-throated Sparrows are common along this stretch. Stop at various places to try a little squeaking and pishing; this technique seems to work well in the close quarters of the boreal forest. In late June and early July two butterfly species, pink-edged sulphur and atlantis fritillary, add their color to the mosses, lichens, and fungus lining the path. This is also a good area in which to brush up on your moose-tracking skills.

This path also provides access to **Moose Bog** via a short side trail to the left. The bog trail is approximately

.5 mile west of the South America Pond Road; however the quickest way to reach the bog is to park at the western end of the main trail. Return to Route 105 and look for the road that is .4 mile east of the Nulhegan River bridge. Park at the entrance (room for one car only) and proceed southeast along the path (boulder near entrance) for approximately .2 mile. Look for a widening in the path at a grassy area with an obscure trail to the south (right). At present it is difficult or impossible to see the bog from the main trail. Follow the spur trail down the slope (.1 mile) to Moose Bog.

Moose Bog is a special place. Seemingly cut off from the rest of the world by a ring of woodlands, the bog's mossy mat creeps out to the quiet, open waters of the center. The subtle hues of bog rosemary, pitcher plant, and cranberry punctuate the saturated sphagnum. You may be able to complete the picture during an early-evening visit by finding a moose feeding at the water's edge. Summer-resident birds include Spruce Grouse, Cape May Warbler, and Lincoln's Sparrow. While the grouse is a rarity in Vermont, the woodlands surrounding Moose Pond provided the majority of records of breeding birds during the Atlas years (1976–1981). This is also an excellent locale for many of the other northern species. Check the woodland perimeter for Northern Saw-whet Owl, the snags for Olive-sided Flycatcher, Gray Jay, and Black-backed Woodpecker, and the open waters for American Black Duck. Common Ravens can also be seen and heard around Moose Bog. If you have the time, plan several trips to the bog at different times of the day. This should increase your chances with the birds and give you the opportunity to enjoy the various moods of the boreal habitat.

Two tenths of a mile east of South American Pond Road another secondary road leaves Route 105 to the south. Go right onto this road and proceed approximately .6 mile to a clearing and a place to park. The mixed forest here has a good variety of birds including Pileated Woodpecker and numerous vireos, warblers, and finches. To explore the area more thoroughly walk south along the old right of way, which ascends a hillside. On your way back to the main road check the dense stands of spruce and fir for boreal species. There are private residences along this road; please respect the owners' property rights. Approximately .25 mile east of here another road intersects Route 105 from the south. This leads to the powerline cut for Hydro–Quebec. Good birding habitat can also be found along this road.

Bird watchers wanting to explore even more of the Island Pond region should take the opportunity to try one or more of the logging roads which lead north from Route 105. Two of these are described below. While the bird life found along the roads is essentially the same as mentioned previously, the logging routes provide access to extensive acreage of good habitat. Detailed descriptions of these and other logging roads can be found in Walter Ellison's *A Guide to Bird Finding in Vermont* (1981).

Just west of Wenlock Crossing the **Lewis Pond Road** goes north into St. Regis Paper Company logging property. In approximately 4.3 miles the road branches. The left branch passes through spruce–fir forest and cut-over areas that can be good for boreal species. The right branch continues on to Lewis Pond through some interesting wetlands. Just under 5 miles east of Wenlock Crossing on Route 105, immediately after crossing the Nulhegan River, the **Black Branch Road** goes north along the Black Branch of the Nulhegan River. Ellison calls this "three-toed road," and it may be the best place to find a Black-backed Woodpecker. Clearcuts along the route have nesting Olive-sided Flycatchers, Mourning Warblers, and Lincoln's Sparrows. In 3 miles the road crosses the river and enters the area known as the Yellow Bogs. This stretch of black spruce forest is particularly good for boreal species including the three toughies: Spruce Grouse, Black-backed Woodpecker, and Gray Jay.

It is often tempting, especially when birding an unfamiliar area, to hurry from one area to the next in an attempt to see everything. While it is only natural to want to find all the specialties, a deliberate pace may actually be more productive. Ellison counsels vigilance in the search for boreal specialties. Add to this a touch of patience and a dose of repellent to ward off the blackflies, and you have the makings of a successful north-woods trip.

In years with an abundant cone crop, the coniferous woodlands around Island Pond are an excellent place to observe numerous winter finches (see species accounts). During migratory periods a variety of waterbirds can be found on Island Pond itself.

The Lakefront Motel (802-723-6507) in Island Pond offers accommodations. There are several restaurants and grocery stores in town. The Buck and Doe Restaurant is touted by one birder as having "legendary portions of old-fashioned, well-prepared food." Campers wanting to reserve a site at the state park should contact:

Brighton State Park
Island Pond, Vermont 05846
802-723-4360

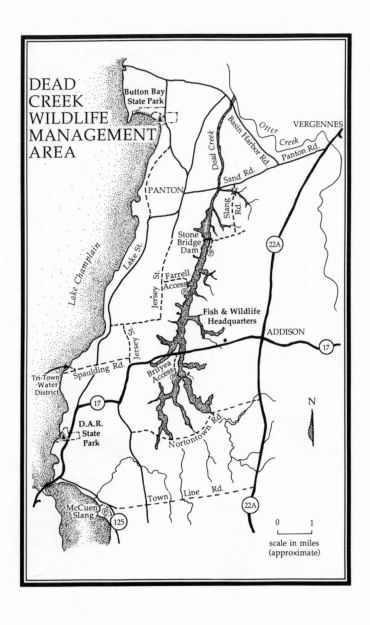

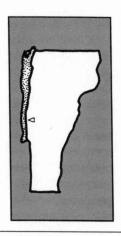

Dead Creek Wildlife
Management Area

SUMMER / FALL

THE CHAMPLAIN LOWLANDS FORM A BROAD
corridor of flat to gently-rolling terrain in northwestern
Vermont. This largely rural landscape is bounded on
the east by the Green Mountains and on the west by
Lake Champlain and the Adirondack Mountains. Although the lowlands receive less precipitation than Vermont's other physiographic regions, the area is well
watered by a series of streams. This natural irrigation
combines with rich soils and favorable topography to
create prime agricultural land. A particularly productive
(from the birder's as well as the farmer's perspective)

section of the region is the Dead Creek drainage, which lies in the central portion of the Champlain Lowlands. The extensive wetlands of Dead Creek, the surrounding farmlands, and Lake Champlain provide an interesting variety of habitats for the bird watcher to explore. Mammal watchers may be rewarded by glimpses of red and gray fox, coyote, otter, or beaver.

Dead Creek Wildlife Management Area (DCWMA) has a well-deserved reputation for its variety of avian summer residents. Marshland nesting species include American Bittern, Least Bittern, Wood Duck, Northern Pintail, Common Goldeneye, Hooded Merganser, Virginia Rail, Sora, Common Moorhen, Black Tern, Northern Harrier, and Marsh Wren. Upland species include Wild Turkey (rare), Upland Sandpiper, Horned Lark, and Grasshopper and Vesper sparrows. While a visit in early summer will increase your chances of finding these and many other species actively engaged in the early stages of the nesting cycle, a late-summer or early-fall visit should produce many of these same species as well as a variety of migrant shorebirds and passerines. On those occasions when one or more of the pools is drawn down to encourage emergent vegetation and discourage carp, a shorebird bonanza may result. Late-summer records, under such favorable conditions, include numbers of Hudsonian Godwits, Baird's Sandpipers, and Red-necked Phalaropes. The beginning of the hunting season (early October) should be avoided.

From Middlebury, Vermont, take Routes 23 and 17 west (approximately 8 miles) to Addison. DCWMA is managed by Vermont's Fish and Wildlife Department, and you will find their headquarters .9 mile west of Addison on Route 17. The refuge manager is a good source for up-to-date information on birds, especially waterfowl and raptors. A map showing the various access points for DCWMA is also available at Fish and Wildlife Headquarters. Three of these access points are described in detail below.

Continue west on Route 17 approximately 1.5 miles to the creek crossing and the **Brilyea Access** on your left. The mile-long access road is bordered by a cattail marsh on the east and agricultural fields on the west. Check the creek for Great Blue Heron, Green-backed Heron, American Black Duck, Blue-winged Teal, Green-winged Teal, and other ducks. If the water is low and mud banks are exposed, this is a good place to look for rails in summer and shorebirds in fall. The access road ends at two parking lots next to open pools. Birds regularly seen over the pools include Osprey, Black Tern, Belted Kingfisher, and various swallows. A path leads away from the second parking lot (check here for Black-crowned Night-Heron in later summer) and along the creek shore. Both Marsh Wren and Swamp Sparrow nest in the dense flags along the creek, and you may be able to tempt them into the open with a little creative "pishing and squeaking." Return to Route 17 and continue west.

The Dead Creek region has a variety of fields, meadows, and pastures that the bird watcher will want to investigate. The farmlands along Route 17 are a good place to start, but because most of this land is privately owned, it is best to work the roadside edges (try to park well off the road). Besides the large flocks of Canada Geese (with an occasional Snow Goose) and Ring-billed Gulls that are commonly seen in the surrounding fields, several smaller, less-conspicuous species are often concealed in the recently tilled areas. A careful investigation of these fields (during migration) will often turn up Horned Lark, Water Pipit, Killdeer, and Lesser Golden-Plover (fall). Check the pastures, hayfields, and fence posts for Upland Sandpiper (May through August). After a heavy rain check the harrowed fields for Black-bellied Plover, Pectoral Sandpiper, and even Buff-breasted Sandpiper. The weedy edges of many of these same fields often harbor Song and Savannah sparrows as well as less-common species such as Lincoln's Sparrow, Grasshopper Sparrow, and Vesper Sparrow. Given the extensive habitat, even the rare Henslow's and Sharp-tailed sparrows are among the possibilities during migration.

To reach the **Farrell Access** turn right (north) at the intersection of Route 17 and Jersey Street. Follow Jersey Street north approximately 1 mile, turn right (east) and proceed for another mile, turn left (north) and continue for one more mile, where you will find an unmarked road on your right leading to the Farrell Access. The parking lot at the end of the access road overlooks Dead Creek and extensive stands of bulrush and flowering rush. This is another good area for herons, bitterns, waterfowl, and rails. You may want to review the various calls and songs of American and Least bitterns as well as Sora, Virginia Rail, and Common Moorhen. These species are normally reclusive, and you are much more likely to hear than see them. While the two bitterns are "in song" primarily in spring and early summer, the rails often remain vocal throughout the summer and even during migration. Sometimes simply clapping your hands will produce a rail chorus.

The Farrell Access road passes through prime agricultural land. The brushy draws along the roadside are nesting habitat for summer-resident Willow Flycatchers from June through early August. Besides checking the fields for those species mentioned previously, you should also be on the lookout for raptors. While the resident and post-breeding red-tails and kestrels are most numerous, you should also be able to find one or more

Turkey Vultures (April through September). Northern Harrier is also a regular feature of this region from spring through late fall, with a few harriers overwintering in the lowlands. Autumn sightings of Sharp-shinned Hawk and Peregrine Falcon are also fairly routine here. Although not common, Bald Eagles are occasionally seen in the Dead Creek region. These same farmlands support a sizable Rough-legged Hawk population during the winter months, when even the rare Gyrfalcon has been seen. Fortunately, many dead trees have been left standing in the Dead Creek region. These not only provide perches for raptors, but serve many other species in a variety of ways.

To reach **Stone Bridge Dam** return to Jersey Street, turn right, and continue north 2.75 miles to Panton. Turn right (east) on Sand Road and continue for a little over 1 mile, crossing Dead Creek. There is room here to park. Check the creek on both sides of the bridge. This is an excellent spot to see resident moorhen and Black Tern. Continue east and take your first right onto Slang Road. Check the slang near the iron bridge for herons and other waterbirds. Follow Slang Road south, turning right toward the creek (a little over 2 miles). From here you can drive along the creek above Stone Bridge Dam to a turnaround. In late summer and early fall the edges and mudflats along the creek are a good spot to check for shorebirds. Regular migrants include Least Sandpiper, Semipalmated Sandpiper, Semipalmated Plover, Spotted Sandpiper, Common Snipe, Killdeer, and Greater and Lesser yellowlegs. Pectoral Sandpiper, Solitary Sandpiper, Short-billed Dowitcher, and Stilt Sandpiper (rare) are also possible. Check the hedgerows and fields along the access road for migrants. Slang Road also passes through some prime raptor territory.

Although the three locales mentioned above (Brilyea Access, Farrell Access, and Stone Bridge Dam) will give the visiting birder a good sample of what Dead Creek has to offer, there are other possibilities. Nortontown Road, south of Addison off Route 22A, crosses farmlands and creeks at several points. The confluence of Dead Creek and Otter Creek, west of Vergennes on Basin Harbor Road, is another good area to check. Several other productive spots are along the eastern shore of Lake Champlain and are described below.

To reach **Lake Champlain** from Addison go south on Route 22A a little over 4 miles to Town Line Road. Go right (west) on Town Line Road another 4.3 miles to Route 125. Turn right onto Route 125 and look for the entrance to **McCuen Slang** ahead on the left. The access road takes you along the marshy delta of Whitney Creek to the shore of Lake Champlain. Check the lakeshore and marsh for waders. A path leading from the southwest corner of the parking lot is lined with dogwoods which often provide cover for migrant passerines.

Return to Route 125 and continue north for 1 mile to Route 17. Follow Route 17 and then Lake Street a total of 4.75 miles to Spaulding Road. Go left on Spaulding Road and then right at the fork to reach the **Tri-town Water District** facility and a view over Lake Champlain. This area is worth checking in late fall and early spring when migrant grebes, scoters, ducks, and gulls are passing through. The hedgerows and trees along the entrance road can be packed with White-throated Sparrows, Cedar Waxwings, and other landbirds.

To reach **Button Bay State Park** (BBSP) return to Lake Road and continue north. In approximately 4.5 miles the main road takes a sharp right. At this point leave Lake Road and continue straight along a secondary road for another 2-plus miles to an intersection with a paved road. Go left and look for the BBSP signs ahead on your left. Follow the signs through the camping area to the picnic grounds and parking lot. A .5-mile walk along the lakeshore will take you to a small nature center. This is a good spot to spend some time investigating the geologic history of the Champlain Lowlands. Exhibits and a self-guiding trail explain the various eras. A fossilized coral reef as well as ancient trilobites give evidence that five hundred million years ago this was a tropical region. Shellfish fossils and glacial striations are representative of the arctic climate of the relatively recent glacial age. In fact, it was the meltwaters of the most recent glacier that formed the immense glacial Lake Vermont. The present-day Champlain Lowlands are the exposed lake bottom which drained 10,000 years ago.

This is also a good area to bird. Check the bay and shoreline for migrant waterfowl and shorebirds. The willows and conifers around the parking lot and boat ramp may have an assortment of woodpeckers, kinglets, vireos, warblers, and other passerines. Great Horned Owl and Eastern Screech Owl nest and are residents of the nearby woodlands.

Campgrounds in the area include Button Bay State Park and DAR State Park, both on Lake Champlain. Vergennes has several inns and guest houses including Emersons' Guest House (bed-and-breakfast). Gas, restaurants, and general stores are also available in Vergennes. The Sugar House Motor Inn is conveniently located in New Haven, Vermont, on Route 7 between Vergennes and Middlebury. A fairly wide choice of accommodations and restaurants is available in Middlebury.

Visitors to the Dead Creek region may want to visit Fort Ticonderoga. The fort can be reached by taking the short (six minutes) ferry ride across Lake Champlain at Larrabee's Point or by crossing on the toll bridge to Crown Point, another place of historical interest. In and around Middlebury are the Vermont State Craft Center at Frog Hollow and the Sheldon Museum. If you are traveling east of Middlebury along Route 125 through the Green Mountains, look for the memorials to Robert Frost. One roadside park commemorating the poet has a short trail and a spot to picnic.

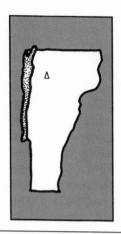

Mount Mansfield

LATE SPRING / EARLY SUMMER

IN NEW ENGLAND, ACCESS TO THE BREEDING
habitat of Gray-cheeked Thrush is restricted. The **Mt.
Mansfield Toll Road** is one of the more convenient
ways for birders to visit the summer territory of this
species. On its way to the summit, the road passes
through northern hardwood, transitional, and spruce–
fir forest. On the summit ridge, a section of the Long
Trail traverses the stunted fir forest and the arctic–alpine
zone above timberline. Because the toll road is a relatively easy drive (as compared with other secondary
summit-access roads reaching timberline) and the ridge
trail undemanding, even those birders lacking an interest in mountaineering should find this trip to their
liking.

To reach Mt. Mansfield take Route 89 north to the

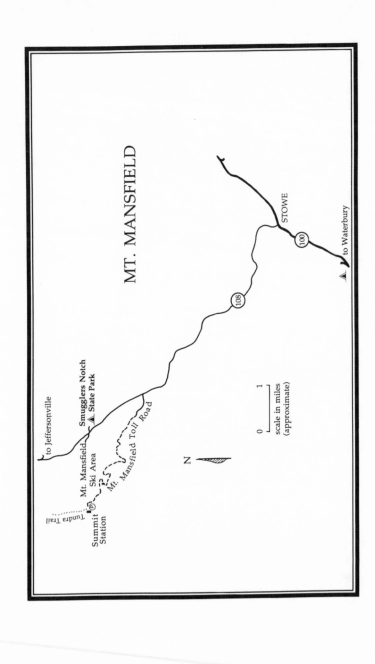

exit for Waterbury, Vermont. Follow Route 100 north to Stowe, and take Route 108 toward Smuggler's Notch and Jeffersonville. The Mt. Mansfield Toll Road entrance is 6 miles northwest of the intersection of Routes 100 and 108 in Stowe. The toll road is open daily (weather permitting) from 9:30 A.M. to 5:00 P.M. between May 23 and October 19. There is a $6 fee per vehicle.

Perhaps the best way to work the toll road is to drive to the summit, do the ridge trail, then work your way down the mountain, stopping at the various pull-offs and picnic areas. The summit parking lot (3,849 feet) is the sight of the former Mt. Mansfield Summit House. It was here that Olin Sewall Pettingill, Jr. in his pioneering *A Guide to Bird Finding East of the Mississippi* (1951) suggested that bird watchers take in the evening chorus of Gray-cheeked Thrushes. Unfortunately the hotel no longer exists; fortunately the thrushes are still in residence. Your best chance to hear their veerylike song may be in the late afternoon, so time your trip accordingly. On days when the ridge is in the clouds, the sunrise chorus may continue late enough to allow for a successful morning trip.

The **Tundra Trail** (self-guiding booklet available at Summit Station) leads out from the Summit Station and passes through dwarf conifers of the Krummholz zone and on to the arctic–alpine zone. Tundralike habitats include the alpine meadows and peat bogs. Bird life along the trail is limited to Dark-eyed Juncos and White-throated Sparrows. Occasionally a Common Raven will pass by, as these large songbirds are right at home around the treeless summit.

If you don't see (more likely *hear*) Gray-cheeked Thrush around the stunted conifers near the Summit Station, you may want to walk part of the maintenance road that leads to the Nose. The upper portion of the toll road can also be productive. Half a mile below the parking lot, at the top of the Haselton Trail, there is a convenient pull-off. This is a good place to look and listen for Blackpoll Warbler. Other stopping spots in the blackpoll habitat are at .9 mile from the summit parking lot and at 1.6 miles. Additional birds to look for in the conifer zone include Yellow-bellied Flycatcher, Winter Wren, Swainson's Thrush, Golden-crowned Kinglet, and Yellow-rumped Warbler.

Back in the northern hardwood forest an even greater variety of birds is possible. Take advantage of the convenient parking areas to explore the woodlands and ski-trail edges. Summer residents include Yellow-bellied Sapsucker, Least Flycatcher, Wood Thrush, Hermit Thrush, Black-throated Blue and Black-throated Green warblers, and Ovenbird. Even the area at the base of the toll road can be productive. A walk along the initial .25 mile, which is paved, may produce such species as Yellow-billed Cuckoo (uncommon), Eastern Phoebe, Cliff and Barn swallows, Cedar Waxwing, Red-eyed Vireo, Black-and-white Warbler, American Redstart, Northern Oriole, Indigo Bunting, and Chipping Sparrow.

Hikers visiting Mt. Mansfield may want to take the Long Trail up the mountain. An overnight at the Taft Lodge (bunkhouse) is a good bet for hearing the thrush chorus. Details on this and other trails in the area can be found in the Green Mountain Club's *Guide Book of the Long Trail*.

Once strictly a winter resort, Stowe is fast becoming a summer playground. While the tourist bureau won't be able to give you much information on Gray-cheeked Thrushes, they can point the way to a variety of activities including alpine sliding, ballooning, canoeing, and dining. Accommodations and services are plentiful in and around the town. Campers have a choice of staying at Nichols Lodge—Gold Brook Camping (2 miles south of Stowe on Route 100) or at the Smuggler's Notch State Park Campground on Route 108 north of the Mt. Mansfield Toll Road entrance.

Most birders planning a trip to Mt. Mansfield will travel north on either Route 89 in New Hampshire and/or Route 91 in Vermont. This provides an opportunity to visit the **Vermont Institute of Natural Science** (VINS) in Woodstock, Vermont. To reach VINS follow Route 4 from White River Junction, Vermont, west into Woodstock. At the end of the village green in downtown Woodstock take Church Hill Road (left of the stone church) 1.5 miles to VINS headquarters. VINS runs extensive programs focusing on natural-history education and research. Their library and bookstore are both excellent resources for visiting naturalists. The newly opened **Vermont Raptor Center** on the premises is a unique living museum with most of New England's native owls, hawks, and eagles in spacious flight habitats. Even bird watchers with a passing fancy for the birds of prey will enjoy this innovative facility. VINS is open daily from May through October from 9:00 A.M. to 5:00 P.M. The Vermont Raptor Center is open daily (closed Tuesday) during the same months from 10:00 A.M. to 4:00 P.M. Call ahead for winter schedule: 802-457-2779.

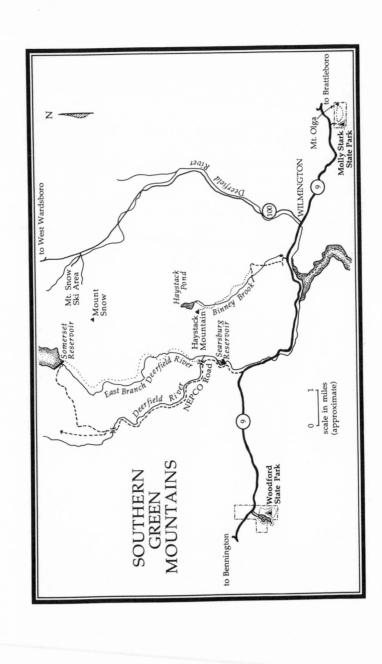

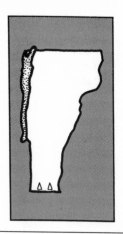

Southern Green Mountains

SUMMER

UNLIKE HER FEMINIST COUNTERPARTS IN THE twentieth century, Molly Stark seems to have gained notoriety, at least in part because of her husband. She was married to General John Stark, the Revolutionary War hero. But Ms. Stark definitely had a mind of her own and made a lasting impression on this region of Vermont (then a part of the New Hampshire Grants). Besides raising a family of 11 children, she rallied the troops for the Battle of Bennington, organized and ran a field hospital, and wasn't above stepping out to a dance *without* her famous husband. The Molly Stark

Trail (Route 9), which crosses southern Vermont, preserves the memory of this independent lady.

Bird watchers will find the Molly Stark Trail a good route for exploring the southern Green Mountains. Here, the high plateau, scattered ponds and streams, northern hardwoods, and spruce–fir forests attract a variety of summer-resident birds. In addition to several species of northern affinity, various flycatchers, thrushes, and warblers highlight the list.

Woodford State Park is 10 miles east of Bennington (c. 28 miles west of Brattleboro) on Route 9. At 2,400 feet above sea level, the park's woodlands provide a good representation of the nesting birds in this section of Vermont. The forest surrounding the Adams Reservoir, in the center of the park, is largely composed of hardwoods. Some spruce and fir occur on the borders of the reservoir and especially at the southwest end of the park. Pick up a trail guide at park headquarters. A good introductory walk is the **Atwood Nature Trail** (self-guiding booklet available), a short loop path near the entrance. Birds which can be seen along the trail include Yellow-bellied Sapsucker, Eastern Phoebe, Winter Wren, Wood and Hermit thrushes, Red-eyed and Solitary vireos, and White-throated Sparrow. Typical warblers along this and other park trails are Magnolia, Black-throated Blue, Black-throated Green, Blackburnian, American Redstart, and Ovenbird. You can reach the southwestern section of the reservoir by following the hiking trail or driving to the end of the road through the campground. The borders of the stump pond are a good place to look for birds. Often there is an active beaver colony here.

A little less than 5 miles east of Woodford State Park the **New England Power Company (NEPCO) Road** goes north from Route 9 to the Searsburg and Somerset reservoirs. This 9-mile-long secondary road follows the Deerfield River for 5 miles and then heads northeast to the Somerset Reservoir. It is a delightful route to explore, normally having little traffic and many opportunities to stop and bird. Try the woodlands and swinging bridge at 2 miles (from Route 9), the riparian habitat at 2.5 miles, the area of the bridge across the Deerfield River at approximately 5 miles, the Somerset Reservoir itself, and any other appealing roadside habitats. Typical birds along the route include Spotted Sandpiper and Belted Kingfisher on the river, Alder Flycatcher, Cedar Waxwing, Common Yellowthroat, Rose-breasted Grosbeak, Scarlet Tanager, and American Goldfinch around streamside shrubs and forest edge, and Least Flycatcher, Golden-crowned Kinglet, Swainson's Thrush, and Yellow-rumped, Blackburnian, and Canada warblers in the hardwood and/or conifer stands. You may even find Evening Grosbeak along the road, although their occurrence here in summer is erratic. Check Somerset Reservoir for Common Loon, Common Merganser, and Bald Eagle.

For hikers, the 1.2-mile (one way) trail to the summit of **Haystack Mountain** (3,420 feet) offers a good way to see several of the "northern" birds of this region. Actually it may be more difficult to find the trailhead than to climb the mountain. The following directions should be helpful. From Wilmington go west on Route 9 for 1.1 miles to the sign for Chimney Hill. Follow this road north 1.2 miles to Chimney Hill Road. Go left onto Chimney Hill and right onto Binney Brook Road in .2 mile. Stay on Binney Brook for 1 mile, passing Howe's Loop, Doe Run, Lila Lane, and Howe's Loop (again). Take a right at the sign for Upper Dam Road and left onto Upper Dam Road. In .2 mile look for the Haystack Mountain trail sign on the right. On your way up the trail you should see many of the birds mentioned previously. The spruce–fir habitat around the summit has summer-resident Yellow-bellied Flycatcher, Winter Wren, Golden-crowned Kinglet, Gray-cheeked Thrush, Blackpoll Warbler, and Dark-eyed Junco. A spur trail leads to **Haystack Pond**, where a variety of warblers as well as Olive-sided Flycatcher and Rusty Blackbird may be found. Heather and Hugh Sadlier's book, *fifty hikes in Vermont* (1985 edition, revised by the Green Mountain Club) contains a section on the Haystack trail which offers specifics about the hike.

Nine miles north of Wilmington on Route 100 is **Mt. Snow** (3,556 feet). This is another choice spot for bird finding. Hiking the ski trails or riding the chair to the summit offers some productive birding. The **Thomson Nature Trail** (self-guiding booklet available at base headquarters) leads down from the summit through a variety of habitats. On the upper reaches of the mountain look for typical subalpine species including Yellow-bellied Flycatcher, Gray-cheeked Thrush, and Blackpoll Warbler. Canada Warblers can be located in the transitional zone. Brushy areas of secondary growth along the trails frequently harbor Mourning Warblers.

Molly Stark State Park is located 3.4 miles east of Wilmington center (c. 15 miles west of Brattleboro) on Route 9. There are some good birding areas right around the campgrounds. Nesting species in deciduous woods and shrubs behind the picnic shelter include Ruby-throated Hummingbird, Veery, Chestnut-sided Warbler, American Redstart, Rose-breasted Grosbeak, and Indigo Bunting. In the coniferous woodlands on the western side of the park you should be able to find Red-breasted Nuthatch, Brown Creeper, and Golden-crowned Kinglet. The loop trail up **Mt. Olga** (2,415 feet) is approximately 1.5 miles long and passes through deciduous and coniferous woodlands. A hike along the trail will likely produce Hermit and Swainson's thrushes, Solitary Vireo, and a good variety of warblers. See the Sadliers' book for details of the trail.

Birders continuing on to Brattleboro may want to check out the **Retreat Meadows** north of the city (off Route 30) and the **riparian habitat** south of Brattleboro (off Route 142) along the Connecticut River.

Another profitable way to extend your explorations of southern Vermont is to spend some time along the **Kelly Stand** road. This National Forest Service secondary road runs between West Wardsboro and East Arlington roughly paralleling Route 9 but 10–12 miles to the north. From the east go north on Route 100 approximately 5 miles from Mt. Snow to West Wardsboro and take the road west toward Stratton. In addition to the typical summer residents of the southern Green Mountains, this route offers the possibility of seeing species of more northerly association including Black-backed Woodpecker (rare), Common Raven, Ruby-crowned Kinglet, Blackpoll Warbler, Rusty Blackbird, and Lincoln's Sparrow. Although a good variety of birds can be found all along Kelly Stand road, **Branch Pond** is one of the better locales. To reach Branch Pond go north on the fire road which is approximately 9.5 miles west of West Wardsboro. In 2.5 miles there is a parking lot with a trail leading west to the southern edge of the pond. For hikers, two other worthwhile ponds in the vicinity are Bourne Pond and Stratton Pond. For details of the hike see the Green Mountain Club's *Guide Book of the Long Trail.*

Southern Vermont does a sizable summer tourist trade. Restaurants, accommodations, and services can be found at various places along Route 9 between Brattleboro and Bennington.

VERMONT
SUPPLEMENTAL LIST

Missisquoi National Wildlife Refuge: Alburg
resident and migratory marshbirds, waterfowl, passerines; Gray
    Partridge

Barton River Marsh and South Bay: Newport and Coventry
nesting and migratory marshbirds and waterfowl, migrant
    shorebirds and passerines

Grand Isle County: Lamoille delta, South Hero, and Grand
    Isle
migrant waterfowl, Gray Partridge, marshbirds

Winooski River Delta: Burlington
migratory waterfowl, herons, marshbirds, shorebirds, and
    passerines

Groton State Forest: Groton
summer-resident northern passerines

Mount Equinox: Manchester
summer-resident northern passerines

Herrick's Cove: Rockingham
migratory birds

SEE:

–*A Guide to Bird Finding in Vermont.* 1981. Walter G. Ellison.
    Vermont Institute of Natural Science.

–*The Atlas of Breeding Birds of Vermont.* 1985. Sarah B. Laughlin
    and Douglas P. Kibbe, editors. University Press of New
    England.

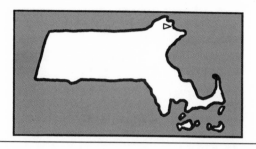

MASSACHUSETTS

Newburyport, Plum Island, and Salisbury

YEAR ROUND

It was January 12th, late Sunday afternoon. We had already finished the day's birding and were ready to go home. Actually we were looking for a Black-headed Gull when we saw a flock of Bonaparte's, and we thought that there might be a Black-headed among them. We stopped by the Clam Shack and got out with our binoculars—not our scope—because the birds were so close. As we looked at the flock, I immediately noticed one of the birds as being smaller and said, "There's no Black-headed, but there's a Little Gull." Then Phil [Parsons] replied, "It's too big to be a Little Gull." I said, "Well, he's too small to be a Bonaparte's—and look how pink he is, very pink, too pink for a Little Gull."

HERMAN WEISSBERG
NEWBURYPORT HARBOR
JANUARY 1975

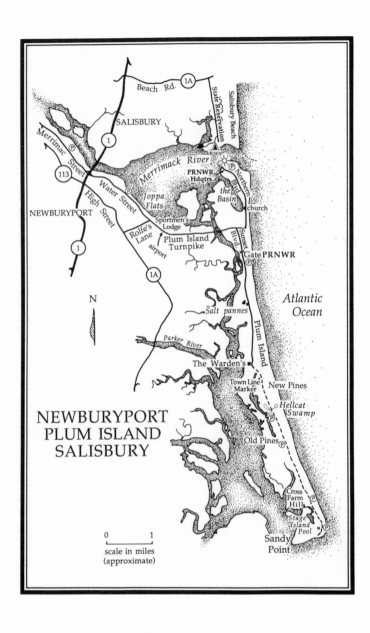

Beach Rd. 1A

SALISBURY

State Reservation

Salisbury Beach

Merrimac Street

113

1

Water Street

High Street

NEWBURYPORT

Merrimack River

PRNWR Hdqtrs.

Joppa Flats

Sportmen's Lodge

Rolfe's Lane

airport

Plum Island Turnpike

1A

N

1

the Basin

church

Northern Blvd.

Sunset Blvd.

Gate PRNWR

Salt pannes

Parker River

Atlantic Ocean

The Warden's

Plum Island

Town Line Marker

New Pines

Hellcat Swamp

Old Pines

NEWBURYPORT
PLUM ISLAND
SALISBURY

Cross Farm Hill

Stage Island Pool

Sandy Point

0   1
scale in miles
(approximate)

OF COURSE, THE PINK GULL TURNED OUT TO be a Ross' Gull, a species never before recorded in the contiguous United States. After a period of initial disbelief, the stampede was on, complete with national news coverage and attendance by many of the country's leading birders. While this event firmly established Newburyport on the bird watcher's map, the ornithological reputation of this coastal locale was well documented a quarter-century before the Ross' Gull sighting. In 1947 Rachel Carson, in an article about the newly established Parker River National Wildlife Refuge (Plum Island), noted that "Probably there is no section of our whole country that has been studied by a larger number of competent bird specialists than this one." Ms. Carson went on to name Edward Howe Forbush, John Charles Phillips, Charles Wendell Townsend, Arthur Cleveland Bent, John Bichard May, and Ludlow Griscom, all of whom devoted a good deal of time to the birds of Plum Island. Indeed, the procession of bird watchers to the thickets, marshes, tidal flats, and dunes of northeastern Essex County began nearly a century ago when C. J. Maynard led regularly scheduled bird walks to Plum Island. Today, there is still ample reason to join in this tradition.

There are three general areas to cover: Newburyport, Plum Island, and Salisbury Beach. Seasonal considerations and time should help you to set your itinerary. To reach Newburyport, take Route 95 to Route 113 (Exit 57) and go east to High Street. Follow High Street to Rolfe's Lane (3.6 miles from Exit 57); go left on Rolfe's Lane and left again at the intersection with Water Street at the edge of the harbor. Continue along Water Street to a parking area on the right next to a **sea wall**.

This brings you to a vantage point overlooking the Merrimack River and the **Joppa Flats**. Depending on the season, this is an excellent place to look for water-fowl, shorebirds, or gulls. During the winter and early-spring months check for Common Goldeneye, Buffle-head, Red-breasted Merganser, and Oldsquaw. From late April through May and mid-July through October shorebirds are found feeding on the flats. It is best to bird this area on a falling tide, just as the flats begin to emerge. One way to estimate the best time to arrive here is to determine high tide for Boston and add four hours. Shorebirds occurring regularly in both seasons include Black-bellied and Semipalmated plovers, Greater Yellowlegs, Semipalmated and Least sandpipers, Dun-lin, and Short-billed Dowitcher. Other, less-common species that occur in spring and fall are Ruddy Turn-stone, Red Knot, and White-rumped Sandpiper. Rari-ties to keep an eye out for include Marbled Godwit, Curlew Sandpiper, and Ruff. While Hudsonian Godwit is a rarity here in spring, the species is a regular feature of the flats between mid-July and mid-September.

Turn around and go east on Water Street looking for places to pull out and view the harbor. One of these, called simply the **Clam Shack**, is where Ross' Gull was first seen. Although you probably won't be able to du-plicate this feat, there are numerous other gull species to look for here and in Newburyport Harbor in general. While Herring Gull and Great Black-backed Gull are the predominant species, Ring-billed Gull can also be com-mon. Perhaps more interesting are the less-common gulls. A few Bonaparte's Gulls may be found in any season, but this species is regularly seen in the spring and fall. In May and October your chances are fairly good of finding one or two Little Gulls, and with luck in fall or winter, you may come across a Common Black-headed Gull. The winter months are the time to look for the white-winged gulls.

Continue along Water Street to the **Sportsmen's Lodge** (less than 1 mile east of the sea wall). A large parking lot here provides another good vantage point for observing the ducks, shorebirds, and gulls in the harbor. Shortly, Water Street becomes the Plum Island Turnpike (PIT), which in turn takes you to Plum Island. Continue east, stopping to check the fields across from the airport. During migratory periods a variety of shorebirds may be found here, including Lesser Golden-Plover (fall), Upland Sandpiper (nests here), and Pectoral Sandpiper. The rare Baird's and Buff-breasted sandpipers have also been recorded here in fall. East of the airport look for a pink house on the right and then (before reaching the bridge) an obscure "road" (path is more like it) leading onto the marsh. At high tide, a walk (wade!) through the salt marsh should produce Savannah and Sharp-tailed sparrows, and perhaps a Seaside Sparrow. During the breeding season, Willet can often be located here. Proceed east along the turnpike, crossing the bridge to **Plum Island**.

Plum Island can be roughly divided into two unequal portions: the north end of the island includes the main residential and commercial areas, and, more importantly for birders, it provides access to the Atlantic Ocean, the mouth of the Merrimack River, and "the basin"; the larger, south end of the island comprises the **Parker River National Wildlife Refuge** (PRNWR) and Plum Island State Reservation.

In winter and early spring the northern section is well worth investigating. Continue straight on PIT and take a sharp left onto Northern Boulevard. A parking lot at this intersection overlooks the ocean. Winter-resident Common and Red-throated loons, Horned Grebe, eiders, and scoters are often seen here. While Northern Gannet are regularly recorded here during

migratory periods, November northeasters may produce a variety of other pelagics (see chapter on pelagic
birding for details). Follow Northern Boulevard north
1.4 miles to a parking lot adjacent to the Coast Guard
Station. Check the harbor for the wintering ducks mentioned previously, as well as for rarities including King
Eider and Barrow's Goldeneye. A walk along the beach,
eastward toward the jetties at the mouth of the river,
should increase your species count. Purple Sandpiper,
Iceland Gull, and Horned Lark are all reasonable expectations during the winter months. Retrace your tracks
along Northern Boulevard watching for a church on the
right. Park here to investigate the basin (an inlet of the
Merrimack River). Continue through town, picking up
the PIT, and go left on Sunset Boulevard to the **Parker
River National Wildlife Refuge** entrance.

Stop at the gatehouse (fee) to pick up a bird list, map,
and regulations. It is a good idea to arrive early on
"beach days," as refuge capacity is limited to 350 vehicles. Also, you may want to obtain a bird-watching
permit (at the gatehouse or PRNWR headquarters at the
north end of the island) which allows you to enter
certain restricted areas. Most of the good spots can be
birded without this permit, however. Portions of the
main access road may be closed during the winter (call
headquarters for updated information: 508-465-5753). Bird
watchers should also anticipate that during the nesting
season sections of the outer beach will be closed to
protect resident Least Terns and Piping Plovers. Finally,
from July through mid-August, the greenhead flies are
voracious. These little beasts will literally drive you off
the island unless you protect yourself with hat, long
sleeves, long pants, and repellent.

Plum Island's beaches front the Atlantic Ocean on the
east. Inland from the shore are various dune commu-

nities and thickets as well as freshwater, brackish, and saltwater marshes. These habitats, together with several pitch pine stands and manmade impoundments, create nesting and foraging areas for many species of birds. A sizable white-tailed deer population also inhabits the island. As you drive along the main road you will find many convenient pull-offs and parking areas which provide access to most of the island. The following account highlights the traditional birding stops; investigating other areas may well turn up something interesting.

Shortly after passing through the entrance gate you will come to the main parking lot on the left (restrooms and water available here except in winter). The panorama of the marshes to the west may include a Snowy Owl or Rough-legged Hawk in winter. During migratory periods check the two hillocks at the south end of the parking lot for passerines. Continue on for .8 mile to the first major birding stop.

The **Salt Pannes** are an excellent place to study feeding and roosting shorebirds. When the tide is high in the harbor, both birders and birds congregate here. Dick Forster, a present-day chronicler of bird life on Plum Island, notes that the species seen here constitute a veritable " 'Who's Who' of the shorebirds of Massachusetts." The best time for finding a majority of the shorebirds is during the fall migration. Beside the species mentioned above, Stilt Sandpiper (July through mid-August), Hudsonian Godwit (July through mid-September), and Long-billed Dowitcher (late July through late September) are regularly seen here. Western Sandpiper, White-rumped Sandpiper (in numbers during late August–early September), and Wilson's Phalarope also occur here. Herons are another feature of the Salt Pannes. From midsummer through early fall look for Great Blue Heron, Great Egret, Snowy Egret, Green-backed Heron, and Black-crowned Night-Heron. By September the duck populations are increasing, and many of the freshwater species, including both teal species, Northern Pintail, Northern Shoveler, Gadwall, and American Wigeon, are often seen. As you scan the far shore for various ducks, keep an eye out for Lesser Golden-Plover along the grassy bank. Before you leave this area be sure to check the southern portion of the pannes for other species lurking in the relatively heavier cover.

Continue south a little over a mile to **The Warden's** (a subheadquarters of the refuge). If you plan to park here and leave your car, make sure you have a permit, otherwise make a quick swing through the area. You should be able to find Purple Martins and perhaps Cliff Swallows here during the nesting season. In fall, look for sparrows, including Clay-colored, Field, and White-crowned. Lark Sparrow has also been found here. Check the perches in the field for American Kestrel and Merlin.

Just south of The Warden's (after the pavement ends) are two areas worth investigating. On the left you will see an extensive stand of pines and on the right, fields. In winter, roadside parking is permitted in order to explore the **New Pines** to the east. Both Long-eared and Northern Saw-whet owls have been found roosting in the pines during the colder months. Other winter specialties that are here from time to time include Red-breasted Nuthatch and Golden-crowned Kinglet. If it is a good finch year you may also find Pine Grosbeak, Purple Finch, either of the crossbills, Common Redpoll, and Pine Siskin. The west side of the road is good habitat for certain shorebirds in fall. Check the area around the granite **Town-line Marker** for Lesser Golden-Plover, Whimbrel, Pectoral Sandpiper, or even Buff-breasted Sandpiper.

Continue south to **Hellcat Swamp**. The parking lot

here provides access to a variety of habitats including dunes, thickets, salt marsh, and freshwater impoundments. Take the path from the west end of the parking area that leads along the dike to the observation tower. South of the dike is the Bill Forward Pool, a good spot at which to observe waterfowl, shorebirds, and herons in the spring and fall. The observation tower provides a vantage point from which to look for raptors, including Northern Harrier and falcons in the spring and fall and Rough-legged Hawks in winter. Check the marsh edge to the north for Virginia Rail and Sora as well as other marshbirds. Another feature of the impoundments is the mid- to late-summer movement of herons to their evening roost. Besides species mentioned previously, Little Blue Heron, Tricolored Heron, and Glossy Ibis can be seen around the marsh.

Back at the Hellcat Swamp parking lot, a boardwalk system (self-guiding booklet at trailhead) takes you northward, shortly dividing into westward and eastward branches. The left fork leads to a freshwater marsh and observation blind. During migratory periods, check the thickets and openings along the beginning section of the trail for various warblers. Farther along, among the dense stands of cattails, Marsh Wren and Least Bittern (rare) nest; because of their secretive habits, both species are more often heard than seen. A loop path off the main trail provides access to more of this freshwater marsh and a variety of waterfowl.

Following the boardwalk to the right (eastward) takes you through thicket habitat which can be excellent for migrant landbirds during late May and early June and again in late August and early September. Numerous flycatchers, thrushes, kinglets, vireos, and warblers occur here during migratory waves. Species (some are recorded only occasionally—see check list for relative abundance) include Yellow-bellied, Least, and Olive-sided flycatchers, Hermit, Swainson's and Gray-cheeked thrushes, and Golden-crowned and Ruby-crowned kinglets. While relatively uncommon, warbler species such as Tennessee, Northern Parula, Magnolia, Cape May, Blackburnian, and Bay-breasted are regularly recorded in spring and fall. Rare migrants include Cerulean (spring), Kentucky, Mourning, Connecticut (fall), and Hooded warblers as well as Yellow-breasted Chat. The eastward branch of the boardwalk eventually crosses the road and loops around the back dunes. In April and during the fall migration, the dune tops offer a good spot at which to pause and look for hawks. Sharp-shinned Hawk, American Kestrel, Merlin, and Peregrine Falcon have all provided some exciting moments here.

Just south of Hellcat is an area on the west side of the road known as the **Old Pines**. A parking lot here provides access to a short trail through the pines and views to the marsh.

Two miles south of the Hellcat Swamp is **Cross Farm Hill**. More than once, the rare Gyrfalcon has put in a winter appearance in this vicinity, although you are much more likely to find an American Kestrel. Groups of Canada Geese (sometimes joined by a lesser number of Snow Geese) are regularly seen here as they browse on the hillside grasses.

Continue south along the main road to parking lot number 6. This is one of two accesses to **Stage Island Pool**. Depending on the water level and season, this site is a prime area for waterfowl, herons, shorebirds, and terns. During April and October look for Gadwall, Northern Pintail, both teal species, and Northern Shoveler. During the nesting season you may find Ruddy Duck, American Bittern, Common Moorhen, and American Coot. Another access to the pool is a path across from parking lot number 7. This leads to an observation tower overlooking Stage Island. With a scope, you should have good views of the various birds in and around the pool. Many of the same species of shorebirds which occur at the Salt Pannes can be found here if the flats are exposed. Possible tern species here include Forster's Tern (fall), Common Tern, and Black Tern.

Just south of Stage Island is the **Plum Island State Reservation**. This area tends to be most productive in late summer when flocks of shorebirds and terns can be found along the beach. From the parking area walk out around Sandy Point, scoping the shoreline as you go. Besides the summer-resident Least Terns, you may find a few Roseate Terns or even a Royal Tern. Piping Plover, Sanderling, and Dunlin are also found here.

Salisbury Beach is well worth a visit during the fall and winter months. From Plum Island, take PIT to Water Street and follow this through downtown Newburyport to Route 1. Cross the Merrimack River on the Route 1 bridge and follow the signs to Salisbury Center. Go right (east) on Route 1A (Beach Road) for 2 miles and look for the entrance to Salisbury Beach State Reservation on the right. The areas to bird here are the access roads and adjacent marshes, the campgrounds, and the river front. In September and October, Salisbury Beach State Reservation campground is a prime spot for observing passerine migrants. The isolated clumps of shrubs and trees offer cover for a variety of transients. One group that is always well represented is the sparrows. While Chipping, Savannah, Song, and White-throated sparrows can be common, Clay-colored (rare), Vesper, Lark (rare), Lincoln's, and White-crowned sparrows can also be found. Check the weedy thickets, building perimeters, and various perches around the campground. Warblers can also be numerous here. Later in the season (late September through mid-November) Lapland Long-spurs and Snow Buntings may be present.

During the winter months, carefully check the marshes west of the access road for Northern Harrier, Rough-legged Hawk, Snowy Owl, and Short-eared Owl. Bear right at the campground and follow the road down to the boat-launch area. This is a good spot from which to see most of the wintering ducks. Scan the waters of the inlet and the Merrimack River. Gulls are another winter feature of the boat-launch area. Iceland and Glaucous gulls occur here with some regularity, and both Ivory Gull and Ross' Gull have been seen from this vantage point. A walk eastward along the beach front should add to your species list. The Ipswich race of the Savannah Sparrow winters among the dunes.

One final winter site worth investigating is the Merrimack River west of Route 1. Return to Newburyport via routes 1A and 1. Stay right as you come down the Merrimack River bridge and go right onto Merrimac Street. In less than .5 mile go right at the Municipal Boat Launch sign. This takes you to Cashman Park and a view over the river. The park is a good place to observe the numerous waterfowl in the river, and there are often wintering Bald Eagles in the vicinity. Scope the tree line on the opposite side of the river for the eagles, Red-tailed Hawks, and Rough-legged Hawks. The gulls should also be checked for Iceland and Glaucous gulls. Often one or both species of the white-winged gulls can be seen along the near bank or on the passing ice floes.

Downtown Newburyport, especially the restored Market Square District, is an enjoyable place to browse or shop. There are numerous eating establishments as well as inn and bed-and-breakfast accommodations in town. Standard motel fare can be had at the Susse Chalet in Amesbury.

Cape Ann

FALL / WINTER

CAPE ANN IS AN IDEAL PLACE TO SAMPLE BOTH the fall seabird migration and the winter-resident bird life of the New England coast. From September through mid-November the seabird migration, which includes pelagics, is underway; later in the season, the typical winter residents are on hand. Here, amidst the granite, ice, and green-cold ocean, scores of loons, grebes, waterfowl, and gulls pass the winter. Visiting bird watchers can poke along the coast investigating the numerous harbors, headlands, and seascapes at their leisure. While a midwinter circuit of Cape Ann is certain to provide the opportunity of seeing a majority of the common species, the bonus of rare ducks, white-winged gulls, and alcids adds to the anticipation of such a tour.

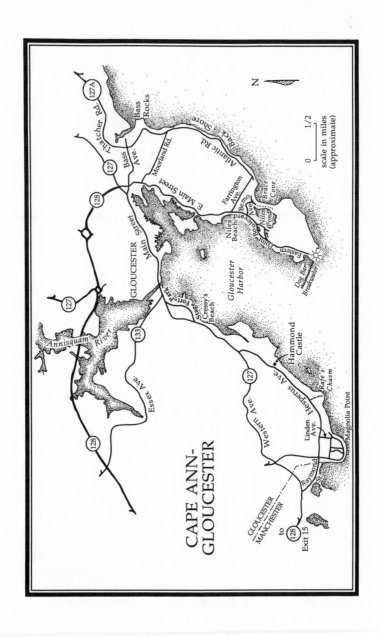

CAPE ANN-
GLOUCESTER

N

0   1/2
scale in miles
(approximate)

To reach Cape Ann follow Route 128 north to Exit 15 (School Street). Follow the signs to Magnolia, joining Route 127 North, and in 3.5 miles (from Route 128 exit) turn right at Raymond Street. Go right again onto Shore Road at the Magnolia Variety store. Shore Road loops around **Magnolia Point**, and there are several stops to make here. A parking lot on your right provides an overlook to a sand beach, Magnolia Harbor, and Kettle Island to the southwest. Check the beach for lingering shorebirds and the harbor for American Black Duck and Red-breasted Merganser. While you should have no trouble spotting the ubiquitous Herring and Great Black-backed gulls, look for the diminutive Bonaparte's Gull as well. As you continue around Magnolia Point there are pull-offs opposite Oakes and Lexington avenues. Scope the ocean for Red-throated and Common loons as well as rafts of Common Eider. This locale offers your first chance of finding Harlequin Duck. Carefully scan the waters along the shoreline and around the offshore rocks. Follow the narrow road down a slight hill (there is a good view to the ocean here), and as you leave the point turn left and then quickly right onto Linden Avenue (no sign). Follow Linden to Hesperus Avenue and turn right again.

In approximately half a mile you will come to **Rafe's Chasm** (unmarked) parking lot on your right beside a chain-link fence. Follow the path along a wood fence through the woodlands down to a rocky bluff that over-looks the Atlantic Ocean. If you missed Harlequin Duck at Magnolia Point, Rafe's Chasm is an even better spot to find this colorful wintering species. Scope the shore-line and in particular the inlet to the west. Often the harlequins are seen actively feeding in the surf or sun-ning on the rocks. This is also a good spot to find Common Goldeneye and Bufflehead, and perhaps a Horned Grebe.

Continue north on Hesperus Avenue. You may want to make a stop at the Hammond Castle Museum just ahead on the right. The castle overlooks a group of rocks called "Norman's Woe" which Longfellow memorialized in *Wreck of the Hesperus*. Follow 127N and turn right into **Stage Fort Park** (2.1 miles from Rafe's Chasm). There is ample parking here, and you may want to take some time to explore the western shoreline of Gloucester Harbor from this access. The waters off Cressy's and Half Moon beaches often attract waterfowl and gulls. Check any goldeneyes for a possible Barrow's Goldeneye and the gulls for white-winged species. Both Iceland and Glaucous gulls are reasonable expectations for any midwinter trip around Cape Ann.

Follow the park road around to where it rejoins 127N and turn right toward Gloucester Center. Continue through town, passing the statue of the *Man at the Wheel* on your right and eventually Gorton's of Gloucester on your left. Shortly, look for East Main Street on your right (at traffic lights). At this point you will leave 127N and follow East Main Street up a hill to the right. Continue along East Main for approximately 1.5 miles to a parking area for **Niles Beach**. Common Loon, Horned Grebe, and many of the typical wintering ducks can be found here.

Just ahead is the gate to **Eastern Point**. Eastern Point is open throughout the winter months (access is restricted from Memorial Day through Labor Day). Follow Eastern Point Boulevard to the Coast Guard station and lighthouse. From a parking lot at the end of the road you will look out over the entrance to Gloucester Harbor and the **Dog Bar Breakwater**. There is normally a variety of wintering seabirds here, including loons, Common Eider, Common Goldeneye, Bufflehead, and Red-breasted Merganser. Check the breakwater for Great

Cormorant, Purple Sandpiper, Iceland Gull, and Glaucous Gull. The concentration of gulls on the breakwater can be impressive. Perhaps it was just such a sight that led T. S. Eliot, in his poem *Cape Ann*, to say, ". . . resign this land at the end, resign it / To its true owner, the tough one, the sea gull." As you return along Eastern Point Boulevard, the exit road swings right and soon passes **Niles Pond.** Look for a spot to pull over where the road comes closest to the pond. If there is open water, this is an excellent locale in which to find many of the freshwater ducks. Mallard, Northern Pintail, Green-winged Teal, Gadwall, American Wigeon, and Ruddy Duck are often seen here, while Eurasian Wigeon is a possible rarity. Both of the white-winged gulls are regularly found at Niles Pond during the winter months, and gull enthusiasts occasionally turn up a Lesser Black-backed Gull among the ever-changing flocks of larids.

Continue north on Eastern Point Boulevard and take your first right onto Bemo Avenue (unmarked). A quick left and then a right will take you to a small parking lot which provides an alternate access to Niles Pond. To explore this area, walk out the path between **Brace Cove** and the pond. Depending on the light, this side of the pond may or may not provide a better look at the waterfowl and gulls. Even if you decide not to walk out the path, you can continue along the road which skirts the cove. This is another good area from which to observe the gulls. Although the great majority will be Ring-billed, Herring, and Great Black-backed, Bonaparte's gulls can be fairly common here. In late winter (February and March) the concentrations of white-winged gulls can be impressive. Check the beach for wintering shorebirds including Sanderling and Dunlin. After exploring the cove, retrace your tracks along Bemo Avenue back to Eastern Point Boulevard. Exit Eastern Point and go right onto Farrington Avenue. This eventually joins Atlantic Road which takes you along **Back Shore**.

The 2-mile drive along Back Shore would be worth the time even if it were devoid of birds. The bold rocky shore, surf, and sea present a dramatic panorama. Fortunately, the birds seem to approve of this setting. You will find several places to pull off the road that provide overlooks to the shore and ocean. Local birders favor the area near the end of this stretch, but don't be in a rush. Check the ocean for Red-throated and Common loons, Red-necked and Horned grebes, and all three species of scoter. White-winged and Surf scoters can be common, but you may have to work a little harder for Black Scoter. The rafts of Common Eider may produce the rare King Eider. Shortly after passing Moorland Road (on your left), you will see **Bass Rocks** cove on the right. Check here for Purple Sandpipers, ducks, and gulls. Rare and uncomon species, including Eared Grebe, King Eider, Harlequin Duck, and Barrow's Goldeneye, have all been recorded here.

At Bass Rocks bear left on Atlantic Road and continue to the next main intersection. Cross Bass Avenue to Thatcher Road (Route 127A), which takes you to Rockport (see Rockport map). From this intersection continue approximately 2.8 miles and go right onto an inconspicuous side street called Tregony Bow. Take your first right onto South Street (unmarked) and left onto Penzance Road. Two places worth checking are **Henry's Pond** on the left and **Pebbly Beach** on the right. If the pond is open scan the edges for ducks; check the beach front and cove for gulls and waterfowl. There are normally eider, scoter, Bufflehead, and goldeneyes along this section. The rocks at the north end of the beach may produce cormorants and/or Purple Sandpipers; Harlequin Ducks are occasionally found here as well.

Follow Penzance Road past Land's End and Emerson Point and go right onto Eden Road (unmarked). There are several areas worth investigating along this stretch. Scoping the coastal waters may turn up a Black Guillemot or even a Thick-billed Murre. Continue along Eden Road to the spot where it makes a sharp left and then rejoins Thatcher Road (Route 127A). Go right, and in .4 mile go right again onto Marmion Way. In .6 mile there is an overlook of Gap Cove. Continue on Marmion Way and take a right onto Old Garden Road. Shortly you will see a convenient parking lot on the right above **Old Garden Beach**.

Follow Old Garden to Norwood Avenue and into "downtown" Rockport. In winter, the traffic is usually sparse enough to permit a quick trip out **Bearskin Neck**. This is the shop-filled peninsula in the town center. The turnaround at the end of Bearskin Neck provides a good vantage point from which to study the various waterbirds. Return to Route 127A and follow the signs to Pigeon Cove. Two stops on the way to Pigeon Cove are **Back Harbor**, where the beach is adjacent to the road, and **Granite Pier**, reached by taking Wharf Road to the right. Continue through Pigeon Cove, following the road up the hill. Go right on Phillips Avenue at the sign for the Ralph Waldo Emerson Inn. Follow Phillips Avenue to Point DeChene Avenue and go straight ahead to **Andrews Point**. Andrews Point often provides the highlights of a Cape Ann trip. In fact, if good fortune or planning have brought you to Cape Ann during a November northeaster, try to be at Andrews Point close to dawn (much of the action here seems to occur in the early-morning hours). As these powerful storms roll up the coast, the migrants, pushed landward by onshore winds, stream by in impressive numbers. Even under less-violent conditions the bird watching is interesting. In early November, Red-throated and Common

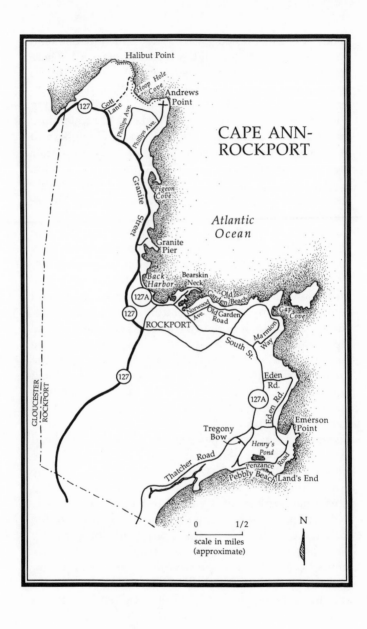

Halibut Point

Hoop Hole Cove

Andrews Point

Gott Lane

127

Phillips Ave.

Phillips Ave.

CAPE ANN-ROCKPORT

Granite Street

Pigeon Cove

Atlantic Ocean

Granite Pier

Back Harbor

Bearskin Neck

Old Garden Beach

127A

127

Norwood Ave.

Old Garden Road

Gap Cove

ROCKPORT

Marmion Way

South St.

Eden Rd.

127A

Eden Rd.

Emerson Point

127

Tregony Bow

Henry's Pond

Penzance Road

GLOUCESTER
ROCKPORT

Thatcher Road

Pebbly Beach

Land's End

0   1/2

scale in miles
(approximate)

N

loons, Northern Gannet, Common Eider, Oldsquaw, all three scoters, and Red-breasted Merganser are normally all well represented. This variety is often complemented by Red-necked and Horned grebes, other ducks, and gulls including Bonaparte's and Black-legged Kittiwake. If you hit the flight on just the right day, the pelagic possibilities are many. Thick-billed Murre, Razorbill, and Black Guillemot are seen fairly regularly during November northeasters, Dovekie, Common Murre, and Atlantic Puffin less often (see chapter on pelagic birding for more details).

Even on a fine day in January, however, you will do well to spend some time at Andrews Point. There are three vantage points to check out. A small parking area (space for one car) will be found at the northern end of Point DeChene Avenue, while the eastern end of Longbranch Avenue overlooks the ocean, and the western end offers a view to Hoop Hole Cove. For the hardy, a path follows the shoreline west to Hoop Hole Cove and then around to Halibut Point (see below). The luxuries of in-car viewing often result in bird watchers recording a good variety of winter specialities at Andrews Point. One or two Black Guillemots are normally on one side of the point or the other. Eiders can be carefully checked for King Eider and goldeneyes for Barrow's Goldeneye. Patience and a good scope will help you to find the various scoters, ducks, and gulls (including white-wings) in the immediate vicinity. Once you have checked off all the regulars you can still entertain the hope that an Ivory Gull may happen by. When you have exhausted the possibilities here, return to Phillips Avenue and then to Route 127.

Less than .5 mile north on Route 127 look for Gott Avenue on the right. This leads to parking for the .5-mile trail that goes out **Halibut Point**. One longtime Cape Ann birder has suggested this is *the* place to take in a November northeaster. While this may be true for the purist, mere mortals should be advised that a visit to Halibut Point during a northeaster is more akin to 12-meter racing or survival school than to a day at the beach. If you decide to visit during a blow, be well prepared (oilskins, warm clothing, and rolls of paper toweling for starters). In less inclement weather, Halibut Point can be a pleasant jaunt offering one of the more spectacular coastal vistas in Massachusetts.

As you continue west and south around the cape you will find several other obvious places to stop and check for species you may have missed earlier. Eventually, Route 127 rejoins Route 128 and the road south to Boston.

There are ample services, accommodations, and restaurants in and around Gloucester which are open throughout the year. Rockport tends to be more seasonal, with many shops and restaurants closed during the winter months. Those anticipating a ration of grog, or the like, after a hard day in the field, should be forewarned that Rockport is a dry town.

Gloucester is the oldest seaport in North America. The earliest European settlement was established at Stage Fort (1623). While the magnificent nineteenth-century fleet of Gloucester fishing schooners represented a high point in the community's vitality, the town is still an important port for the fishing industry. A visit to the Cape Ann Historical Society (27 Pleasant Street) and a stroll around the docks will provide a good introduction to Gloucester, past and present.

Both Gloucester and Rockport have long been associated with the visual arts. Artists' colonies thrive here, particularly during the summer months. Activities are centered around the North Shore Arts Association in East Gloucester and the Rockport Art Association on Main Street in Rockport.

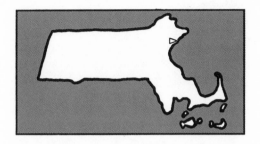

Marblehead Neck
Wildlife Sanctuary

SPRING / FALL

"HEADS," "HARBORS," "BIGHTS," "BAYS,"
"necks," and "narrows." The language used to describe
the shoreline is as varied as the New England coast
itself. Marblehead Neck, which pokes out into Massachusetts Bay just north of Boston, is one of many pen-
insulas along the irregular coastline. During spring and
fall migrating landbirds are attracted to such areas as
resting and feeding spots. Unfortunately, many of these
coastal locales have been preempted for human habi-
tation. As development and habitat fragmentation continue, the number of good lay-over sites for birds decreases. Thanks to the foresight of local residents and
the Massachusetts Audubon Society, the **Marblehead**

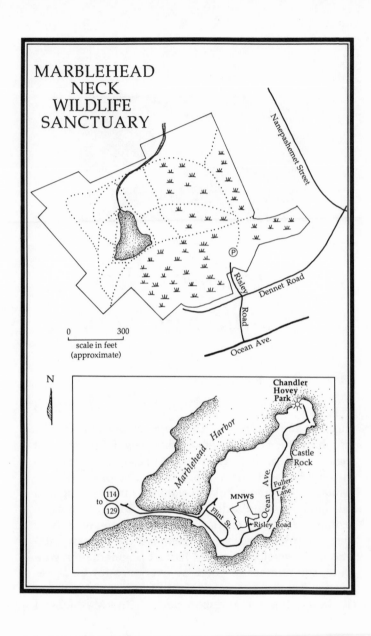

MARBLEHEAD NECK WILDLIFE SANCTUARY

Nanepashemet Street

P

Risley Road

Dennet Road

Ocean Ave.

0   300
scale in feet
(approximate)

N

Marblehead Harbor

Chandler Hovey Park

Castle Rock

Ocean Ave.

Fuller Lane

to 114
129

MNWS

Flint St.

Risley Road

Neck Wildlife Sanctuary (MNWS) offers over 15 acres of suitable habitat for the migrants. Between late April and early June and from late August through the third week in October, the sanctuary can be a bird watcher's delight. Over 235 species have been recorded here, with various flycatchers, thrushes, vireos, and warblers packing the list.

To reach Marblehead Neck take Route 128 north to Route 114 to Salem. Continue through Salem on Route 114 following the signs to Marblehead and Marblehead Neck. Turn right (south) onto Ocean Avenue (at the intersection with signs to Route 129), which takes you across the **causeway** to Marblehead Neck. At the eastern end of the causeway there is room to pull off and scope the harbor for shorebirds, ducks, and seabirds. The view (in clear weather) of downtown Boston from this spot is excellent and emphasizes the neck's proximity to the metropolitan area. Continue on Ocean Avenue (right at fork) to Risley Road, which goes left (north) to the sanctuary parking lot.

Although the neck was once heavily wooded, seventeenth-century cutting for house and ship timber as well as continuous farming resulted in a treeless landscape for well over two centuries. No doubt most migrant passerines passed by during this era. The fields did, however, provide suitable habitat for certain migrant shorebirds. In the middle of the nineteenth century the neck was recommended to sportsmen as "the favorite resort of Plover and Curlew." During the latter part of that century the farms were gradually abandoned, while at the same time interest in the neck as a summer resort grew. Twentieth-century improvements in the causeway encouraged more development. By the early 1950s the entire perimeter and much of the interior had been "improved." It was at that point that the conservation efforts, which ultimately led to the establishment of the Marblehead Neck Wildlife Sanctuary, were begun.

Today the thickets formed by second-growth woodland and shrub communities offer a variety of habitats for birds and birders. The sanctuary is crisscrossed by a series of trails, most of which run generally north–south or east–west. A few steps from the parking lot you will find the main east–west trail. Walking back and forth over the length of this trail several times may give an idea of the activity level for the day of your visit. You should plan to canvass the entire sanctuary, however, as its relatively small size makes it easy to cover during a half-day visit. Warblers that occur on a regular basis in the spring and fall include Black-and-white, Blue-winged, Tennessee, Nashville, Northern Parula, Yellow, Magnolia, Cape May, Yellow-rumped, Black-throated Green, Blackburnian, Chestnut-sided, Bay-breasted, Blackpoll, Prairie, Palm, Ovenbird, Northern Waterthrush, Mourning, Common Yellowthroat, Yellow-breasted Chat, Wilson's, Canada, and American Redstart. Other, rarer, warblers which have been recorded at the Sanctuary include Prothonotary, Worm-eating, Orange-crowned, Cerulean, Yellow-throated, Kentucky, Connecticut (fall), and Hooded. While no one should expect to see most of these birds on any one visit, good days often produce lists of 15 or more species of warblers. Most migrant warblers are found moving through the canopy and understory feeding in mixed flocks (often in association with chickadees and titmice). In addition to the sanctuary's woodlands, birders should also investigate the pond edge for waterthrushes, as well as ground-level tangles on the hillside and elsewhere for the *Oporornis* (Mourning and Connecticut) warblers. It may be especially profitable to arrive at the pond early and scout the entire perimeter; this locale often attracts many of the migrants.

Marblehead Neck Wildlife Sanctuary also provides a good opportunity to see many nonwarbler species during migration. One of the specialties of the sanctuary is the fall flight of Philadelphia Vireos (a few are noted in spring). From the last week in August through late September your chances of seeing this bird are fairly good. Much less regular are the Yellow-throated Vireo and the White-eyed Vireo, although both species are normally recorded in fall. Red-eyed and Solitary vireos are seen regularly in both seasons. While the common flycatchers are Eastern Kingbird, Great Crested Flycatcher, and Eastern Phoebe, Marblehead Neck is a good spot to find Olive-sided (check the bare snags on the back side of the hill) and Yellow-bellied flycatchers. Besides the Yellow-bellied Flycatcher, which can be identified with some confidence even in fall, other *Empidonax* species recorded in the sanctuary are Acadian, Willow, Alder, and Least flycatchers. While the members of this latter group are readily identified in spring through their distinctive vocalizations, their silence in fall leaves most undetermined. Migrant thrushes seen in the sanctuary include Veery, Gray-cheeked Thrush (uncommon), Swainson's Thrush, Hermit Thrush, and Wood Thrush.

Places such as Marblehead Neck sanctuary are touted as "migrant traps" because of the regularity with which large groups of birds appear in certain seasons. And while one is perfectly correct in assuming that flocks of warblers, vireos, and thrushes will pass through this sanctuary during the fall and spring migrations, predicting the best day to visit is difficult at best. In fall, northwest winds accompanying the passage of a high-pressure system favor the passage of south-bound migrants. Unfortunately this does not allow us to predict with precision where a "wave" of birds will settle on any given day. Some of the best lists are made under very localized conditions, e.g., on those cloudy, misty days when weather fronts are stalled and the birds remain active throughout the day. Suffice it to say that a visit to the Marblehead Neck sanctuary during migration puts you in the right place; you will know if you have chosen the right day! **Flint Street**, west of the sanctuary, is another place you may want to check for migrants.

If you happen to be visiting the neck during the winter months check the vistas to Massachusetts Bay at the end of Fuller Lane and at **Castle Rock Park**. Both of these areas are off of Ocean Avenue to the east. At the northern end of Marblehead Neck are the **Chandler Hovey Park** and the Marblehead Lighthouse. There is public parking here as well as a place to picnic. The bluffs overlooking the bay and harbor provide another spot from which to scope for ducks and seabirds (see Cape Ann chapter for relevant winter species).

A recommended side trip for visitors to this area is the Peabody Museum in Salem. While the major focus of the museum is the maritime history of Massachusetts, the Peabody also devotes a considerable amount of space to natural history. The bird collection includes a comprehensive display of the birds of the Essex County region. A fairly wide choice of accommodations and restaurants is available a short distance from the Neck. Salem's Hawthorne Inn and Marblehead's Pleasant Manor Inn are both convenient. Two of Marblehead's best-known restaurants are Rosalie's and Maddie's Sail Loft.

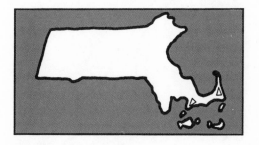

Cape Cod and Monomoy

SUMMER / FALL / WINTER

ROBERT FINCH CHARACTERIZES CAPE COD AS
"a place by the sea that has been explored, settled,
visited, studied, and written about more than almost
any other stretch of the North American coastline."
Naturalists are well represented in this perennial crowd
of Cape Cod chroniclers. Useful books on the Cape's
geology, marshes, beaches, plants, birds, marine mammals, reptiles, and amphibians are readily found in
bookstores from Falmouth to Provincetown. This lavish
attention to the Cape's natural history gives even the
first-time visitor a sense of being on well-worked, if not
familiar, soil (or in this case, sand). Here bird watchers
partake of a tradition dating back four centuries. The
Great Auks and the Black Skimmers described by the

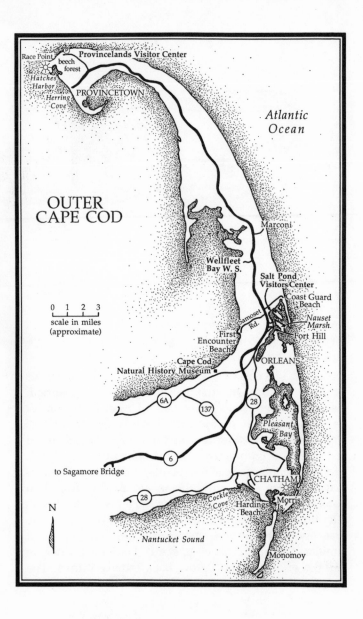

explorers Gosnold and Champlain in the early 1600s mark the beginning of an interest in the Cape's bird life that is carried on today by scientists studying Piping Plovers on Nauset Beach and boatloads of bird watchers heading for Monomoy.

Certainly there is much to anticipate while planning a birding trip to Cape Cod. If this is your first visit, however, there may be a temptation to do too much. The Cape is a relatively large area that takes one or two days to cover in even cursory fashion. If your time is limited, you would do well to concentrate on the Outer Cape (the north-south forearm), which has the majority of prime bird-watching areas. Seasonal considerations will also help you to select certain stops and omit others. Perhaps the optimal time for a visit is September. During the two or three weeks following Labor Day the crowds decrease, and the migration is in full swing. Birding on the Cape can be excellent any time from midsummer through late fall, however. Due to the maritime climate and extensive shoreline, the winter birding also offers some interesting possibilities.

On the assumption that most bird watchers will be visiting the Cape between midsummer and early fall, this account begins with a representative tour of the Outer Cape.

Many devotees of the Cape's bird life are content to spend most of their time in the Chatham area. William Brewster and Ludlow Griscom, two of Massachusetts's more famous ornithologists, did extensive work here. Even today, a cadre of astute ornithologists have residences in and around Chatham—and with good reason. The annual movement of birds through the local marshes, freshwater ponds, coastal thickets, and offshore islands is as diverse as it is anywhere in New England. One birder can point with pride to the 24 species of warblers he recorded one September morning; another recounts the 46 species of shorebirds that have been seen on Monomoy. While you will probably have to settle for somewhat fewer shorebirds and warblers, Chatham is a good place to start a birding tour of the Cape.

To reach Chatham take Exit 11 off Route 6 and follow Route 137 south to Route 28. Go left (east) on Route 28, and in less than .5 mile go right onto Cockle Cove Road. Continue straight, to the parking lot at **Cockle Cove** (fee). Three areas worth exploring here are the flats to the east of the parking area, Nantucket Sound to the south, and the marshes to the west. From August to early autumn a variety of shorebirds frequent the flats. Semipalmated Plover, Greater Yellowlegs, Semipalmated Sandpiper, and Least Sandpiper are common; Ruddy Turnstone, Pectoral Sandpiper, and Short-billed Dowitcher are also regular migrants. Laughing and Ring-billed gulls, as well as Common and Least terns, often roost on the edge of the flats. While Nantucket Sound is most productive during the late-fall and early-winter season, you may be able to find Common Eider, White-winged Scoter, and Red-breasted Merganser even in summer. Walk westward down the beach to the inlet where you can look over the marsh behind the shore-front cottages. (At high tide the marsh can be reached via Clark Metters Way just north of the parking lot off Cockle Cove Road.) This is a good area to find Great Blue Heron, Snowy Egret, Green-backed Heron, Glossy Ibis, Black-bellied Plover, Willet, and Whimbrel. No doubt the Whimbrel are attracted to the many fiddler crabs living in the marsh. Before leaving, check the perches on the back side of the marsh for Osprey and American Kestrel.

Returning to Route 28 go right for a little over a mile to Barn Hill Road. Turn right onto Barn Hill and right at the fork onto Harding's Beach Road and continue to **Harding's Beach** (fee) parking lot. This is a good winter site because of its view to the sound. A walk out the barrier beach (southeast) in winter may produce Snow Bunting, Lapland Longspur, the Ipswich race of Savannah Sparrow, or even a Short-eared Owl. In August you will have to arrive in the early morning before the beach crowd moves in; rainy or foggy days, at the height of the tourist season, can be productive even at the most popular beaches. Many of the birds mentioned in the Cockle Cove section occur along Harding's Beach; also look for Piping Plover, American Oystercatcher, and Sanderling along the beach and cormorants in the sound.

To reach **Morris Island Beach** go east on Route 28 to the rotary; continue straight ahead on Main Street through Chatham Center. At the end of Main Street go right on Shore Road and left at the sharp curve just past the lighthouse onto Morris Island Road. After a turn to the right Morris Island Road crosses the causeway. Parking is permitted along the east side of the causeway; with luck you may find a parking space at the Monomoy Refuge Headquarters (up the hill and to the left). The developed sections of Morris Island are private and non-residents are unwelcome. As you walk out the beach path from the causeway look for the muted gray-green *Hudsonia* (Thoreau's "Poverty Grass") and the bright golden aster. Eastward from Morris Island Beach are the thoroughfare and a new island, formerly the southern tip of Nauset Beach. During the summer months gulls and terns are constantly plying the thoroughfare. While Laughing Gulls and Common and Least terns are among the common species, with diligence you may find a Bonaparte's Gull or a Roseate Tern. Check the flocks following incoming fishing boats; occasionally a

Parasitic Jaeger is seen harassing the terns and gulls. Walk south along the beach toward the point that looks out to Monomoy Island. At the tip of the peninsula, an incoming tide and a scope should provide excellent shorebirding. Besides the species mentioned earlier, look for Red Knot (early August peak) and Dunlin (late summer and throughout the fall). American Oystercatchers are regularly seen here through late September. In July and August the chances are good of seeing one or two Hudsonian Godwits. With luck you may even find a Black Skimmer. Be sure to walk out and around the point to see the birds feeding along the western shore. Roseate and Forster's terns are a good bet here, and there are occasional reports of Royal Tern.

Several paths lead back through the dunes of Morris Island to the thickets and oak–pine scrub (be sure to stay out of restricted areas and to respect private-property lines). This habitat can be excellent for passerines during the late summer–fall migration. A variety of flycatchers, vireos, and warblers are regularly seen here. Common migrants include Great Crested Flycatcher, Red-eyed Vireo, and Cape May, Yellow-rumped, Black-throated Green, Bay-breasted, Blackpoll, and Black-and-white warblers. Indeed few, if any, of New England's warblers have not been recorded on Morris Island. Prothonotary, Worm-eating, Connecticut, Mourning, and Hooded warblers as well as Yellow-breasted Chat are normally seen each year. Species such as Blue-gray Gnatcatcher, Red-breasted Nuthatch, and Philadelphia Vireo are also features of Morris Island.

When you return to the beach you will, no doubt, notice the flocks of cormorants, shorebirds, gulls, and terns lining the beaches of **Monomoy**. With a scope, you might even make out a Short-eared Owl, Northern Harrier, or perhaps an eagle in the skies above the island. Monomoy is at once tantalizingly close yet frustratingly far away. The best way to resolve this dilemma is to plan a trip to Monomoy.

A quarter-century ago birders walked to Monomoy. The constantly shifting sands of the island have now separated from the mainland, and you will need to take a short boat ride to reach Monomoy. Plan your visit to be on the island at high tide. Also make sure to bring water, snacks, and proper clothing; Monomoy is a wilderness area devoid of services. Contact Monomoy Refuge Headquarters for up-to-date information on ferry services (508-945-0594) or try one of the following:

Art Gould's Boat Livery
Reservations: Call John W. McGrath, Jr.
508-945-9378

Monomoy Island Tours
Reservations: Call Bird Watcher's General Store
508-255-6974

Massachusetts Audubon Society
Wellfleet Bay Wildlife Sanctuary
508-349-2615

Monomoy is actually two islands, North Island and South Island. North Island, the closest to the mainland, is the destination of most bird watchers. Although you can arrange a trip to South Island, the charter will be expensive. While the variety of birds (and habitats) is greater on South Island, as is the list of vagrants, North Island is more convenient and offers spectacular concentrations of waterbirds from mid-July to mid-September. North Island also attracts its share of surprises, with such species as Eurasian and Long-billed curlews, Little and Rufous-necked stints, Bar-tailed Godwit, and Reddish Egret leading the list.

The prime birding area on North Island is the sand- and mudflats region along the northwestern shore. From the tip of Monomoy to the Godwit Bar (.25 mile to the south), the birder can expect to find hundreds, if not thousands, of sandpipers in late summer. Certainly one of the highlights is the concentration (peak numbers in early August) of Hudsonian Godwits. This is the best spot in New England to see large numbers of this species. The Monomoy shorebird list includes all the common migrants with substantial numbers of American Oystercatcher, Willet, Whimbrel, Red Knot, and Short-billed Dowitcher. A few "rare" species such as Wilson's Plover (spring), American Avocet, Marbled Godwit, Curlew Sandpiper, and Ruff occur with some regularity on Monomoy.

The north end of Monomoy is also a good spot to observe terns. Mixed flocks of Common, Least, and Roseate terns often roost on the beach. While Arctic Tern is a rare nester on Monomoy, numbers of subadult nonbreeders (*portlandica* type) are present in June and July. Forster's Tern and Black Tern are also regularly seen here.

For landbirds, including nesting Sharp-tailed Sparrow, check the marsh in the vicinity of Godwit Bar. While hiking around North Island keep an eye out for Bald Eagle, Short-eared Owl, and later in the season, hawks including sharp-shins, Merlins, and peregrines. Monomoy, almost invariably, has something special to offer the bird watcher. Blair Nikula, the current "dean of the Moy," calls every trip to Monomoy "a voyage of discovery." What you discover on Monomoy may be the highlight of your Cape Cod visit.

Return to Shore Road which connects with Route 28; this route takes you north along Pleasant Bay (worth checking for bay ducks in winter) and eventually joins

Route 6A in Orleans. Soon after reaching Route 6A you will come to Route 6 (Mid-Cape Highway) at the traffic circle. Follow the signs to Provincetown, and in a little over 1 mile go right at the entrance to **Fort Hill**. Drive to the parking lot at the top of the rise. The view from Fort Hill to Nauset Marsh and the ocean beyond is one of the finest on the Cape. Take at least a few minutes to enoy the unique combination of natural sights and sounds that give Cape Cod its special character. While you are scanning the horizon you may even spy a harrier working the tops of the marsh grasses. In late summer, the hillside meadows often attract flocks of Bobolinks; another feature of Fort Hill at this season is the Eastern Kingbirds. Follow the path down the hill to the large boulders (glacial erratics) at the edge of the tidal creek. If the mudflats are exposed you may see a few shorebirds; Greater Yellowlegs and Short-billed Dowitchers often feed along the banks. Follow the path north (left) along the marsh watching for herons as you go. You may also discover one or two brightly marked land snails along this path. In late September and October a walk along the marsh's edge at high tide can be productive. Possibilities include rails and Seaside Sparrow. The thickets between the marsh and the uplands sometimes produce a variety of migrant landbirds; occasionally even a Yellow-breasted Chat tees up in one of the shrubs. Retrace your steps to your car and drive down the hill to the parking lot on the right. A trail here leads out into old–field–red-cedar habitat and then through a red maple swamp. Although normally unremarkable for its bird life, it can be an enjoyable walk and might even produce a few birds.

Return to Route 6 and continue north. In less than .5 mile, you will come to Hemenway Road on your right. **Hemenway Landing** at the end of the road is the site of one of the Cape's time-honored bird-watching rituals. At dusk each evening the nocturnal herons leave their daytime roosts; a steady stream of Black-crowned Night-Herons, and the occasional Yellow-crowned Night-Heron, exit the dark groves and spread out across Nauset Marsh to feed. At the same time, Great Blue Herons, Snowy Egrets, and Green-backed Herons are moving out of the marsh. In late summer this procession of herons is complemented by flocks of terns and gulls, many of which will soon migrate south. When the sunset cooperates, the pastel colors of the marsh and sky provide a perfect backdrop for this impressive movement of birds.

Less than 1 mile north of Hemenway Road on Route 6 is Samoset Road. Go left here, following the signs to **First Encounter Beach** (fee). Park in the second parking area. From this location the beach and Cape Cod Bay are to the west, the extensive Eastham marshes are to the east, and southward the Herring River inlet cuts through the beach. The best birding on the bay side involves pelagics in late summer and fall, with northwest winds following northeasters (see Sandy Neck, Barnstable, below, and the chapter on pelagic birding). The flats (low tide) off the beach normally attract large numbers of shorebirds, gulls, and terns. The birds are often widely dispersed, however, and in summer bathers make the birding somewhat difficult. You will probably have more success on the marsh side. At high tide many shorebirds gather in flocks to roost on the marsh. Large numbers of Black-bellied Plovers and Greater Yellowlegs often congregate here. Also look for Lesser Golden-Plover (late summer and fall), Willet, Spotted Sandpiper, Upland Sandpiper (rare), Whimbrel, Ruddy Turnstone, Least Sandpiper, and Short-billed Dowitcher.

This is a good spot to study many of the Cape's typical plants and animals. Characteristic vegetation includes coastal beachgrass on the upper beach and dunes, black grass on the drier portions of the marsh, and the spartinas: salt-meadow grass and saltwater cord-grass. In the numerous drainage ditches crisscrossing the marsh look for green crabs, salt-marsh snails, ribbed mussel, and "mummichogs" or common minnows. Horned Larks often nest and forage in the beachgrass and black-grass zones. A walk (wade!) out across the marsh at high tide should produce Sharp-tailed Sparrows in the tall salt-water cord-grass lining the creeks and ditches.

A variety of herons, and American Bittern, are regularly seen on the marsh; rarely a Clapper Rail is spotted. There is often a good flight of harriers and sharp-shins in fall. In October, with luck, you may see a Red-headed Woodpecker or even a Yellow Rail. Concentrations of waterfowl and seabirds (see Provincetown, below, for species) are noted in late fall and winter on Cape Cod Bay.

Just north of Samoset Road on Route 6 is the Cape Cod National Seashore's **Salt Pond Visitor Center**. This facility is open from March through December and is a worthwhile place to visit. A large relief map of the Cape, exhibits on the natural and cultural history of Cape Cod, and an introductory film are the main attractions. A check list of Cape Cod's birds is available at the bookstore. During the summer months, park rangers offer a variety of programs and activities on natural history (including bird walks). A copy of the weekly newspaper gives the schedule of events.

From June through August shuttle buses run from the visitor center out to Coast Guard Beach. A bike path also leads to the beach and can be a productive route to hike or pedal. Although the buses are mainly used to transport the beach crowd (no public parking is available at the beach in summer), this is a good trip for visiting birders. The 10-minute ride takes you to the Coast Guard Station overlooking the Atlantic Ocean and Nauset Marsh. West of the beach are the extensive flats of **Nauset Bay**. If you position yourself at the head of the bay on a rising tide, large numbers of shorebirds, gulls, and terns will be pushed your way. (A narrow cut through the dunes behind the restroom-shower area takes you to the right place. Check with a ranger for current regulations and access; you may have to walk down the beach a way before crossing to the bayside.) In late summer, large flocks of Black-bellied and Semipalmated plovers, and Semipalmated Sandpipers, are regular. Other common migrants include Greater Yellowlegs, Ruddy Turnstone, Least Sandpiper, and Short-billed Dowitcher. A careful check of the peep should also produce an occasional Western or White-rumped sandpiper. A variety of terns, often including Forster's Tern, can be seen feeding in the bay and roosting on the flats.

One of the largest concentrations of nesting Piping Plover on the east coast is on this beach. If you decide to look for this species keep in mind that it is threatened, and stay out of all restricted areas. South on Coast Guard Beach is the site of Henry Beston's "Outermost House." Although the house was destroyed in the blizzard of 1978, park rangers lead pilgrimages to the area in summer. In the fall and winter parking is permitted at the Coast Guard Station, and this a good spot for hawks (mainly accipiters and falcons) in the earlier season, and for seabirds and waterfowl later.

North on Route 6 just past the Eastham–Wellfleet town line is the entrance to Massachusetts Audubon's **Wellfleet Bay Wildlife Sanctuary** (WBWS). The sanctuary's Goose Pond Trail (guide book with bird list available) passes through a variety of habitats. In the oak–pine scrub are resident Northern Bobwhite, Eastern Wood-Pewee, Pine Warbler, and Rufous-sided Towhee. The edge of Goose Pond (photo- and viewing blind) and nearby salt pannes are good spots to observe shorebirds and herons. Besides the regular migrants, less-common species, including Lesser Yellowlegs, Solitary, Pectoral, and Stilt sandpipers, and Long-billed Dowitcher, are occasionally found here. Whimbrel are commonly found on the marsh from midsummer on and Clapper Rail (rare) and Sharp-tailed Sparrow are nesters. The sanctuary's bird list is an impressive one, as the varied habitat attracts its share of rare migrants and vagrants. A recent sighting of a Rufous-type (*Selasphorus*) hummingbird at the headquarters building is just one example. During migratory periods it's a good idea to double-check the thickets for warblers and other landbirds, and the marshes, tidal creeks, and beach front for waterbirds. A list of current sightings is kept at headquarters.

Wellfleet Bay Sanctuary is staffed by knowledgeable naturalists who will be able to answer your questions. The staff also conducts programs that may be of interest. A gift shop with books and other natural-history items is located in the main sanctuary building.

Approximately 1.5 miles north of WBWS on the right side of Route 6 you will see the entrance to **Marconi Beach**. Two areas are of interest here: the sand plain community, and the white cedar swamp. Near the entrance in the vicinity of the headquarters building are extensive areas of oak and pitch pine barrens. Summer-resident Vesper Sparrows can often be found here with a little searching. In fall various warblers and sparrows including Palm and Yellow-rumped warblers, and Chipping, Field, and Savannah sparrows are common. Rarely a Yellow-breasted Chat, Clay-colored Sparrow, or Lark Sparrow is found.

Follow the access road to the parking area at the Marconi Wireless Station. The Atlantic White Cedar Swamp Trial (1.2 miles) has interpretive markers, and an explanatory booklet is available at the trailhead. Besides the relic white cedar, stands of broom-crowberry, huckleberry, and other interesting plants are on the path. The thickets lining the path and the cedar swamp itself sometimes produce a reasonable variety of birds. Red-breasted Nuthatch, Ruby-crowned and Golden-crowned kinglets, and Cape May, Bay-breasted, Black-poll, Black-and-white, and American Redstart warblers are typical migrants. Northern Saw-whet Owls occasionally nest in the cedar swamp and can often be heard calling in the evening. In the area of the Marconi monument, paths lead along the tops of the high coastal bluffs. Horned Larks are commonly found here, and occasionally there is a major movement of Sharp-shinned Hawks in the fall (late September–mid-October). The observation platform is an excellent spot from which to watch for hawks in fall and spring.

Continue north on the Mid-Cape Highway (Route 6) to Provincetown and turn right onto Race Point Road. In approximately .5 mile you will come to the parking lot for the **Beech Forest** on the left. Although this area is normally most productive in spring, it is worth checking in late August and throughout September for land-bird migrants. A trail that begins to the right of the restrooms leads out between two ponds and is a good place to start looking. If there seems to be good bird activity also check that section of the main trail that parallels Race Point Road.

The Provincelands Visitor Center (open mid-April

through Thanksgiving) is farther along Race Point Road. You may want to stop here, especially if you haven't been to the Salt Pond center in Eastham. Orientation exhibits and materials are available. Park rangers are on duty here and are willing to answer your questions. The rooftop observation deck is a good hawk-watching site.

In fall you may want to check the thickets around the **airport** for passerine migrants.

Continue to the **Race Point** (fee) parking lot. This is one of the best sites in New England for land-based viewing of pelagic birds. From August through December, northeast winds result in a variety of seabirds occurring here. From August through October you may have some luck even under less than ideal conditions. Scope the offshore waters for Greater Shearwater, Wilson's Storm-Petrel, and Northern Gannet. Race Point is also a good location to find jaegers in late summer and early fall. Parasitic Jaeger is by far the most common species, although Pomerine Jaeger occurs fairly regularly, and even the rare Long-tailed Jaeger has been noted here. Alcids, especially Razorbill, are regular in early winter. While you are scanning the waves you may sight a whale. Humpback, fin, and minke whales are regularly seen off of Provincetown. In fall, an added bonus to the bird watching at Race Point is the movement of hawks, especially Merlins and Peregrine Falcons, along the beach. A walk westward along the point may be productive.

Follow the park road to **Herring Cove**. This area may produce many of the same birds seen from the Race Point parking area. Flocks of feeding terns are a feature here, and they are often close enough for good observation. For the ambitious, a walk (approximately 1 mile) northwest along the beach to **Hatches Harbor** is definitely worthwhile. The marshes and flats of this silted-in harbor attract a few shorebirds and often one or two rarities. In September there is always the possibility of finding Baird's or Buff-breasted sandpiper. This is a good place to see Roseate Tern, and Lesser Black-backed Gull occurs here fairly regularly in fall. For the truly hardy, a winter trek to Hatches may even produce a Mew Gull. Wintering harbor seals are commonly found here.

Proceed to downtown Provincetown and Commercial Street (one-way east to west) which runs alongside the harbor. McMillan Wharf (between Conwell and Shank Painter on Commercial Street), offers a good view of the harbor and excellent winter birding. Glaucous and Iceland gulls, and Black-legged Kittiwake are among the winter specialties. Besides the various sea ducks, Great Cormorants are found here in winter. At the south-western end of Commercial Street is a public parking lot with another good view to the harbor. Black Guil-lemot has been seen from here in winter. Occasionally in January and February one or two other alcids, most often Thick-billed Murre, can be found in Provincetown Harbor, often right around the wharf.

Besides the birds, P'town offers a variety of other interesting sights. People watching is high on the list. The various morphs of *Homo sapiens* wandering the streets at any given time may be cause for wonder. Once you are "peopled-out" try the Portuguese baked goods, soup, or sausage before leaving town. A note of caution: Beware of P'town on rainy days at the height of the tourist season. Under these conditions, everyone on the Cape seems to arrive here at the same time.

Accommodations should not be a problem on Cape Cod. Even in winter, some motels remain open. If your visit coincides with the tourist season you may want to

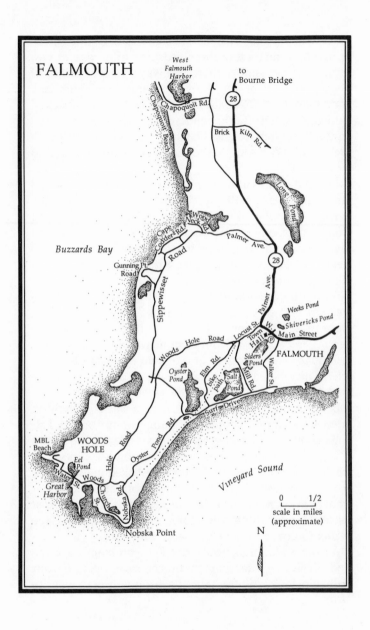

FALMOUTH

West Falmouth Harbor

to Bourne Bridge

28

Chapoquoit Rd.

Chapoquoit Beach

Brick Kiln Rd.

Long Pond

Wood Neck Rd.

Cape Codder Rd.

Palmer Ave.

28

Buzzards Bay

Gunning Pt. Road

Road

Sippewisset

Weeks Pond

Shivericks Pond

Locust St.

W. Main Street

Town Hall

Palmer Ave.

Woods Hole Road

FALMOUTH

Oyster Pond

Elm Rd.

Siders Pond

bike path

Salt Pond

Mill Rd.

Walker St.

Surf Drive

Woods Hole Road

Oyster Pond Rd.

MBL Beach

WOODS HOLE

Eel Pond

Water St.

Woods

Church St.

St.

Nobska Rd.

Great Harbor

Vineyard Sound

Nobska Point

0   1/2
scale in miles
(approximate)

N

make reservations; contact local chambers of commerce for recommended motels and inns. The only state campground on the Cape is the R. C. Nickerson State Park on Route 6A in Brewster. Nickerson State Park and the various private campgrounds are often full during the summer months. Cape restaurants run the gamut from fast food to nouvelle cuisine. If you are interested in more traditional fare, the Eastham Lobster Pool on Route 6 in North Eastham is a regular stop for many seasoned Cape goers. A visit to **The Cape Cod Museum of Natural History** on Route 6A in Brewster is recommended. Nature trails, exhibits, and a gift shop should be of interest to birders and naturalists of all ages. The Bird Room contains over 250 mounted specimens of local birds. The Bird Watcher's General Store on Route 6A in Orleans is another stop you may want to make. Besides birding supplies, a blackboard with updated bird sightings is kept by the proprietors.

Falmouth is of interest to bird watchers primarily as a late fall to early winter stop. The ponds, many of which remain ice-free well into winter, offer an excellent variety of ducks. In addition to the waterfowl, semihardy landbirds are often present in the coastal thickets. Finally, Buzzards Bay and Vineyard Sound provide an opportunity to search for seabirds and gulls.

From the Bourne Bridge go south on Route 28 approximately 14 miles to West Main Street in Falmouth. Go left here (where Route 28 turns east) and look for the Falmouth Town Hall set back on your right. There is parking behind the town hall. From the parking lot you will see greenbrier and bramble thickets at the northern end of **Siders Pond**. This is a good place to begin your search for wintering passerines. Carolina Wren, Northern Mockingbird, Northern Cardinal, White-throated Sparrow, and House Sparrow are common here, and a little diligent searching may turn up Gray Catbird, Rufous-sided Towhee, or even a Yellow-breasted Chat. Trees and shrubs lining the near side of the pond, and thickets along the brook to the northwest, are also good spots for landbirds. Siders Pond normally has a variety of ducks including Canvasback, scaup (both species, with a preponderance of Greater Scaup), Common Goldeneye, and Bufflehead. Hooded Merganser, Redhead, Ruddy Duck, and American Coot are also good possibilities. The best light for viewing waterfowl from this vantage point is in early morning.

After leaving the Town Hall go left on West Main Street and take your first right onto Post Office Road. Continue straight to a parking lot beside **Shivericks Pond**. Pied-billed Grebe, American Black Duck, Mallard, American Wigeon, Redhead, and Ring-necked Duck occur here. **Weeks Pond**, a short distance to the northeast, may also be worth checking.

Return to West Main Street and go left; turn right on Walker Street and follow this to **Surf Drive**. There are several places along Surf Drive to park and scope Vineyard Sound. Species to be expected in winter include Common and Red-throated loons, Horned Grebe, Common Eider, and Red-breasted Merganser. Follow Surf Drive west to Mill Road; a parking lot at this intersection offers a view over **Salt Pond**. Many of the species mentioned previously can be found here. Rarities occurring from time to time include Eurasian Wigeon, Tufted Duck, and Barrow's Goldeneye. Also check the gulls for possible Little Gull or Common Black-headed Gull.

Continue west on Surf Drive to Elm Road; go right on Elm and park where the **bicycle path** crosses the road. Taking the bicycle path toward the sound (south) will lead you to **Oyster Pond**. This is a good spot to find Mute Swan as well as species of waterfowl you may have missed at the other ponds. The thickets along the bike path north of Elm Road are often packed with landbirds. Wintering Hermit Thrush, Yellow-breasted Chat, Orange-crowned Warbler, and Northern Oriole are all possible.

Return to Surf Drive and turn right (west). Check the various roadside thickets as you proceed, making sure to respect residents' private property. Also, be careful not to block the road by stopping along the narrower sections. Continue on Surf Drive to Oyster Pond Road and follow this toward Woods Hole. Take Nobska Road left to the Coast Guard Station overlooking **Nobska Point**. Scan the sound for rafts of Common Eider (perhaps a King Eider), and smaller groups of Surf, White-winged, and Black scoters. On the offshore islands look for wintering Great Cormorants as well as the occasional Double-crested Cormorant. You may also find Old-squaw, Purple Sandpiper, or Iceland Gull in this area.

Two areas worth checking in Woods Hole are **Great Harbor** and **Marine Biological Laboratory** (MBL) **Beach**. From Nobska Point take Church Street to Woods Hole Road and go left to the Woods Hole Steamship Authority main building. Park on the street and walk down to the slips where the ferry boats dock. Check here for white-winged gulls; scope Great Harbor for seaducks and the rocks for Purple Sandpiper. After you finish here, follow Woods Hole Road to Water Street which crosses Eel Pond. Turn right at the end of Water Street and take your next left. Follow this less than .5 mile and go right looking for a dirt parking lot with stone pillars. Park here to bird MBL Beach. Oldsquaw and a variety of other seaducks can usually be found off the beach. Return to Woods Hole Road and follow the signs back toward Falmouth.

Woods Hole Road will bring you to Locust Street and eventually back to Route 28. Take Route 28 north 1 mile to Palmer Avenue; go left on Palmer to **Sippewisset Road**. Several good birding locales in this vicinity are the terminus of Wood Neck Road, the bluff at the end of Cape Codder Road (behind the inn), and the loop around Gunning Point Road. Check the marshy areas, overlooks to Buzzards Bay, and roadside thickets. Species that may be found are American Bittern, Great Blue Heron, and Belted Kingfisher in the marsh, seabirds and waterfowl at the overlooks, and Northern Flicker, Brown Thrasher, Yellow-rumped Warbler, and various sparrows in the thickets.

There are numerous other locales in the Falmouth area that may provide good winter birding. West Falmouth Harbor and Chapoquoit Beach (Brick Kiln Road exit, north on Route 28), and Great Pond in East Falmouth are just two of the other choices. A local map will indicate the numerous ponds and beach fronts that can serve as focal points for your investigations.

Sandy Neck, Barnstable, is another favored birding site on the lower Cape. In Massachusetts, Sandy Neck is best known among birders as a place to visit during northeast storms in September, October, and November. When conditions are right, excellent pelagic birding can be enjoyed from the beach parking lot.

To reach Sandy Neck, cross the Sagamore Bridge and follow Route 6 to Exit 4, taking a left onto Chase Road. Bear right at the fork and continue on to Jones Lane. Go left onto Jones Lane and then right onto Route 6A. Turn left at the Sandy Neck Motel and follow the road to the Sandy Neck Beach parking lot.

During a northeast blow in late summer or fall you can sit right in your car and enjoy the show. The species present will depend on the date (see chapter on pelagic birding), but a variety of loons, grebes, shearwaters, storm-petrels, scoters, phalaropes, jaegers, and alcids are all possible. Northern Gannet and Black-legged Kittiwake are regularly seen here during November storms, and occasionally Northern Fulmar puts in an appearance. The regime followed by the local birders is to stay at Sandy Neck while the wind is northeast and move to First Encounter Beach, Eastham, when the wind goes northwest.

The extensive marshes and flats of Sandy Neck are excellent habitat for a variety of herons and shorebirds; unfortunately, to reach the best areas requires an off-road vehicle or a long hike. In fall, however, the thickets and dunes adjacent to the parking area should be checked for landbird migrants.

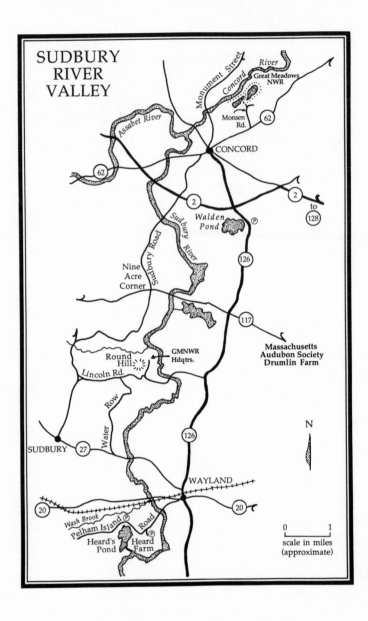

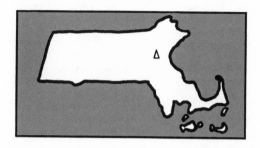

Concord and the Sudbury River Valley

SPRING / FALL

THE BIRDER'S FIRST TRIP TO THE CONCORD region should prove a rewarding experience. If your plans allow for an autumn visit you will be treated to a surprising diversity of birds and also have the opportunity to acquaint yourself with many local spots that are rich in birding lore. Of course it all started with Thoreau over a century and a half ago. In fact, you should probably begin your tour of the region at the Thoreau cabin site at **Walden Pond**. This is easily reached from the Boston area via Route 128 and Route 2 westbound. Soon after entering Concord turn south on Route 126 and in less than .5 mile look for Walden Pond State

Reservation (parking and Thoreau cabin replica on left). Although the Walden woods and pond may offer a variety of migrants in the spring and fall, the main point here is the Thoreau connection. Thoreau provided one of the first in-depth looks at the bird life of a New England town. His "travels" in Concord led to hundreds of journal entries that were later compiled by Francis H. Allen. Thoreau's Concord bird list includes over 100 species, and the naturalist enjoyed many of these birds right at Walden Pond. His playful chasing of the Common Loon on Walden led to Thoreau's account depicting this species' grace and agility. As you stroll around the trails and pay your respects at the cabin site, recall that the Concord area had barely 10 percent forest cover at the time Thoreau was wandering the region. The relatively heavy forest cover (50 percent) of today reflects a major change. Thoreau buffs will want to visit the Thoreau Lyceum (156 Belknap Street) and the Antiquarian Museum (200 Lexington Road) in Concord.

For those anxious to get to the birding action, proceed directly to the **Great Meadows National Wildlife Refuge** (GMNWR) impoundments off Monsen Road in Concord. To reach GMNWR go north on Route 126 (from Walden Pond) for 1.5 miles to Concord Center. Turn right onto Main Street and jog left and right around the green onto Route 62 (East to Bedford). Follow Route 62 for 1.3 miles to Monsen Road. Go left onto Monsen and proceed less than .5 mile to GMNWR. Although 3,000 acres of refuge property extends up and down the Concord and Sudbury rivers, this section provides the best bird watching.

The Great Meadows impoundments consist of wetlands dominated by two large open pools as well as upland, second-growth forest. A dike and trail system provide good access throughout. Typical plants found in and around the pools include sacred bean (American lotus), water-chestnut, buttonbush, cattail, and purple loosestrife. From the parking lot (see the display board and map) a walk out the main dike, around the north (lower) pool, and back through the mixed forest will present a good introduction to the possibilities here. Herons, waterfowl, and shorebirds (in years of low water) are the fall specialties. As you proceed out the dike, stop frequently to scope the pools, banks, and flats. Wood Duck, American Wigeon, both teal species, Northern Pintail, Gadwall, and Northern Shoveler are all good possibilities in the fall. You should have no difficulty finding Great Blue Heron, Black-crowned Night-Heron, and Green-backed Heron. American Bittern is an uncommon summer resident on the refuge but is often found here in the autumn. You'll need considerably more luck to see Least Bittern, but this rare summer resident is a distinct possibility. Regular shorebird migrants (late summer–fall) include Least Sandpiper, Common Snipe, Spotted Sandpiper, both yellowlegs, and Pectoral Sandpiper. Exceptional years (low water and exposed flats) have produced Western Sandpiper, Baird's Sandpiper, and Hudsonian Godwit. Lesser Golden-Plover is a fairly good possibility. Make sure to check out the cattail stands for Marsh Wren, a common summer resident that often lingers well into fall. Common Moorhen is also a breeding bird at the Great Meadows and should be looked for in the pools on either side of the dike. For rail fans, the chances are good that you will either hear or see Virginia Rail and/or Sora. Look and listen for these uncommon summer residents in the cattail sections and particularly along the water's edge. Although large hawk flights are seldom recorded at Great Meadows, common fall migrants include Osprey, Northern Harrier, and Broad-winged Hawk. Occasionally a Merlin, and more rarely a Peregrine, will move through the meadows. Resident Red-tailed Hawks can be found in this area throughout the year. Once you reach that point where the trail reenters the woodlands, keep an eye out for migrating warblers and other passerines. Blackpolls, yellowrumps, black-and-whites, and yellowthroats can be common, while 20 other warbler species, including Nashville, Northern Parula, Magnolia, and Canada, are occasionally recorded. During the nesting season, Yellow Warblers are easily found between the parking lot and the dike trail. Willow Flycatcher also nests here. The fall is a good time to see the roving flocks of blackbirds, particularly toward sunset as they fly to roost. Besides the hundreds of red-wings, cowbirds, and grackles, look for small groups of Rusty Blackbirds from the dike trail as you enjoy the fading light.

The only record for Gyrfalcon (don't get your hopes up) in this area was recorded by William Brewster on November 21, 1896. Brewster (1851–1919) followed Thoreau in the line of estimable Concord naturalists. Originally from Cambridge, Massachusetts, Brewster owned property across the river from the Great Meadows. He achieved national prominence in the ornithological community by being an early advocate of bird protection, and he was a founder of the American Ornithologists' Union. But Brewster's heart was in Concord. Besides his October Farm (the main house can still be seen from Monument Street), he built a cabin and a boat house on the bank of the Concord River. From here, he and many of Massachusetts's noted ornithologists made excursions to various locales in the valley. Many of William Brewster's bird notes are compiled in *October Farm* and *Concord River*. Although both books are now out of print, a trip to one of Concord's used bookstores should turn up one or both of these volumes.

The Great Meadows National Wildlife Refuge head-quarters is adjacent to Round Hill in Sudbury, Massa-chusett. Bird lists, books, interpretive displays, and maps are available there. On your way to the refuge center you should stop at **Nine Acre Corner** (NAC). To reach NAC return to Concord Center and follow Main Street to the brick library. Bear left here and follow Sudbury Road south for 3 miles to NAC. This is primarily an agricultural area and is particularly productive at the height of the fall mi-gration. You're almost certain to see flocks of Canada Geese moving in and out of the fields as well as a few American Black Ducks and Mallards. Check the fields in fall for Lesser Golden-Plover, Killdeer, Pectoral Sandpi-per, and Common Snipe. You might even find a Solitary Sandpiper at the edge of one of the sloughs or farm ponds. The Nine Acre Corner area is a good place to watch for hawks, and sharp-shins are common migrants during September and October. The various weedfields are worth checking for sparrows, including Lincoln's and White-crowned. Because this land is privately owned, birders should ask permission to walk the fields. This is a good area in which to find Water Pipit. Also, the blackbird flocks can be impressive; although they are rarities, both Yel-low-headed and Brewer's blackbirds have been recorded here. Nine Acre Corner's latest claim to avian fame is the Fieldfare which spent a week there in April of 1986.

To reach GMNWR headquarters continue south on Sudbury Road turning left in 2.4 miles and left again in less than 1 mile onto Lincoln Road. Follow this for 1.3 miles to the entrance road. After you have spent some time at the Great Meadows headquarters you may want to check **Round Hill** just west of the headquarters on Lincoln Road. Look for the sign for Lincoln Meadows conservation area and park in the adjacent parking lot. Round Hill, the community gardens, and the agricultural fields across the street can be productive during migratory periods when a variety of thrushes, warblers, and sparrows may be found here.

Continue west on Lincoln Road less than .5 mile and go left onto Water Row. Follow this for 1.9 miles to Route 27. Go left onto Route 27 and proceed 1.8 miles into Wayland Center. In Wayland Center turn right onto Route 20 and take your first left onto Pelham Island Road. Follow this road for 1.4 miles to a parking lot opposite **Heard's Pond**. Park here and explore the woods and trail. Summer residents of these woodlands include Great Crested Flycatcher, Eastern Wood-Pewee, Brown Creeper, Blue-gray Gnatcatcher, Wood Thrush, Warbling and Yellow-throated (occasionally) vireos, Scarlet Tanager, and Rose-breasted Grosbeak. The trail will take you to the edge of **Wash Brook Marsh**, one of the finest freshwater marshes in Massachusetts. Nesting birds include American Bittern, Least Bittern, Green-backed Heron, Wood Duck, Virginia Rail, Sora, Common Moorhen, Willow Flycatcher, and Marsh Wren. (For an alternate access to the marsh take Route 20 west from Wayland Center to the railroad tracks; park and walk west on the abandoned track bed.)

As you continue around the loop trail you will come to a rock bearing a memorial plaque to one of Massachusetts's greatest field ornithologists. Ludlow Griscom (1890–1959) was largely responsible for making ornithology accessible to the hoards of modern-day bird watchers. As a boy in Central Park, New York, he astounded many "museum men" (who were accustomed to doing their ornithology across a gun sight) by demonstrating that birds could be identified accurately and consistently with binoculars. Many of Griscom's techniques were later to be popularized by Roger Tory Peterson. Ludlow Griscom spent the last three decades of his life in Massachusetts, where he nurtured and prodded a generation of capable field naturalists. Griscom's *Birds of Massachusetts* (with D. Snyder) and *Birds of Concord* are just two of his many publications.

A walk along the road bordering Heard's Pond can be particularly productive during the spring and fall and will provide vantage points from which to scan the pond. Look for waterfowl, swallows, and warblers. Rusty Blackbirds frequent the red maple swamp in April and from late September through mid-October. The **Heard Farm** area (.5 mile east of Heard's Pond off Heard Road) is town conservation property which includes agricultural land, weedfields, and thickets. This is another good spot to check for passerine migrants. Incidentally, this is where Cattle Egret was first collected in North America.

If your travels bring you to the Sudbury River Valley in the spring, I would suggest you start at this end of the valley and work your way northward to the Nine Acre Corner area and then the Great Meadows. The March–April period usually produces a good flight of waterfowl migrants on the ponds and rivers, including Ring-necked Duck, Common Goldeneye, and Common and Hooded mergansers. Mid-May is the height of the passerine migration.

If time allows, be adventurous and check out the spots along the rivers that appear promising to you. Chances are your instincts will prove sound, and it's always more fun to make your own discoveries.

Two side trips may be of interest to naturalists visiting this area. The Massachusetts Audubon Society's headquarters and their Drumlin Farm Wildlife Sanctuary are in Lincoln, Massachusetts. The visitor will find a library, bookstore (heavy emphasis on natural-history books), working farm, and wildlife exhibits here. The New England Wild Flower Society maintains gardens, a library, and a bookstore at its center in Framingham, Massachusetts. Their Garden in the Woods provides interpretive trails through many habitat gardens representing most of New England's floral communities.

In the Concord area there are plenty of opportunities to enjoy the cultural as well as the natural history. Minute Man National Historical Park has a visitors' center that will provide a host of suggested activities. Certainly the Old North Bridge, the Old Manse, and the Orchard House will be good for starters. A Howard Johnson's motel in Concord provides standard lodging, while the purist might want to look into a night at the Colonial Inn (Concord) or the Wayside Inn (Sudbury). Bed-and-breakfast accommodations are also available. There is a KOA Campground in Littleton.

Mt. Greylock: North Adams
summer-resident passerines

Berkshire Lakes: Berkshire County: Routes 7 and 20 (Pittsfield)
    Pontoosuc Lake
    Onota Lake
    Richmond Pond
Migrant waterfowl and shorebirds

Connecticut River Valley:
    Stebbins Memorial Wildlife Refuge: Longmeadow
    Arcadia Sanctuary: Easthampton
    Barton's Cove: Gill
These three sites offer a good sampling of Connecticut River
Valley habitat. All are particularly interesting for their va-
riety of migrant and wintering waterfowl.

Mt. Auburn Cemetery: Cambridge
spring passerine migrants

Plymouth Beach: Plymouth
summer-resident terns and migrant shorebirds

SEE:

–*Birds in Massachusetts: When and Where to Find Them*. 1955.
Wallace Bailey. Massachusetts Audubon Society.

–*Where to Find Birds in Eastern Massachusetts*. 1978. Leif J. Robinson and Robert H. Stymeist. Bird Observer of Eastern
Massachusetts.

–*Birding Cape Cod* (scheduled for 1988). Cape Cod Bird Club.
Massachusetts Audubon Society.

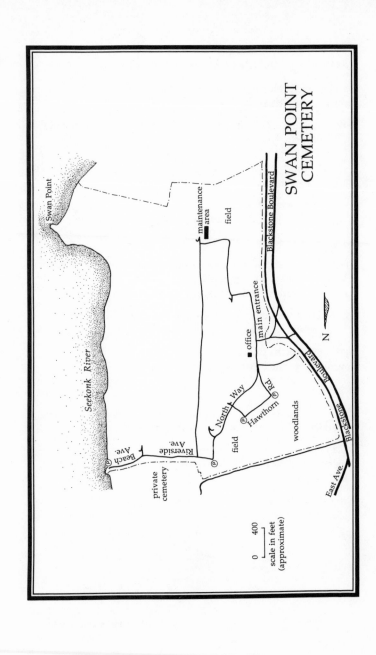

SWAN POINT
CEMETERY

Swan Point

Seekonk River

Beach Ave.

Riverside Ave.

private
cemetery

North Way

Hawthorn Rd.

field

field

office

main entrance

maintenance
area

Blackstone Boulevard

woodlands

Boulevard

Blackstone

East Ave.

N

0   400

scale in feet
(approximate)

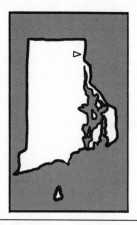

RHODE ISLAND

Swan Point Cemetery

SPRING

THE WOODED REFUGIA OF URBAN CEMETERIES
are a favored destination for birders in springtime. Across
North America from Fort Rosecrans National Cemetery
in San Diego, California, to Mount Auburn Cemetery
in Cambridge, Massachusetts, flocks of birds and bird
watchers arrive during the northward migration. A particular passion of observers on both sides of the con-
tinent is the wood-warbler family. Soon after Califor-
nians have delighted in the passage of Orange-crowned,
Black-throated Gray, Townsend's, and Hermit warblers, New Englanders are treated to such gems as Blue-
winged, Black-throated Blue, Blackburnian, and Bay-
breasted warblers. Swan Point Cemetery in Providence,
Rhode Island, is a fine locale in which to take part in
this spring tradition.

Swan Point Cemetery is located in East Providence just south of the Massachusetts–Rhode Island border. To reach the cemetery take Route 95 south to Exit 27 (North Providence and Pawtucket). Go left (south) at the first set of lights after the exit ramp onto George Street. In .2 mile bear left onto East Avenue and follow this 1 mile to the intersection with Blackstone Boulevard. Go left onto Blackstone Boulevard and look for the entrance to Swan Point Cemetery ahead on the left.

As you enter the gate to the cemetery, the main office will be on your left. Visitors who take time to go into the office will be greeted by two of J. J. Audubon's famous prints: the *Whistling (Tundra) Swan* and the *Trumpeter Swan*. Investigation of the chapel will turn up additional evidence of the avian theme. Here, two stained-glass windows are decorated with likenesses of birds commonly found about the grounds. Incidentally, these windows were inspired by similar ones at the Selborne Chapel in England. The Selborne Chapel is dedicated to Gilbert White, the eighteenth-century curate-naturalist who did pioneering work in field ornithology. Another sign of the interest in birds is Charles Wood's book *The Birds of Swan Point Cemetery*. Published in 1981 by the proprietors of the cemetery, this volume includes a check list of the birds occurring at Swan Point as well as reminiscences of 50 years of birding here. Truly the cemetery is, as Wood points out in his introduction, "a sanctuary for people and also for wildlife."

Large sections of the grounds of Swan Point are, as in so many cemeteries, carefully designed, creatively planted, and impeccably manicured. In spring a variety of flowering trees, shrubs, and herbaceous plants lend an air of ordered beauty to the area. It is, however, the wilder, more natural sections of the cemetery that offer the best birding. Most birders head directly to the woods and field in the **northwest corner** of Swan Point. Here within a relatively small area are mixed woodlands of oak and maple, groves of paper birch, and a second-growth field. On "big days" during May this part of the cemetery can be swarming with migrants. And the warblers are a highlight.

Common migrant warblers at Swan Point include Black-and-white, Blue-winged, Tennessee, Nashville, Northern Parula, Yellow, Yellow-rumped, Black-throated Green, Chestnut-sided, Magnolia, Blackpoll, Prairie, Palm, American Redstart, and Canada. Other less-common, though regularly occurring warblers are Cape May, Black-throated Blue, Blackburnian, Bay-breasted, Pine, Northern Waterthrush, and Wilson's. After you have checked off all these species you can start looking for a few of the rarer warblers to have been recorded at Swan Point. One or more of the rarities seems to appear each year, so keep an eye out for Prothonotary, Golden-winged, Orange-crowned, Cerulean, Yellow-throated, Kentucky, Mourning, and Hooded warblers. Chances are you won't repeat the 1974 and 1975 records of Black-throated Gray Warblers.

While warblers form the focal point of the migration at Swan Point, a variety of flycatchers, swallows, wrens, kinglets, thrushes, vireos, finches, and blackbirds add their voices to the spring chorus. Listen (and look!) for Great Crested Flycatcher and Eastern Wood-Pewee, Carolina and House wrens, Ruby-crowned Kinglet, all five spotted-breasted thrushes, Solitary and Red-eyed vireos, Scarlet Tanager, Rose-breasted Grosbeak, Chipping Sparrow, and Northern Oriole. Other less-common or rare species include Yellow-bellied Sapsucker (April), Olive-sided Flycatcher (late spring), White-eyed Vireo, Yellow-breasted Chat, Blue Grosbeak, Lincoln's Sparrow, and Orchard Oriole.

Riverside and Beach avenues traverse the northern border of the cemetery and lead to the bank of the **Seekonk River** in the northeast corner of the cemetery. This stream flows into Narragansett Bay to the south. Tidal currents along the Seekonk alternately cover and expose muddy banks and flats. The river is worth checking for migratory herons, ducks, and shorebirds. In spring, species such as American Black Duck, Spotted Sandpiper, and Greater Yellowlegs are regularly observed here. Another spot local birders visit is the **field and maintenance area** in the southwest corner of the cemetery. Migrant sparrows can be found around the disturbed areas and dirt piles; swallows are often seen hawking in the vicinity.

If you arrive early, before the main gate is open, park on Blackstone Boulevard (north of the entrance) and look for a place to go over the stone wall. Otherwise, once the gate is open, park in one of the areas indicated on the map. During the height of the spring migration (first three weeks in May), personnel from the Audubon Society of Rhode Island (ASRI) lead a series of morning walks on most weekdays. Joining one of these groups will give you a good introduction to Swan Point Cemetery. Contact ASRI for exact schedule.

Southern Shore: Point Judith to Watch Hill

LATE FALL / WINTER

SPECULATORS INCREASE THEIR TAKE BY HEDG-
ing their bets. Bird watchers searching for New England's late-fall migrants and winter-resident bird life
can gain a similar edge by coming to the southern shore
of Rhode Island. While there may be more Snowy Owls
and Common Eider along the Massachusetts coast and
more Carolina Wrens and Eastern Bluebirds in Connecticut, each of these species can also be found in
Rhode Island. From Point Judith's bold exposure to the
open Atlantic, to the sheltered coves of numerous salt
ponds, the south coastline of "Little Rhody" offers a
variety of excellent birding habitats. A day-long tour

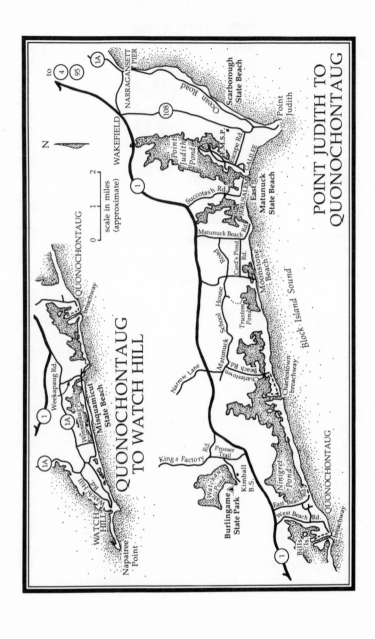

will take you to the majority of the top spots. Once you've been introduced to the area, the possibilities are nearly endless.

Take Route 95 south from Providence to Exit 9 (Route 4). Follow Routes 4 and 1 south for 17.5 miles to Wakefield. At Wakefield take 1A North (east) 1.4 miles to **Narragansett Pier**, and go south on Ocean Road. Between mid-November and the end of April, the jetties and rocks along this section of the coast are a reliable spot for Purple Sandpiper. Check the Pier 5 vicinity and the east end of Newtown Avenue. As you continue south on Ocean Road look for other wintering or lingering shorebirds. Species occurring with some regularity include Black-bellied Plover, Sanderling, and Dunlin. **Scarborough State Beach** is particularly accessible, and a walk to the south end often produces one or more of these species.

Continue south to the intersection with Route 108. Proceed straight (south), across the intersection, and in a little less than 1 mile you will reach **Point Judith**. There are three good observation points in this vicinity. The Lighthouse Restaurant parking lot offers the best in-car viewing on stormy days. In fact, this is perhaps the top spot in Rhode Island from which to observe the fall (mid-October through early January) and spring (February through April) seabird migration. Under ideal conditions—a coastal storm in November with onshore winds—you will be treated to a spectacle of birds including Red-throated and Common loons, Horned Grebe, Northern Gannet, Common Eider, Oldsquaw, scoter (three species), and Red-breasted Merganser. Pomarine and Parasitic jaegers, white-winged gulls, and Black-legged Kittiwake are also possible. Although it is a rare occurrence, Point Judith also produces a fair number of alcids when timing and weather are right. Thick-billed

Murre, Dovekie, and Razorbill have all been seen in numbers from this parking lot. Also, Manx Shearwater is regularly seen here from April through June. Even if you haven't won the weather lottery on the day of your visit, a careful search of the ocean should produce loons, a grebe or two, and various seaducks and gulls. During the winter months Horned Grebe, Common Goldeneye, and Red-breasted Merganser are consistently found here. The Coast Guard Station (park outside the fence—visitors welcome between 8:00 A.M. and 7:00 P.M.) offers another vantage point over the ocean. Set up your scope on the rise west of the station. As you head back the road you came in on, look for the entrance to Pt. Judith State Park (.2 mile) on the left. A crude road leads down to the west-facing shore and a jetty. The view to the southwest may produce many of the same species mentioned above.

Return to the intersection of Route 108 and Ocean Road and take 108 north (left) toward **Galilee**. Follow the signs which direct you left onto Escape Road. In approximately .5 mile look for a place to pull off with an overlook to the extensive marsh and tidal flats to the north. Migrant shorebirds and waterfowl are a feature of this area in fall and spring. During the winter months look for Mute Swans, other waterfowl, flocks of seagulls, and lingering shorebirds. Laughing Gulls are present in numbers through mid-November, while at least a few Bonaparte's Gulls overwinter here. From December on, however, the majority of seagulls will be Ring-billed, Herring, and Great Black-backed. At the end of Escape Road take a left onto the road that passes the fish piers. The local flocks of gulls, which are constantly patrolling the area in hopes of an easy meal, sometimes include Iceland and Glaucous gulls. Try the parking lot at the south end of the shorefront road.

Because the road passing the piers is one-way, you will need to drive around behind the waterfront to return to the intersection with Escape Road. An optional side loop crosses the bridge to Great Island. This affords closer views of Point Judith Pond (flats and tidal waters) where you can inspect the ever-present swans, ducks, and gulls. From mid-February to mid-May your chances are excellent of finding Brant in this area.

Just north of the intersection of Escape Road and Route 108 you will find the entrance to **Fisherman's Memorial State Park** (FMSP). While this park is most productive during periods of landbird migration, a variety of lingering or overwintering passerines can be found here between November and March.

Once you are satisfied that you have found what Point Judith and Galilee have to offer, return to Wakefield via Route 108 north. This will put you in place to begin your exploration of the balance of the south shore. At Wakefield follow the signs to Route 1 (south) and in a little over 4 miles take the **Jerusalem/Snug Harbor** exit. This will take you south along Succotash Road where in 1.5 miles you will find the Succotash Salt Marsh on your left. Sharp-tailed and Seaside sparrows are summer residents here. In late fall, check the marsh for lingering shorebirds and herons as well as resident gulls. Great Blue Heron, Mute Swan, and American Black Duck are found here throughout the winter, occasionally Snowy Owl or Short-eared Owl. You may also find a Northern Harrier working this area. A little farther on look for East Matunuck State Beach parking lot on the right. Park and walk across the beach for another view of Block Island Sound. Red-necked Grebe is a possibility here. Continue along to the village of Jerusalem where there are views across the breachway to Galilee. Return to Route 1.

After going south on Route 1 for 1.2 miles, exit onto the **Matunuck Beach Road**. This will take you through the first of several agricultural areas. In fall and winter this is prime sparrow and raptor habitat. Wintering species include Northern Harrier, Rough-legged Hawk, American Kestrel, Short-eared Owl, and Vesper Sparrow. Continue south on this road, passing through a residential area, to the Deep Hole parking lot (just to the right of "Private Road" sign) overlooking the sound. Both Red-throated and Common loons, Common Goldeneye, and Red-breasted Merganser are regularly seen here in winter. Check the goldeneyes for a possible Barrow's Goldeneye. From this parking lot return along Matunuck Beach Road for .7 mile and go left onto **Card's Pond Road**. In winter, the fields along this stretch may contain flocks of Horned Larks, Lapland Longspurs, or Snow Buntings. Stop to check Card's Pond on the left, and shortly thereafter go left onto **Moonstone Beach Road**. Follow this to the beach parking area. A small section of Card's Pond to the west should be checked for migrant shorebirds in the fall, and later for wintering waterfowl. In early spring this pond may afford close-up views of the courting behavior of one or more species. A path takes you across the beach for another view offshore. Walking west on the beach (.5 mile) will put you in place to scope the ducks on Trustom Pond (see species below). The light from this vantage point is often better than from the north side of the pond.

Return along Moonstone Beach Road and take the first left onto Matunuck School House Road. In .7 mile you will reach **Trustom Pond National Wildlife Refuge**. A trail (1.9 miles round trip) will take you south through alfalfa fields, old orchards, and thickets to a peninsula extending into Trustom Pond. An observation platform provides a good place to scope the migrant and wintering waterfowl. Besides the numerous Mute Swans and Canada Geese, look for Snow Goose, Green-winged Teal, American Black Duck, Northern Pintail, American Wigeon, Canvasback, Redhead, the scaups, Bufflehead, and Ruddy Duck. During migratory periods the numbers and variety of passerines in the upland section and waterfowl on the pond increases greatly.

Return to Matunuck School House Road and continue west a little over 2 miles to Charlestown Beach Road (unmarked, several stores at intersection). Follow this road south to a bridge crossing and take the dirt road right (west) 1 mile to the **Charlestown Breachway**. While this locale is a particularly productive one for shorebirds and terns in season (see Quonochontaug account), the tidal section and flats in winter normally harbor a variety of waterfowl and gulls with occasional Dunlin.

Return to School House Road and go left and take your second right onto Narrow Lane. Proceed straight across the first intersection and go right onto Route 1. Reverse your direction at the first turnaround and go west until you see a pond on the right. Pull over here to check for wintering waterfowl. Continue south on Route 1 and take the exit for East Beach Road (reversing direction and then turning south onto East Beach Road). Follow East Beach Road 1.5 miles to the **Ninigret Conservation Area**. This is another good area at which to observe wintering ducks, although you (and the waterfowl) may have to share the pond with the sailboarders. Ninigret Pond is one of a string of brackish ponds along Rhode Island's southern shore. Besides being an attractive area for human visitors, these ponds are rich nurseries for both finfish and shellfish. At various times of the year herons, waterfowl, and shorebirds take advantage of this resource. A display on the edge of the parking lot gives an overview of salt-pond ecology.

After leaving the conservation area, take the first left (Overlook Road), then go left again (for one block), and then right to the intersection with West Beach Road. If there has been a hard freeze and a majority of the ponds are iced over, you may want to take West Beach Road (left/south) to the **Quonochontaug Breachway**. Like the Charlestown Breachway, this is a more productive spot during the warmer months; it is also good for ducks in winter, however, if other areas are closed by ice. To reach Quonochontaug marsh go south on West Beach Road and west along the beach, then north to the end of the dirt road.

If you are not taking the Quonochontaug loop (or after doing so), return north on West Beach Road to Route 1 and proceed west. Follow Route 1 approximately 3 miles and turn left onto Route 1A (Scenic Route). In less than 1.5 miles, go left again onto **Weekapaug Road** (unmarked). Follow this south for a short distance to where a culvert passes under the road. Stop here to check for swans, ducks, and gulls. Occasionally Bonaparte's Gull or even Common Black-headed Gull can be found on the pond to the east or on the sandbar to the west. Continue south, passing a bridge on your right and then bearing left, for approximately 1 mile to an ocean overlook. This is yet another good spot from which to watch the seabirds. Besides loons and grebes, also look for King Eider, which has been seen here fairly regularly in winter. Check the surf just offshore of the rocks for wintering harbor seals. Retrace your path along the same road and go left across the Weekapaug Breachway bridge. This road takes you west along the Weekapaug Town Beach toward Misquamicut State Beach. Although you will note a Coney Island atmosphere to part of this stretch, in winter the relatively small crowds permit some good birding. Several spots on the north side of the road provide views to Winnapaug Pond.

Keep an eye out here for Short-eared Owls which may be patrolling the dune line. Continue west to Misquamicut and then go north on Winnapaug Road, back to Route 1A.

Follow 1A and Watch Hill Road to **Watch Hill**. In late fall and winter there is usually ample parking on the main street or in the lot with a view to the harbor. For the ambitious, a walk westward out the beach and then north along Napatree Point (one of Rhode Island's hawk-watching hot spots) may turn up something interesting. Purple Sandpipers winter along rocky sections of the beach. You may also find Black-bellied Plover, Ruddy Turnstone, Red Knot, or Sanderling along the shore.

If you are returning east on Route 1 you may want to spend some time at **Watchaug Pond** in Burlingame State Park. Take Kings Factory Road north off of Route 1 (in Charlestown) and go left on Prosser Trail for just less than 1 mile. Turn right onto an unmarked road which will take you to the Kimball Bird Sanctuary on the shore of Watchaug Pond. Just past the sanctuary a dirt road leads to the pond. The pond is a good spot for migratory waterfowl, and Bald Eagles have wintered here.

You will find basic services, including a few gas stations and variety stores, along most of this route. In winter, however, accommodations are more difficult to locate. The Dutch Inn at Galilee is open year round, and there are other motels in the Westerly area. Seasonal camping is available at Fisherman's Memorial State Park in Galilee and Burlingame State Park in Charlestown.

Two additional areas that birders visiting Rhode Island in winter may want to include on their itineraries are Watchemocket Cove and Sachuest Point.

Watchemocket Cove is located in East Providence and is reached by taking Route 95 to East Providence and then Memorial Parkway south (follows the east shore of Narragansett Bay) less than 2 miles to Metacomet Golf Course (where the water goes under the road). Pull well off the side of the road and look for the birds on either side. A variety of overwintering waterfowl (check particularly for Eurasian Wigeon), are to be found at the cove, which is one of the most consistent spots in New England for Common Black-headed Gull.

Sachuest Point is fast gaining the reputation as *the* place to go to see numbers of Harlequin Ducks (mid-November through mid-April). Counts of over 30 birds have been made here recently. Besides these fancy ducks, you may also find a Short-eared Owl or Snowy Owl on the point. Check the surf for a possible Barrow's Goldeneye or a King Eider. To reach Sachuest Point from the west, cross the Jamestown Bridge and the Newport Bridge; follow Route 138 to Miantonomi Avenue to Green End Avenue and go right onto Paradise Avenue. Go left on Hanging Rock Road past the Norman Bird Sanctuary following the road along Second Beach to the dead end at Sachuest Point.

As you stop at various spots along Narragansett Bay look for large groups of Greater Scaup. This bay hosts one of the largest east-coast wintering populations.

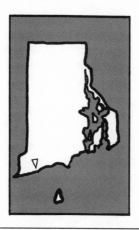

Quonochontaug and Charlestown Beach

SPRING / LATE SUMMER / EARLY FALL

THE SHOREBIRD MIGRATIONS IN SPRING (MAY) and again in fall (mid-July through October) are a highlight of New England birding. Along the southern shore of Rhode Island, numerous salt ponds, tidal flats, and marshes offer various locales at which to watch plovers, peep, and other species as they rest and feed during their epic journeys. Quonochontaug ("Quonie") and Charlestown Beach, in southwestern Rhode Island, are two of the better coastal observation points. The fall season is particularly exciting, as shorebird numbers are at yearly highs. Complementing the numerous sandpipers are a variety of herons, gulls, and terns. Bird watchers willing to get their feet wet (wading is a prerequisite here) are sure to be rewarded with a rich diversity of birds.

To reach Quonie take West Beach Road south from Route 1 in southwestern Rhode Island (see map for Point Judith to Watch Hill). Proceed out the dirt road that parallels the breachway and park on the right. In spring, birders may have this area more or less to themselves. In fall, however, you will have to share Quonie with snapper blue fishermen and shellfish harvesters. If you can arrange a weekday visit it will be to your advantage. Another consideration in birding this area is the tide. Quonie should be birded on a low or incoming tide. Because there are few roosting sites for shorebirds in the immediate vicinity, the birds move elsewhere at high tide. Also, tide charts will quote times for Block Island Sound. High tides on the inside (where most of the birds are) run approximately two hours later than on the sound side. Once you have sorted out the tides and laced on your sneakers, the birding is easy.

East of the access road is an extensive salt marsh with numerous tidal pools and drainage ditches. Stands of phragmites reeds border the marsh. To the north you will see Bill's Island in Quonochontaug Pond. The best shorebirding is in the marsh pools and exposed flats south of Bill's Island. Walk out onto the marsh and approach the feeding shorebirds with the sun at your back. Common migrants in both seasons include Blackbellied and Semipalmated plovers, Greater Yellowlegs, Semipalmated and Least sandpipers, Dunlin, and Shortbilled Dowitcher. Other, less common possibilities are Willet, Ruddy Turnstone, Red Knot, and White-rumped Sandpiper. The fall season typically provides greater variety as well as more rarities. Regular migrants seen in small numbers at Quonie include Lesser Golden-Plover, Lesser Yellowlegs (fairly common), Whimbrel, Western and Pectoral sandpipers, and Long-billed Dowitcher. Birders should also keep an eye out for Hudsonian and Marbled godwits, Baird's and Buff-breasted sandpipers, and Wilson's Phalarope.

The Quonochontaug Pond end of the breachway is a good place to watch feeding terns, particularly in late summer. As the tide comes in, large schools of baitfish run up the channel and attract the birds. Species regularly seen include Common, Forster's, Least, and Black terns. Roseate Tern as well as Royal and Caspian terns are also possible. Ring-billed, Herring, and Great Black-backed gulls are seen here year round. By midsummer these are joined by increasing numbers of Laughing Gulls; by October Bonaparte's Gulls are also likely to be seen.

A number of herons can be found on and around the Quonie marsh. Great Blue Heron, Green-backed Heron, Great Egret, Snowy Egret, and Black-crowned Night-Heron are common, particularly in mid- to late summer during the post-breeding movemeni. Little Blue Heron, Tricolored Heron (rare), and Yellow-crowned Night-Heron also occur. Other species to watch for are Clapper Rail (resident) and Least Bittern.

Two interesting summer-resident passerines can also be found at Quonie. As the tidewaters fill Quonochontaug Pond the marshes flood. This is the ideal time to look for the nesting Sharp-tailed and Seaside sparrows. If you walk (wade) the marsh at high tide you will likely flush one or both of these birds. A particularly good spot to search for these normally secretive sparrows is at the southern end of the marsh around the phragmites stands.

Many of the same species that occur at Quonie can also be found at Charlestown Beach. Because of the sites' proximity, both can easily be visited on the same day. You may want to bird Quonie at dead low tide and then move east to Charlestown at midtide. To reach Charlestown go east on Route 1 to Charlestown Beach Road. The best birding is in the area of the Charlestown Breachway Campground (fee) at the end of the dirt access road. Park in the day parking area and walk along the road that begins at the boat-trailer parking area. Follow the main channel northward to where it divides. The right fork is a straight channel running into Green Hill Pond. Extensive mudflats and sandbars lie to the north of this channel and are utilized by large numbers of shorebirds, herons, gulls, and terns.

To get a better view, continue eastward (some wading will be required) along the channel to a point where you can look directly across to the roosting or feeding birds. Local birders can often find their way across the channel (at low tide) and thus gain access to the north bank. Actually, with a scope, you can cover most of the habitat from the south bank.

The Charlestown Beach area often has numbers of waterfowl as well as herons and shorebirds. Also, this is a good spot to watch for Osprey, Northern Harrier, Sharp-shinned Hawk, Merlin, and occasionally Peregrine Falcon. Common Snipe can, at times, be flushed from the marsh, as can Sharp-tailed and Seaside sparrows. Check the breachway for feeding terns and gulls and the thickets for passerines during migration.

Campers visiting the southern shore of Rhode Island have a choice of staying at the Charlestown Breachway Campground (convenient but rather bleak) or at Burlingame State Park (woodland sites) off Route 1 between Charlestown and Quonochontaug. Motels, groceries, and services are generally available along Route 1 except in winter.

Block Island

FALL

DAWN AT NORTH POINT. A STEADY RHYTHM
of call notes can be heard along the roadside. The Sil-
houetted forms of nuthatches, kinglets, vireos, and warblers drop from the gray sky and seek cover in the
shadows of shrub-covered dunes. While most remain
unnamed in the half-light of dawn, the truncated shape
of the Red-breasted Nuthatch reveals the identity of this
migrant. An irresistible force has moved the nuthatch
from a northern conifer grove and urged him southward. Blown offshore by strong winds, he must now
regain the mainland and continue the risky business of
migration. As the light improves, the identity of other
birds sharing the nuthatch's predicament is revealed:
House Wrens, Ruby-crowned and Golden-crowned

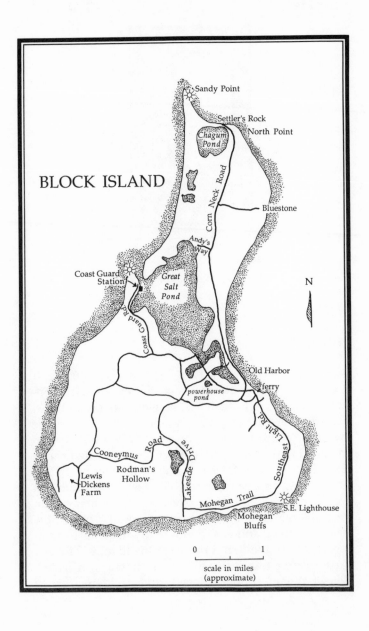

Sandy Point

Settler's Rock
North Point

Chagum Pond

BLOCK ISLAND

Corn Neck Road

Bluestone

Andy's Way

Coast Guard Station

Great Salt Pond

N

Coast Guard Road

Old Harbor

ferry

powerhouse pond

Light Rd.

Cooneymus Road

Rodman's Hollow

Lakeside Drive

Southeast

Lewis Dickens Farm

Mohegan Trail

S.E. Lighthouse

Mohegan Bluffs

0   1

scale in miles
(approximate)

kinglets, Yellow-rumped and Palm warblers, and many others. Not the least of the problems facing these passerines are the Merlins flashing across treetop and dune.

While it may be impossible to fully understand the complex phenomenon of migration, Block Island in autumn offers the bird watcher a microcosm of this dramatic seasonal movement. The best time to join the influx of birds and birders is between the last week in September and mid-October. Block Island can be reached by ferry from the State Pier in Galilee, Rhode Island (401-789-3502) or by air from Westerly, Rhode Island (1-800-243-2460 and 401-596-2460). While many visitors are content to rent bicycles or mopeds for touring the island, a car is recommended for birders wishing to cover the various areas, especially if one's stay is limited to a weekend. The ferry boat carries cars (reservations are a necessity), and a limited number of rentals are available on Block Island.

Block Island, located 10 miles off the Rhode Island mainland, was formed at the end of the last Ice Age and is part of the same terminal moraine that includes Martha's Vineyard and Nantucket. Roughly triangular in shape, the island is nearly 4 miles wide at its base and narrows to a point at its northern end. Rolling moorlands, precipitous bluffs, dunes, and brackish ponds are all typical features of the landscape. Block Island's 11 square miles offer the visitor a variety of possibilities.

Bird watchers traditionally start their day at **North Point**. To reach this area follow Corn Neck Road north approximately 4 miles from Old Harbor Village. You will find a parking lot across from Settler's Rock at the end of the road. Between the road's end and Sandy Point (the extreme northern end of the island) lies a dune community which is crisscrossed by deer trails and walking paths. Much of this area, including the old granite lighthouse, is now part of the Block Island National Wildlife Refuge. Coastal beachgrass, seaside goldenrod, pokeweed, bayberry, and rugosa rose are typical plants growing on the interior of the sandspit. Besides the numerous Song and Savannah sparrows that are regularly found in the dune vegetation, a variety of warblers and kinglets can usually be coaxed from the cover. Common species in fall include Golden-crowned Kinglet, Cape May Warbler, Yellow-rumped Warbler, Black-throated Green Warbler, Palm Warbler, and Blackpoll Warbler.

Although Block Island does not have a lot of good shorebird habitat, a walk along the rocky beach on the east side of Sandy Point may produce a fair variety of birds. Typical fall migrants here are Sanderling, Semipalmated Sandpaper, Least Sandpiper, and Dunlin. Also check the shore for Horned Lark and Water Pipit.

Perhaps the best locale for passerine migrants at North Point is the area between the parking lot and the pine grove on the east side of Corn Neck Road opposite Chagum (Sachem) Pond. The small clumps of rugosa rose, stands of phragmites, bayberry thickets, and the pine grove should all be checked. If there has been a strong northwest blow preceding your visit, you won't have to look for the birds; they will find you. One or two may even try to land on your pantleg! Hundreds of yellow-rumps and kinglets are observed here on a good day. Red-eyed and Solitary vireo, Nashville, Northern Parula, Magnolia, Black-throated Blue, Pine, Bay-breasted, and Black-and-white warblers, as well as many other species, are regularly recorded. These same thickets provide cover for a variety of sparrows, including Chipping, Field, Lincoln's, Swamp, White-throated, and White-crowned, and Dark-eyed Junco.

Block Island is famous for the regularity with which

rarities show up. North Point claims its fair share of these records, so it's a good idea to keep an eye out here for such species as Blue Grosbeak, Dickcissel, and Clay-colored Sparrow. A private driveway with a sign welcoming walkers (no vehicles) leads off the main road to a bluff overlooking Rhode Island Sound. The thickets on either side of the drive are excellent birding habitat, and the view from the bluff is one of the finest on Block Island. Scope the offshore waters and rocks for Double-crested and Great cormorants, Common Loons, and White-winged Scoters.

A word about birding on private land. Traditionally, many of the residents of Block Island have invited birders onto their land. They still do, but make sure to respect the owner's rights and ask for permission. Whenever possible stay on public right-of-ways, and use common sense about where to walk.

Although the south end of Block Island is the place to go to see hawks, a few Merlin and even a peregrine or two are regularly recorded at North Point. Before leaving this area check Chagum Pond for gulls, waterfowl, and herons.

There are numerous spots along **Corn Neck Road** that offer excellent birding. Several locales that have proved productive in the past are described below, but don't hesitate to explore other areas. It is impossible to say what front yard, doorstep, or thicket will be the hot spot on any given day. Connecticut Warblers, Summer and Western tanagers, and even a Say's Phoebe have shown up here before and probably will again.

Less than 1 mile south of North Point parking lot, where Corn Neck Road begins to climb a hill, you will come to an area with several residences and side roads.

Yellow-bellied Sapsucker is frequently found here. Also check the shrubs for kinglets, vireos, and warblers; Carolina and House wrens are regularly heard singing from the thickets. As you continue south along Corn Neck Road keep an eye on the utility poles for Red-headed Woodpecker and the wires for Western Kingbird. These are two more of the "regular rarities" of Block Island. Adjacent to utility pole Number 129 (next to a red house) a secondary road goes east. This road leads to **Bluestone** ("The Maze"), Clay Head, and the **Lapham Banding Station**. Go left at the first fork and look for the parking area on the edge of a field. A trail marked with streamers leads out through the thickets, eventually reaching the bluffs. Cover provided by the dense vegetation usually harbors a good number of passerine migrants, while Merlins and Sharp-shinned Hawks patrol the area looking for a meal. Follow the dirt road (on foot) east from the parking lot and you will soon reach the banding station. The Laphams welcome birders to the station, which is in operation during the spring and fall migrations. Feel free to walk about the grounds, but don't disturb the delicate trapping nets.

Another productive area reached from Corn Neck Road is **Andy's Way**. Look for the sign near utility pole Number 96. From the parking lot you can scan **Great Salt Pond** for herons, swans, geese, ducks, and shorebirds. Better yet, if you don't mind wet feet, a walk (counterclockwise) around the pond's edge should prove even more productive. Species regularly found here include American Bittern, Great Blue Heron, Snowy Egret, Black-crowned Night-Heron, Mute Swan, Green-winged Teal, American Black Duck, Black-bellied Plover, Greater Yellowlegs, Least Sandpiper, Pectoral Sandpiper, and Sharp-tailed Sparrow. With a little luck you may even find a Yellow-crowned Night-Heron or a Buff-breasted

Sandpiper. Another access point to the pond is off Coast Guard Road. Follow this to the **Coast Guard Station** to exlore the inlet from Block Island Sound as well as Cormorant Point Cove southwest of the station. The cove has been a reliable spot for American Oyster-catcher.

The southern section of Block Island also offers some interesting birding. About 2 miles south of Old Harbor on Southeast Light Road you will find **Southeast Light-house** and **Mohegan Bluffs**. The view to the ocean from the lawn of the brick lighthouse is spectacular. Even more dramatic is the landscape along the boardwalk leading to the bluffs. A short walk here reveals steep clay cliffs dropping away to the rocky shorefront and crashing surf. Add a Peregrine Falcon, cruising over the highlands or sweeping up the cliff face, and the setting seems complete. Fortunately for the peregrines, and the birders, this species has shown a definite increase during the 1980s. One recent sighting involved six of these spectacular raptors in the air at once.

Another good spot to see peregrines as well as other hawks is **Rodman's Hollow**. To reach this area follow Mohegan Trail west from the lighthouse, go right on Lakeside Drive, and left on Cooneymus Road. Rod-man's Hollow is a dry kettle hole formed over ten thou-sand years ago. Present-day vegetation includes shad-bush, gray birch, bayberry, and rugosa rose. A main trail descends the steep north side of the kettle hole, eventually branching to the south and west, although you may have a better view of the hawks from the rim. Species regularly seen here are Northern Harrier, Mer-lin, Peregrine Falcon, and Sharp-shinned Hawk. Other possibilities include Osprey, American Kestrel, and rarely a Cooper's Hawk. Continuing west on Cooneymus Road will bring you to the **Lewis–Dickens Farm**. The entrance to Dickens's Road is marked by two large rocks on the left just before the road turns north. In fall these moorlands are covered with bright-flowered herbs which attract butterflies by the hundreds. Besides the ubiquitous cabbage whites and common sulphurs, migrant monarchs are also common here. White-throated Sparrows and Yellow-rumped Warblers pack the thickets at times, and occasionally they are joined by a Yellow-breasted Chat.

As is true elsewhere, birds on Block Island are where you find them. Some days a walk around town will produce a surprising variety as well as one or two rarities. Checking the small ponds, like the one at the powerhouse, a phragmites stand on the edge of town, the waterfront, or a thicket in back of your hotel may all be productive. From the Yellow-headed Blackbirds to the rare Northern Wheatear to the astonishing Phainopepla, the birds of Block Island in fall always provide some excitement.

One way to join the fun is to sign up for Rhode Island Audubon's annual autumn visit (first weekend in October). The price of this package includes round-trip boat fare, room and board, and van transportation around Block Island. A variety of field trips are led by knowledgeable and experienced naturalists. The camaraderie and the birds are both highlights of the weekend. One drawback to this trip is the numbers of participants. The popular weekend leaves little room for solitude. If it's your first trip to Block Island, however, or if you like a lot of companionship, this is a good way to go. Contact Audubon Society of Rhode Island.

No overnight camping is permitted on Block Island. A number of hotels and inns, including the Surf Hotel, Gables Inn, and Blue Dory Inn, are centrally located and frequented by birders. Reservations, particularly during the birding season, are a must and should be arranged well in advance. Restaurants tend to be on the expensive side. Try Tiffany's for good food at reasonable prices.

Great Swamp: West Kingston
nesting waterfowl, raptors, and passerines

James V. Turner Reservoir: East Providence
migrant waterfowl

Sakonnet Point: Little Compton
fall-migrant seabirds, waterfowl, hawks, and passerines

Sapowet Marsh: Tiverton
migrant shorebirds, summer-resident herons and marshbirds

SEE:

–*Field Checklist of Rhode Island Birds.* 1979. Robert A. Conway. Audubon Society of Rhode Island.

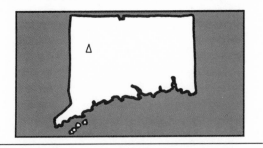

CONNECTICUT

White Memorial Foundation

SPRING / SUMMER / FALL

THE TOWN OF LITCHFIELD, IN NORTHWESTERN
Connecticut, is blessed by a lack of commercial development. An attractive green and numerous houses dating from the eighteenth and nineteenth centuries preserve much of the feeling of old New England. Just
south of the town center, on the shores of Lake Bantam,
is the White Memorial Foundation. Much of this 4,000-
acre property was acquired at the beginning of the century and subsequently given, along with a considerable
endowment, to the foundation. Today, these wetlands,
fields, pastures, and woodlands constitute a valuable
natural resource which is used for conservation, edu-

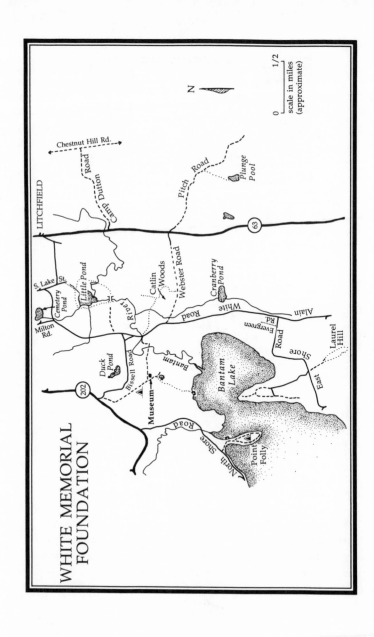

cation, recreation, and research. Among the avian high-lights are 113 species of nesting birds. Woodland birds, particularly forest-interior species, are especially well represented. Summer residents include 7 species of fly-catchers, 5 species of vireos, and 20 species of warblers. During migratory periods, these are complemented by a variety of other birds; the total count of species recorded at White Memorial now stands at 243.

Litchfield can be reached from the Hartford area by following routes 44 and 202 west, and from south-western Connecticut via Route 8 north. From Litchfield take Route 202 southwest a little over 2 miles and go left on Bissell Road. The White Memorial Foundation sign is at this intersection. Take your first right and proceed to the Conservation Center's headquarters and museum.

A visit to the **Museum** will be time well spent. Besides an interesting series of displays and educational activities, bird lists, maps, and natural-history information are available. The foundation's bird list indicating habitat affiliation of many of the breeding species, and its site map showing the extensive network of roads and trails are well worth their small costs. You may also want to look at Frank Egler and William Neiring's book, *The Natural Areas of the White Memorial Foundation*. With luck, Gordon Loery, the White Memorial Conservation Center's director of research, may be on duty. Among other things, Mr. Loery has operated a banding station on foundation property for three decades. His knowledge of the local birds, particularly summer and winter residents, is extensive.

If your visit brings you here during spring (late April through May) or fall (mid-August through mid-October) migration, a walk south from the headquarters to the edge of Bantam Lake should give you a general idea of bird movement. Follow the yellow markings (trail marked G on the foundation map) through cut-over woodlands and along a maple swamp to the lake. Look for such species as Hairy Woodpecker, Great Crested Flycatcher, White-breasted Nuthatch, Veery, and Northern Oriole. Warblers, including Black-and-white, Tennessee, Nashville, Yellow, Common Yellowthroat, Wilson's, Canada, and American Redstart, as well as White-throated, Lincoln's, and Swamp sparrows can all be found here. This is also a good area at which to keep an eye out for Blue-gray Gnatcatcher and White-eyed Vireo. The observation platform, built on the old ice house foundation, provides a vantage point from which to search for waterfowl; over 20 species occur during migration. Ducks are most numerous in fall, with large groups of American Wigeon, American Coot, and Common Merganser. Other spring and/or fall species include both teal, Ring-necked Duck, scaup, Common Goldeneye, and Bufflehead.

If a good movement of migrants seems to have occurred, your next destination should be **Laurel Hill**. This area is in the southern section of foundation property off East Shore Road. Park on the shoulder of the road and hike the trail up Laurel Hill. The main trail follows the west flank of the hill through deciduous woodlands. A short distance from the trailhead a path leads off to the east (left) and passes through dense stands of mountain laurel. Both routes ascend the hill to the summit where there are extensive open fields bordered by woodlands. You may want to go up one trail and come down the other. During a good day in spring you may see many of the 36 species of warblers which are on the foundation's list. Alas, like any migrant spot, Laurel Hill can be "quiet" even in mid-May. Fortunately, one of the features of White Memorial is the resident population of warblers. At least eight species have nested on Laurel Hill, and chances are you will see or hear Blue-winged, Nashville, Black-throated Blue, Chestnut-sided, and/or American Redstart. Although Golden-winged Warblers have nested here in the past, continuing competition from Blue-winged Warblers makes their status tenuous at best. If the migrants are pouring through, these and other residents will just be the icing on the cake. An early-evening stroll up Laurel Hill is almost sure to produce a chorus of Wood Thrush and perhaps a drumming grouse.

While in the vicinity of Laurel Hill look for the cutover area near the intersection of East Shore Road and Alain White Road. **Evergreen Road** (Number 11 on the foundation's map) crosses an area of second growth that was once a red pine forest. The pines were cut in order to help control a scale disease, and pioneering species are beginning to revegetate the area. This is excellent habitat for Chestnut-sided, Blue-winged and Golden-winged warblers, Common Yellowthroat, and Indigo Bunting. The spruces east of the field are one of the areas where northern species such as Golden-crowned Kinglets have nested.

Another excellent birding area is **Little Pond**. Enter from Alain White Road through the Town of Litchfield Recreation Area or along trails from South Lake Street. A trail, including a raised boardwalk over a marsh and a foot bridge over a stream, circles Little Pond. (As of 1987 portions of the boardwalk are in disrepair. With care, however, many of the sections can be negotiated.) The woodlands and powerline right-of-way on the west side of Little Pond are a good place to start your investigations. Besides any migrants you may come across, resident Broad-winged Hawk, Blue-winged Warbler, Eastern Bluebird, Yellow-throated Vireo, and Warbling

Vireo can be found in the vicinity. South of Little Pond the trail crosses Sutton Bridge over the Bantam River. Stop here to look for herons, waterfowl, and shorebirds. Green-backed Heron, Wood Duck, Spotted Sandpiper, Solitary Sandpiper, and Greater Yellowlegs are regularly seen here. North of the pond listen for Least (rare) and American bitterns and Marsh Wrens; summer-resident Sora and Virginia Rail can also be found here, although populations fluctuate from year to year. Other local residents include Alder Flycatcher (Song: "way-bee-o") and Willow Flycatcher (Song: "fitz-bew") as well as numerous Yellow Warblers, Common Yellowthroats, and Swamp Sparrows.

Certainly one of the most attractive of White Memorial properties is the **Catlin Woods**. Many of the forest's magnificent hemlocks and pines have escaped the woodcutter for nearly two centuries. A walk through the forest is a must. Whether you're inclined toward poetry or quantitative analysis (or both), Catlin Woods is sure to impress. Add to the forest giants the voices of Eastern Wood-Pewee, Ovenbird, Veery, Red-eyed Vireo, Blackburnian Warbler, and Black-throated Green Warbler, and you have the makings for a delightful stroll. While you may have to search the understory for the Ovenbirds and crane your neck for the Blackburnians, the effort is definitely worthwhile. Other, rarer, nesting species of Catlin Woods include Barred Owl, Pileated Woodpecker, Solitary Vireo, and Yellow-rumped Warbler. Try to return to the woods at different times of the day, as the amount of light filtering through the canopy to the forest floor lends different moods to the area.

Many of the wetlands of White Memorial show signs of past or present beaver activity. The **Plunge Pool** area demonstrates the impact these mammals can have on natural habitats. To reach Plunge Pool, follow Webster Road east past Catlin Woods to the intersection with Route 63. Cross 63 and follow Pitch Road approximately .7 mile and park. At the bottom of a short hill, a trail leads off to the right (south), reaching the main beaver pond (Plunge Pool) in .25 mile. This is a delightful walk in spring when trillium and dwarf ginseng are in bloom. The streamside forest includes yellow and black birch, while a steep hillside to the west is covered with mountain laurel. Black-throated Blue Warblers have nested on these slopes. Northern Waterthrush nests along the stream, particularly in those places where the beavers' activity has slowed the water's flow. Black-billed Cuckoo, Great Crested Flycatcher, and Scarlet Tanager can often be seen or heard in the surrounding woodlands. Once you reach Plunge Pool, besides searching for the beaver, look for Green-backed Heron on the snags around the pond.

In the late summer and in the fall, two areas that are especially productive are the **cemetery pond** at the junction of Alain White Road and Milton Road south, and the observation tower on the east side of **Point Folly**. The cemetery pond site attracts post-breeding herons, while migrant waterfowl can be scoped from the observation tower.

There are many possible birding sites at White Memorial which are not covered in this account. Visitors should take full advantage of the extensive road-and-trail network to explore the property. No doubt, you will find your own birding hot spot, and who knows, you may add a new species to the White Memorial Foundation's growing list.

Campers will find a convenient spot to pitch their tents at one of two White Memorial Foundation Family Campgrounds. Reservations may be made by mail: Box

368, Litchfield, Connecticut 06759. Phone reservations are not accepted, but you may want to call ahead to determine availability of camp sites—203-567-0089. The Litchfield Inn and several other establishments offer lodging. During the foliage season, finding a room or campsite without a reservation may be difficult. Those interested in obtaining more information about this locale should write or call The White Memorial Conservation Center, Inc., Box 368, Litchfield, Connecticut 06759. Phone: 203-567-0015.

Norwalk Islands

SUMMER

IN 1614 DUTCH EXPLORER ADRIAN BLOCK (OF
Block Island fame) made the following entry in his ship's
log: "Off the port bow appeared several islands with
trees." Although local Indian tribes had been harvesting
oysters in these waters for centuries, Block's brief note
was the first European reference to the group of islands
that would become known as the Norwalk Islands. In
the four centuries since Block sailed past the Norwalks,
the islands have been part of a series of agricultural
and real-estate ventures. Early island history consists
largely of attempts to fatten cattle and sheep on the
poor-soil grasses. Beginning in the nineteenth century,
a procession of pleasure seekers came to the islands to
establish expensive residences and summer cottages.
Ultimately, both the shepherds and the wealthy with-

drew, leaving several of the Norwalk Islands to return to their natural state.

Sheffield, Shea, Chimon, and Cockenoe islands are located on the north shore of Long Island Sound south of Norwalk, Connecticut. These four major islands, as well as a series of islets and hummocks, constitute the Norwalk chain. Typical habitats include second-growth woodlands, thicket and shrub communities, old fields, and salt marshes. Tidal flats border several of the islands.

From the birder's point of view, John Bull's 1961 visit to the Norwalks was to open a new era in the island's history. Bull's census work on Sheffield Island resulted in the first documented nesting of Snowy Egret and Great Egret for Connecticut. Other firsts for Connecticut ornithology soon followed. In subsequent years, work by Milan G. Bull (no relation to John), of the Connecticut Audubon Society, and others, established the importance of the heronry. Fortunately, these field studies have resulted in conservation efforts directed at protecting the nesting sites and their breeding birds. While in the past such diverse figures as Captain Kidd and Lillian Hellman were the talk of the Norwalks, today the herons and the egrets get most of the press.

In order to ensure the continued success of the heronries, access to the federally owned islands is restricted, and unauthorized landings are illegal. Bird watchers interested in visiting one or more of the Norwalk Islands by boat during the breeding season can make arrangements by contacting:

The Stuart B. McKinney National Wildlife Refuge
U.S. Federal Building—Room 210
915 Lafayette Boulevard
Bridgeport, Connecticut 06604
203-579-5617

Currently the most productive heronry is located on Chimon Island. Chimon, the largest of the Norwalks, is now part of the Stuart B. McKinney National Wildlife Refuge. During the last decade, Great Egret, Snowy Egret, Little Blue Heron, Cattle Egret, Green-backed Heron, Black-crowned Night-Heron, Yellow-crowned Night-Heron, and Glossy Ibis have nested here on a regular basis. Tricolored Heron has also nested on Chimon, although this "southerner" is not a consistent summer resident.

While the herons are sure to be a highlight of a summer cruise to the Norwalks, other interesting birds can be seen as well. Nesting American Oystercatcher is a good possibility, as are a variety of shorebirds and landbirds during migration. The ubiquitous Herring and Great Black-backed gulls, which have sizable nesting colonies on Chimon Island, are also noteworthy.

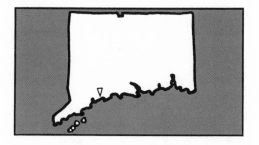

Milford Point

SPRING / FALL

MILFORD POINT ON LONG ISLAND SOUND IS A
favorite stop for Connecticut birders. The area is most
productive during the spring and fall seasons, when
migratory waterfowl, shorebirds, and landbirds com-
plement a variety of herons, gulls, and terns. In May
and June a highlight is the Least Tern colony, which
often harbors scattered pairs of the endangered Piping
Plover within its boundaries. During July, August, and
September the returning flocks of shorebirds include all
the common species and occasionally such rarities as
Baird's or Curlew sandpipers. Recent changes in stew-
ardship and wildlife-management policies at Milford Point
have emphasized the importance of this site both as a
nesting area for summer residents and as a staging area
for migrant shorebirds.

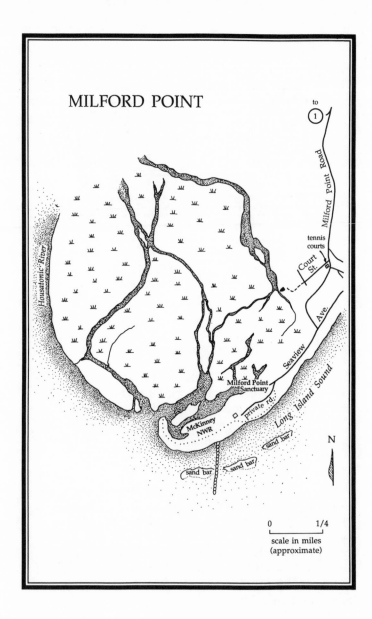

MILFORD POINT

to ①

Milford Point Road

Housatonic River

tennis courts

Court St.

Seaview Ave.

Milford Point Sanctuary

private rd.

McKinney NWR

Long Island Sound

sand bar?

sand bar

sand bar

N

0   1/4

scale in miles
(approximate)

To reach Milford Point take Exit 35 off 95 (Connecticut Turnpike) and go south to Route 1. Turn right on Route 1 and proceed to the first stoplight by Denny's Restaurant (Lansdale Avenue, no sign). Go left at the light and continue to the next light, turning right onto Milford Point Road. Follow Milford Point Road (crossing Naugatuck Avenue in .7 mile) 1.5 miles to Court Street (at tennis courts). Go right on Court Street and proceed straight ahead to the entrance of a boat-launch area (vehicle entry normally restricted by chain and lock).

The deciduous growth around the **boat-launch** area is a good place to search for landbird migrants. In springtime, the flowering blue-eyed-grass, buttercups, and honeysuckle add a touch of color to the parking area. Check the knotweed thickets for sparrows and the shrubs and trees for flycatchers, vireos, warblers, tanagers, and orioles. At the water's edge you will find a good overview of the reed-lined marsh and tidal creeks. If the tide is low and the mudbanks along the creek exposed, a variety of shorebirds can be observed feeding. Also herons, including Great Blue, Great Egret, Snowy Egret, and Green-backed, are commonly observed here. Other, less-common possibilities among the long-legged waders are Little Blue and Tricolored herons (rare) and/or Glossy Ibis. This is also a good vantage point from which to see dabbling ducks. Besides resident Mallard and American Black Duck, look for migrant Wood Duck, teal (both species), Northern Pintail, and Northern Shoveler (fall). Other species to look for, in or over the marsh, are Clapper Rail, Northern Harrier, and Willet. The boat launch provides a good access point for canoeists to explore the marsh and see the birds.

Return to Milford Point Road and go right at the

tennis courts. The road bears to the right and then swings back to the left before reaching a stop sign at the junction with Seaview Avenue. Turn right onto Seaview and proceed .3 mile to the sanctuary entrance. Bear *right* into the sanctuary; do not go left, as this is a private road. Space for parking is available inside the gate on the grounds. The **Milford Point Sanctuary** is on state property which has recently been leased to the Connecticut Audubon Society. Planning is in progress to renovate and preserve the existing buildings and expand facilities for visiting naturalists. The main structure is the once-illustrious Ford Hotel. Diamond Jim Brady, among other figures of the Gilded Age, is closely associated with the hotel's heyday.

Before going out to the beach take a look around the sanctuary. Migrant passerines pass through these thickets and woodlands in good numbers each spring and fall. Common species include Northern Flicker, Great Crested Flycatcher, Ruby-crowned Kinglet, Gray Catbird, Northern Mockingbird (year-round resident), Red-eyed Vireo, Yellow-rumped Warbler, American Redstart, Rufous-sided Towhee, and White-throated Sparrow. Less-common but regular migrants include Swainson's Thrush, Orchard Oriole, and White-crowned Sparrow.

Follow the path past the small shelter (check here for birding information and current sightings) and across the road to the **outer beach**. Do not use the private road. Visitors should be aware that this section of the beach (above mean high tide) is private; continued use by birders depends on our responsible behavior and the owner's good will. At present, there is a Least Tern colony on the right where the path comes out on the beach. In spring and early summer this is a good spot to observe the nesting behavior of this interesting species. You may also find resident Piping Plover at this same locale.

Once on the beach, birders will begin to appreciate the excellence of Milford Point as a shorebird-viewing site. Just plunk yourself down on the sand, set up your scope, and enjoy the birds. The shoreline as well as the mudflats and sandbars all provide excellent foraging and roosting territory for peeps, plovers, and many others. Common species in both spring and fall are Black-bellied and Semipalmated plovers, Ruddy Turnstone, Sanderling, Semipalmated and Least sandpipers, Dunlin, and Short-billed Dowitcher. In spring several of these species will be in breeding plumage.

Continue west along the beach; shortly you will come to a point abreast of where the private road ends. From mid-April to mid-August the western end of the point is fenced to protect nesting terns and plovers. This portion of the point is part of the **Stuart B. McKinney National Wildlife Refuge**. During the nesting season birders can use the observation platform (this is moved out to the point from mid-August through mid-April) here to scope the marsh to the north and Long Island Sound to the south. The common gulls of the sound are Ring-billed, Herring, and Great Black-backed; a few Laughing Gulls may be found here in spring, too, with sizable flocks present in late summer. Check the breakwater for these gulls as well as for Black-crowned Night-Heron and Double-crested Cormorant. Scope the marsh for herons and/or waterfowl you may have missed at Court Street. At low tide, the marsh flats may yield Greater and/or Lesser yellowlegs to add to your shorebird list.

After mid-August you should continue out to the point. Late summer and fall yield a majority of the less-common species. As you walk out the point, carefully check the birds on the flats and at the shoreline; possibilities include Lesser Golden-Plover, Whimbrel, Hudsonian or Marbled godwits, Red Knot, Western Sandpiper, and White-rumped Sandpiper. Even a Buff-breasted Sandpiper may be lurking on the grassy point. During August and early September, Roseate and Common terns, which nest on nearby Falkner Island, join the Least Terns as they take on fuel for the upcoming migration. Your chances of seeing Black Tern are fairly good from late August through September. This is also the time of year to look for American Oystercatcher and Black Skimmer.

Because of the considerable deciduous growth on the outer point, birders visiting in fall should check for landbird migrants. Your reward might even be a Western Kingbird or Yellow-breasted Chat. Noble Proctor, one of Connecticut's foremost birders, relates how six Boreal Chickadees were found here one late October. See Proctor's *25 Birding Areas in Connecticut* (1978).

Another feature of the Milford Point area is the growing population of Mute Swans. Counts of over 120 birds have been made on several occasions. Unfortunately, this species, like many other introduced plants and animals, may ultimately be more of a pest than a boon. Nesting swans require large territories, and many indigenous species have difficulty coexisting with such formidable competitors.

Birding Milford Point in winter can also be rewarding. A variety of loons, cormorants, seaducks, gulls, shorebirds, and passerines can usually be found. Among regularly wintering species are Red-throated Loon, Great Cormorant, Greater Scaup, Purple Sandpiper, and Savannah (Ipswich race) Sparrow. Species such as Common and King (rare) eiders as well as Iceland and Glaucous gulls can normally be counted on to make an appearance sometime during the winter. During the colder months Short-eared Owls often hunt on the point; in big flight years Snowy Owl may occur here.

The Susse Chalet, located off Exit 35 of Route 95, offers lodging at reasonable rates. If you like Italian food, Armellino's at 667 Bridgeport Avenue (Route 1) is a good bet. Fast food is plentiful along Route 1.

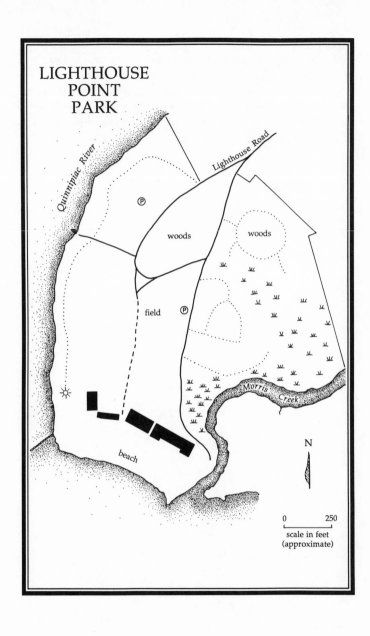

LIGHTHOUSE
POINT
PARK

Quinnipiac River

Lighthouse Road

woods

woods

field

beach

Morris Creek

N

0   250

scale in feet
(approximate)

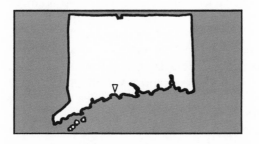

Lighthouse Point Park—
New Haven

LATE SUMMER / EARLY FALL

In the course of a number of years, while collecting ornithological specimens in the vicinity of New Haven, Connecticut, I observed that on certain days early in the fall, almost annually, immense flocks of hawks appeared migrating southward. . . . Several species of hawks were very abundant, especially the Sharp-shinned, in young plumage.

C. C. TROWBRIDGE

ALTHOUGH THESE OBSERVATIONS WERE MADE a century ago, present-day bird watchers can enjoy the same phenomenon. A fall visit to New Haven's Lighthouse Point Park (LPP) provides the opportunity to see not only hawks, but large groups of passerines as well. Indeed, Trowbridge also noted that "The first very large flight of hawks which I ever witnessed occurred on the 18th of September, 1886, and on that day there was also a great flight of Red-headed Woodpeckers and Flickers." Add to Trowbridge's list immense flocks of Bobolinks and Blue Jays, large numbers of American Kestrel and Osprey, and a variety of other hawks and landbirds, and you have some idea of the possibilities at LPP.

To reach LPP take Exit 50 (Woodward Avenue) off Route 95 east (Connecticut Turnpike) in New Haven. Proceed straight to the second set of lights (Townsend Avenue). Take a right on Townsend and continue for 2.3 miles. Turn right onto Lighthouse Road; the entrance to the park is .5 mile ahead. Follow the loop road around to the left to a large parking lot. On most fall days you will find members of the New Haven Bird Club counting hawks.

The view from the parking lot provides a good overview of the park as well as unobstructed lines of sight for hawk watching. While Sharp-shinned Hawks and American Kestrels are the predominant raptor species at this coastal locale, large numbers of Osprey, Northern Harrier, and occasionally Broad-winged Hawks are also recorded. During the 1980s this site has averaged approximately 400 sharpies per day from mid-September through mid-October with peak flights during the last week in September and the first week in October. Other raptors seen regularly, though in lesser numbers, are Turkey Vulture, Cooper's Hawk, Red-shouldered Hawk, Red-tailed Hawk, Merlin, and Peregrine Falcon. An eagle or two is also a fairly good possibility. Bald Eagle observations are made throughout the fall, while

Golden Eagle is most often recorded in October. Although Lighthouse Point's seasonal hawk numbers are impressive by most measures, it is the individual bird that provides the real thrill. A sharpie careening through the treeline, a harrier tilting back and forth over the marsh, a young Merlin harassing a crow on the ballfield, or even a Golden Eagle drifting southward; these are the sights that make the park a special place for hawk lovers.

While watching the hawks, birders will find it difficult not to notice the impressive numbers of certain passerines that occur here. Early in September, thousands of Bobolinks pass by, later in the month Blue Jays put on an equally impressive display, and in early October American Goldfinch numbers peak. Although Northern Flicker numbers don't approach those of Bobolinks, jays, or goldfinches, there is often a steady passage of these woodpeckers. Because LPP is definitely not only a hawk site, you should allow time for exploring its various habitats.

Begin with the thickets and marsh directly across the road from the parking lot. A series of paths cut through a sumac and knotweed thicket. This tangle offers good cover for a variety of passerine migrants. Check the edges for Song and Savannah sparrows, Grasshopper and Vesper sparrows (occasional), or even a Dickcissel. Goldfinches and White-throated Sparrows are commonly found in the thicket, as are a variety of thrushes. This same area frequently has catbirds and wrens as well as a few warblers. A slight rise across from the parking lot provides a place at which to watch the hawk-trapping and -banding operation that is often in progress on the marsh. Next to the mound another path leads out into the phragmites marsh. Swamp and White-crowned sparrows, Yellow Warblers, Palm Warblers,

Common Yellowthroats, Common Snipe, and Virginia Rails (rarely) can be found here. At the points where you can see through the grasses to the marsh and tidal creek look for Belted Kingfisher, Great Blue and Green-backed herons, and American Bittern.

Another excellent place to search for passerines is the oak–hickory woods next to the park's exit road. A loop path winds around these woods through patches of greenbrier and stands of sassafras. Common migrants include Ruby-crowned and Golden-crowned kinglets, Red-eyed and Solitary vireos, and a variety of woodland warblers. A spur path (off the loop) leads out toward the marsh and ends in a dense thicket. Check here for the skulkers (Kentucky, Mourning, and Connecticut warblers). A feature of LPP is the October migration of Red-headed Woodpecker. If you are visiting during that month, a careful check of this and the other woods may turn up this species. Then again, a red-headed may fly by as you scan the skies for eagles. Another spot to check for woodpeckers, flycatchers, thrushes, kinglets, vireos, and warblers is the woods on both sides of the entrance road. Parking is available near the boat launch, or you can walk over from the hawk-watching area.

Because LPP occupies a relatively small area it is possible to visit all of the birding spots in the park in several hours. As you walk around check disturbed areas, weedy edges, and fields for sparrows. Also investigate any isolated stands of trees; these often harbor migrants. Besides the more common species, the list of "vagrants" that have been recorded in the park includes Western Kingbird, Blue Grosbeak, and Lark Sparrow. On almost any day in autumn the list could get longer.

Wawa's convenience store at the corner of Townsend Avenue and Lighthouse Road is open 24 hours and has coffee, sandwiches, picnic supplies, and a variety of other goods. Motel accommodations can be found north of New Haven on Route 91 and east of New Haven along Route 95.

While visiting the New Haven area, birders should definitely take the opportunity to visit Yale's Peabody Museum. Billed as "the largest natural-history museum in New England," the Peabody houses several impressive displays. Besides their famous dinosaur collections and murals, mammal exhibits, and various dioramas, the museum devotes considerable space to Connecticut's bird life. A comprehensive exhibit, titled Connecticut Birds, is well displayed and highly informative. The birds are arranged by families and include juvenile as well as male and female plumages. This is a great spot to bone up on your identification skills; shorebirds, gulls and terns, warblers, and sparrows (and all the rest) are just standing there awaiting your inspection. The exhibit also contains a series of Golden-winged X Blue-winged warbler hybrids. Be sure to take a few minutes to inspect the display on the evolution of birds and the reconstructed Dodo, both of which are in the dinosaur hall. The museum gift shop has a variety of books, records, and other materials which may be of interest to the naturalist. The Peabody Museum is open Monday through Saturday 9:00 A.M.–4:45 P.M., Sunday 1:00 P.M.–4:45 P.M.. Admission is $2.00 per adult (free on Tuesday). To reach the museum from LPP return to Route 95 and take the highway west to Route 91 north. Take Exit 3 (Trumbull Street) off Route 91, to Whitney Avenue. Go right on Whitney. The museum is located at 170 Whitney Avenue.

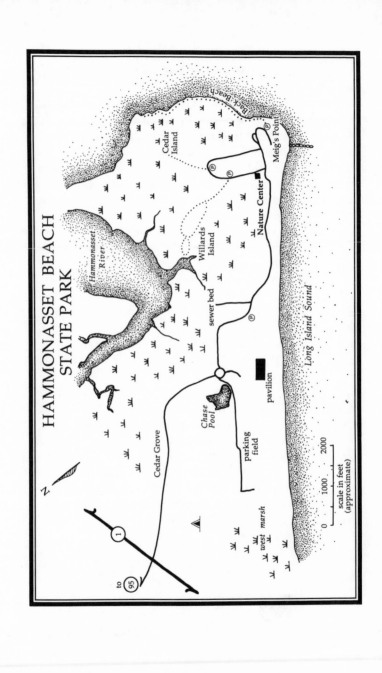

HAMMONASSET BEACH
STATE PARK

Hammonasset River

Cedar Grove

Chase Pool

parking field

west marsh

pavilion

sewer bed

Willards Island

Cedar Island

Back Beach

Meig's Point

Nature Center

Long Island Sound

N

to 95

1

0   1000   2000
scale in feet
(approximate)

Hammonasset Beach
State Park

SPRING / SUMMER / FALL

EXPERIENCED BIRDERS LEARN TO READ THE
landscape. Their search for a specific habitat or combination of habitats is guided by their understanding of
birding possibilities. Occasionally they come across an
area that causes their expectations to leap. Willard's
Island, located at the eastern end of Hammonasset Beach
State Park (HBSP), is just such a spot. Happily, the
birding history of the "island" demonstrates that here,
more often than not, reality lives up to expectation.
Willard's Island, actually an oval-shaped highland bordered by salt marsh, was once an orchard. Over the
last several decades natural succession has led to a mixed
habitat consisting of weedy fields interspersed with ce-

dars, bayberry thickets, and mixed woodlands. The seeds and fruits of the various grasses, herbs, shrubs, and trees provide an abundant natural food crop for migrant granivores and frugivores. Other passerines take advantage of the diverse insect populations. These birds, in turn, attract a variety of hawks and falcons. By itself, Willard's Island would be reason enough for a visit, but other attractions of Hammonasset Beach State Park include ocean, beach, marsh, and pond. This rich combination makes the park one of the premier birding locations on the northeast coast.

To reach HBSP take Exit 62 south from Route 95 (Connecticut Turnpike). The exit road leads to the Hammonasset Connector which in turn crosses Route 1 shortly before entering the park (fee). May, August, September, and October are the best birding months, although the summer residents and wintering seabirds and waterfowl also offer some interesting possibilities. Be prepared for hoards of bathers on good beach days in summer.

To reach **Willard's Island** follow the park road to the rotary and head toward Meig's Point. Take a left after passing the Nature Center and follow the secondary road around behind the picnic area to a small parking lot. The access road (pedestrians only) to Willard's Island is across from the parking area. The paved surface eventually reaches a loop path which circles the island. In spring and fall, Willard's Island provides welcome food and cover for migrating landbirds and thus acts as a natural "trap." Check the shrubs lining the road leading out to the island for catbirds and mockingbirds. Once you reach the island you can go right or left around the loop path. Make sure also to cover the central areas, which contain good sparrow habitat. Song, Field, Savannah, Swamp, and White-throated sparrows as well as Dark-eyed Juncos can be common; also be on the lookout for the occasional Lincoln's, White-crowned, or Clay-colored sparrow (fall). During migratory periods the cedars attract flocks of robins and waxwings and, at times, good numbers of kinglets and yellow-rumps. If things seem a little slow on the day of your visit, work your way to the northern tip of the island where the birds tend to congregate. A variety of thrushes, vireos, and warblers can often be found here. Common migrants include Hermit and Swainson's thrushes, Solitary and Red-eyed vireos, and Black-and-white, Nashville, Northern Parula, Blackpoll, Common Yellowthroat, and American Redstart warblers. Scarlet Tanager, Rose-breasted Grosbeak, and Northern Oriole should also be expected. With a little luck you may even scare up a Yellow-breasted Chat.

One of the beauties of Willard's Island is its proximity to the salt marsh and tidal river. Take advantage of the overlooks to search for herons, rails, bitterns, shorebirds, and both Sharp-tailed and Seaside sparrows. Five species of rail have been seen or heard in the adjacent wetlands including King and Clapper (summer resident) as well as the rare Yellow Rail. At low tide check the exposed flats of the Hammonasset River, which can be seen from the north end of the island. Common migrants include Black-bellied and Semipalmated plovers, both yellowlegs, and Least and Semipalmated sandpipers. In fall, the raptors found on and around Willard's Island (and the park in general), add still another dimension to the bird watching. An early-morning walk along the loop path may turn up a Merlin or a Peregrine Falcon perched in one of the trees bordering the marsh. Species such as Osprey, Northern Harrier, Sharp-shinned Hawk, and American Kestrel are regularly seen throughout the park.

Another good birding area is the **Cedar Island Trail** east of Willard's Island. Return to the parking lot, cross through the picnic area, and look for a trailhead across from the access road. The first part of the trail passes through woodlands that may have many of the same birds that are present on the island. This is also a good spot for Eastern Phoebe, Carolina Wren, Brown Thrasher, and Rufous-sided Towhee. The trail soon reaches a boardwalk. At present the boardwalk is in disrepair. Because of nesting birds, including the endangered Piping Plover, however, it is likely the boardwalk will be repaired and made to end in a viewing platform partway out the marsh. From here you will be able to scan the marsh to the north and east. Willet nest in the eastern portion of the marsh.

Although Hammonasset does not have easy access to extensive mudflats usually associated with good shorebird habitat, the park's shorebird list is impressive. At high tide, fields, parking lots, and pond edges may be productive. A good area at which to start your search is on the picnic grounds and fields south of Willard's Island and the Cedar Island Trail. During migration check here for Killdeer, Pectoral Sandpiper, and Lesser Golden-Plover (fall). After a heavy rain, standing pools of water may attract other shorebirds including plovers, peep, snipe, and Dunlin.

Meig's Point is a favored spot for bluefish anglers. While it is worth checking at any time of year, this rocky headland overlooking Long Island Sound is at its best during winter and early spring. Loons, grebes, cormorants, and seaducks are regularly seen here, while winter storms sometime result in an alcid flight. On low tides in fall you can park at the fisherman's parking lot, walk along the rocky beach, and then follow either of two paths, over the top or along the marsh side of the glacial moraine. Check the rocks at the end of the moraine for Royal Tern. Once you reach the Back Beach, you can bird the estuary and flats to the east. This area is closed during spring and summer to protect nesting species.

Return to the main park road and proceed west. Look for the **Sewer Bed Road** on your right. Although you are not allowed to drive down this road, a convenient parking lot is just ahead on the left. Walk in the service road. The thickets along the road and the stands of sumac around the sewer beds are often packed with migrants. Thrashers and mockingbirds, Savannah and Song sparrows, as well as a few House Wrens can usually be found. This is also an excellent location for White-crowned Sparrow. In fall rarities, including Western Kingbird and Blue Grosbeak, have occurred here. The fence around the sewer beds not only provides a good perch for the birds but allows the bird watcher to carefully study the perchers. This is an ideal spot to work on sparrow identification. At low tide check the river for shorebirds and the ditches for rails.

Just west of the rotary, on the road leading to the main bathhouse and concessions, you will find **Chase Pool** (known to birders as The Swan Pool). True to its nickname, the pool has a resident pair of Mute Swans; rarely, migrant Tundra Swans put in an appearance. Purple Martins and Willow Flycatchers nest here. The pond is a good spot to look for herons, waterfowl, rails (mainly Sora), and shorebirds. Species commonly found here include Snowy Egret and Green-backed Heron, American Black Duck, Green-winged and Blue-winged teal, American Wigeon, and Bufflehead, both yellowlegs, Solitary, Spotted, and Pectoral sandpipers, and Common Snipe. This is just one of several spots in the park where rarities have occurred. One of Swan Pool's contributions to the record book is a Black-necked Stilt. Gulls commonly seen resting on the pond include Ring-billed and Laughing gulls (late summer).

The **Picnic Areas and Parking Lots** in the vicinity (both sides of the road) of The Swan Pool are definitely worth checking. Clay Taylor, a local expert, calls these areas "the best places in the park." Any standing water on the grassy fields may attract shorebirds. Besides species already mentioned, less-common shorebirds, including Upland Sandpiper, Hudsonian Godwit, Western Sandpiper, White-rumped Sandpiper, Baird's Sandpiper, Stilt Sandpiper, and Buff-breasted Sandpiper, have all been found here in the fall. You will find other, similar grassy areas as you drive around the park. If conditions are right (flooding after heavy rain), be sure to investigate these spots. In late fall and winter many of these same fields have flocks of larks, longspurs, and buntings. While the gull congregations in the parking areas will consist mainly of Laughing Gull, Ring-billed Gull, Herring Gull, and Great Black-backed Gull, rarities such as Mew Gull have been recorded. In 1985 a Northern Wheatear spent five days in this area.

Continue west along the park road as far as you can to a dirt parking lot on the edge of the west marsh. A tidal inlet from Long Island Sound floods this spartina wetland at high tide. In fall, American Bittern, Great Blue Heron, and Green-backed Heron can often be found here. Whimbrel sometimes feed in the marsh, and Belted Kingfisher often patrol the creek. If the throngs of sun worshippers are not on hand you may want to take the path leading out to the beach. In late October and early November this is a good overlook for scoter flights.

Another autumn (mid-October onward) birding attraction of the park is owling. Birders have had most success in finding the various species in the **Cedar Groves** on both sides of the road between the rotary and the park's entrance gate. Common Barn-Owl, Great Horned Owl, Barred Owl, Long-eared Owl, and Northern Saw-whet Owl have all been found roosting in the cedars. Owl seekers should also check the north end of Willard's Island.

Because Hammonasset Beach State Park covers almost 1,000 acres there are numerous spots to stop and bird. Other areas worth investigating are the edges around the campgrounds, the trees and shrubs near the bathhouses and the Main Pavilion, and the various service roads. No doubt you will find other productive sites, and perhaps just that rarity you were looking for.

The campgrounds in the park, while not beautiful, are convenient and comfortable, particularly in the off-seasons. Food and other supplies are available in Clinton (east on Route 1). The Audubon Shop in Madison (871 Boston Post Road—Route 1) has a full range of birding supplies.

CONNECTICUT
SUPPLEMENTAL LIST

New Haven Harbor: New Haven
migrant and wintering birds

East Rock Park: New Haven
spring passerine migrants

Devil's Hopyard State Park: East Haddam
summer-resident Acadian Flycatcher, Eastern Bluebirds, and
various warblers

SEE:

–25 *Birding Areas in Connecticut.* 1978. Noble S. Proctor. The Pequot Press.

PART TWO

Seabirds & Hawks

Hawk Watching in
New England

FALL / WINTER / SPRING

HAWKS HAVE FASCINATED MANKIND THROUGH-
out recorded history. In fact, the first bird book, *De arte
venandi cum avibus*, written by Frederick II of Hohen-
staufen in the thirteenth century, treats the popular
subject of falconry. Frederick's interest in raptors went
well beyond hunting and included detailed studies of
bird behavior. Unfortunately for the hawks, however,
an attitude more akin to that of the Dark Ages prevailed
well into the twentieth century in North America. In
New England, the eras of colonization and agriculture
were characterized by a combination of habitat destruc-
tion and hunting that resulted in significant decreases

in bird populations. Many species of hawks were particularly hard hit. Every family that kept a few chickens tended to see all hawks as inimical to its livelihood. Apart from the concern for chickens, hawks were large, attractive targets, and they became subjects of a seemingly endless barrage.

The phenomenon of hawk migration was well known to hunters, who used these flights to sharpen their skills. The following account from Lake Erie, reported by A. C. Bent, is typical.

> When I saw the flight in 1882 it was probably greater than in 1905. There were more Sharp-shins than one would suppose were in Ontario, and one day my brother and I stood thirty paces apart, facing each other, with double-barrel, breech-loaders, and for a short time the hawks passed so thick that we had to let some go by unmolested because we could not load fast enough to fire at each as it came by.

This annual slaughter of hawks continued well into the third decade of the present century. One of the first significant conservation efforts was made in Pennsylvania. Documentation of the fall hawk kill along the Kittatinny Ridge by Richard Pough and Henry Collins led to the establishment of the Hawk Mountain Sanctuary in 1934. During the last half-century, effective conservation and education programs have led to the virtual elimination of hawk hunting as well as to a growing interest in hawk watching.

Hawk watching is basically a seasonal activity. In New England, the autumn flight is far and away the most spectacular in terms of numbers of hawks. While the spring flight involves the same variety of raptors as is seen in the fall, the hawks often move northward singly or in small groups rather than in large concentrations. A third seasonal hawk-watching activity involves raptors on their wintering grounds.

AUTUMN. Excellent fall hawk-watching areas are located at inland, coastal, and island sites. New England hawk watchers have tallied up to a quarter of a million birds in this season. Turkey Vultures, Broad-winged Hawks, Sharp-shinned Hawks, American Kestrels, Red-tailed Hawks, Ospreys, and Northern Harriers constitute the majority of migrants. Other species seen regularly, although in lesser numbers, are Bald Eagle, Cooper's Hawk, Northern Goshawk, Red-shouldered Hawk, Merlin, and Peregrine Falcon. Occasionally a Rough-legged Hawk flight occurs. Rare migrants include Golden Eagle and Gyrfalcon.

While timing (see chart p. 252) and luck each play a part in determining what raptors an observer will see at a given spot on a given day, several generalities may be useful in scheduling your hawk watching. Normally, the mid-September broad-wing flight is best observed at inland locales. Coastal sites in late September and early October provide an excellent opportunity to see large numbers of sharp-shins, kestrels, Ospreys, and harriers. The prime locales for observing the late September through mid-October flight of Merlin and Peregrine Falcon are several of the coastal islands, although mainland barrier beaches can be productive as well. A late (October through November) movement of eagles, goshawks, red-shoulders, red-tails, and rough-legs normally occurs across a broad front.

Serious hawk watchers are invariably amateur meteorologists. In autumn they are particularly interested in the arrival of cold fronts and the attendant northeast or northwest winds. In general, these conditions favor hawk flights. Variables, including specific wind direction and velocity and upper atmospheric conditions, make "calling the day" an art as well as a science. Not

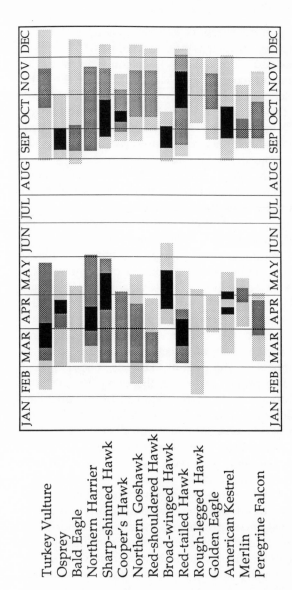

	JAN	FEB	MAR	APR	MAY	JUN	JUL	AUG	SEP	OCT	NOV	DEC
Turkey Vulture												
Osprey												
Bald Eagle												
Northern Harrier												
Sharp-shinned Hawk												
Cooper's Hawk												
Northern Goshawk												
Red-shouldered Hawk												
Broad-winged Hawk												
Red-tailed Hawk												
Rough-legged Hawk												
Golden Eagle												
American Kestrel												
Merlin												
Peregrine Falcon												

(adapted from Paul Roberts,
Eastern Massachusetts Hawk Watch 1986)

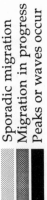

Sporadic migration

Migration in progress

Peaks or waves occur

a few inveterate watchers have taken vacation time on the wrong day. On occasion hawks break all the rules and move even under adverse conditions. The only foolproof way of assuring that you will be there for the big flight is to bird every day.

SPRING. As noted previously, the spring hawk flight is normally more a trickle than a wave. Coastal locales, however, on April and May days with westerly winds, may produce fairly good hawk movements. Although inland sites tend to be less productive during this season, there are occasional reports of fairly large (50 to 1,000 birds) concentrations of broad-wings. The spring migration gets under way in March when Turkey Vultures start north. Other early migrants include Northern Harrier, Red-shouldered Hawk, Red-tailed Hawk, and American Kestrel. The kestrel migration continues throughout April and into May. During these same two months Osprey, Sharp-shinned Hawk, and Broad-winged Hawk are on the move in New England. Other migrants, adding to the springtime variety, include Bald Eagle, Cooper's Hawk, Northern Goshawk, Rough-legged Hawk, Merlin, and Peregrine Falcon. Although extremely rare, Black Vulture, American Swallow-tailed Kite, and Mississippi Kite are possible at this time of year. The spring migration continues throughout May and even into June for broad-wings and harriers.

WINTER. Wintering Red-tailed Hawks and American Kestrels, as well as the occasional Northern Harrier, Sharp-shinned Hawk, Cooper's Hawk, Goshawk, or Red-shoulderd Hawk, can be found in many New England locales. At several sites, one or more of these raptors are found in association with wintering populations of Turkey Vultures, Bald Eagles, or Rough-legged Hawks. In certain years this variety of raptors is further enhanced by Snowy, Long-eared, Short-eared, and Northern Saw-whet owls. While no one site holds the promise of all of these species, several coastal locales as well as inland river valleys and lowlands regularly attract birders because of their interesting variety of wintering raptors. The ultimate excitement in winter hawk watching, however, is reserved for those rare occasions when a Gyrfalcon (or two) visits New England.

For some individuals, bird watching means hawk watching. Certainly their passion is understandable. Hawks are generally large, graceful birds that often maintain a high profile. As well as being exciting and beautiful, raptors are also good subjects to study. The traditional link between the professional and amateur ornithologist is maintained through a variety of raptor projects. One of the most popular endeavors is the hawk watch. This activity provides valuable information on population trends and species distribution and creates an educational forum for the participants. Individuals interested in joining seasonal hawk counts should contact one or both of the organizations listed below.

National
Hawk Migration Association of North America
Diann MacRae, Chairman
22622-53 Avenue S.E.
Bothell, Washington 98021

New England
Hawks
P.O. Box 212
Portland, Connecticut 06480

The following listing of New England hawk-watching sites consists of traditional locales with proven productivity. Many of these sites are covered by hawk-watching teams, particularly during the fall migration. A visit to one or more of these spots offers the beginning or visiting birder the opportunity to gain useful information from individuals familiar with the area.

STATE HAWK-WATCHING SITES

MAINE:

- Cadillac Mountain, Mt. Desert Island (Fall)*
  Directions: Take Rt. 3 south from Ellsworth to entrance for Acadia National Park on Mt. Desert Island. Follow the loop access road to the summit road.

- Beech Mountain, Mt. Desert Island (Fall)*
  Directions: Take Rt. 3 south from Ellsworth to Mt. Desert Island. Go south on Rt. 102 to Somesville. Go right on Pretty Marsh Rd. and then left onto Beech Hill Rd. following signs to Beech Mountain. Hike the .4-mile trail to the summit.

- Monhegan Island (Fall)*
  Directions: Take the ferry from Port Clyde (no cars allowed on island). Hike to Lobster Cove.

- Mount Agamenticus, York (Fall)
  Directions: Take Exit 1 off Rt. 95 (Maine Turnpike) at York. Follow Rt. 1 north to Cape Neddick and go left on the (Cat) Mountain Road to Agamenticus Village. Take Mt. Agamenticus Rd. west approximately 1.5 miles to Mt. Agamenticus access road on right.

- Fort Foster, Kittery Point (Fall)
  Directions: Take Rt. 103 east from Kittery to Kittery Point. Go right onto bridge to Gerrish Island. Take a right onto Pocahontas Rd. and drive out the point to Fort Foster.

NEW HAMPSHIRE:

- Little Roundtop, Bristol (Fall)
  Directions: Take Rt. 3A south from Bristol. Go right at fork

* See site maps for locations.

up hill and right again at next fork. Follow this road straight to Slim Baker Conservation Area. Park and hike trail (5–10 min.) to lookout.

· Blue Job Mountain, Farmington (Spring)
Directions: Take First Crown Point Road northwest out of Strafford Corner. In just under 4 miles look for a parking area on the edge of a field. From here a trail leads to the summit (15–20 min.).

· Pitcher Mountain, Stoddard (Fall and Spring)
Directions: From Stoddard go west on Rt. 123 for 2 miles to small parking lot on right-hand side of road. The hike to the summit of Pitcher Mountain takes 5–10 min.

· Pack Monadnock, Peterborough (Fall and Spring)
Directions: Take Rt. 101 southeast out of Peterborough. Go left to Miller State Park (just before Temple Mountain Ski area). Take road to summit of South Pack.

VERMONT:

· Dead Creek Wildlife Management Area, Addison County (Winter)*
Directions: Take Rt. 22A from Vergennes to Addison, or Rts. 23 and 17 from Middlebury.

· Rockingham/Springfield (Spring)
Directions: Take Rt. 91 north to the rest area at the Rockingham/Springfield line.

· Putney Mountain, Putney (Fall)
Directions: From Rt. 5 in Putney take the secondary road northwest toward Westminster West. After passing a school turn left opposite a cemetery. Cross the intersection at 1.8 miles and bear right on road up Putney Mountain. From here go 1.7 miles, bearing right at the next intersection, and turn right, proceeding north on a dirt road. Continue as far as the surface allows, park, and walk to a large clearing. (You can normally drive to within 1 mile of the site.)

· Mount Tom, Easthampton (Fall and Spring)
Directions: Take Exit 17W off of Rt. I91 north onto Rt. 141. Follow Rt. 141 for 1.7 miles to Christopher Clark Rd. on the right. This road leads to park headquarters. For Bray Tower, turn left onto Reservation Rd. at headquarters. To reach Goat's Peak Tower continue on Christopher Clark Rd. past headquarters to a parking lot on the right. Hike road to base of tower. In springtime Bray Tower is the better location.

· Quabbin Reservoir, Belchertown (Winter)
Directions: Take Massachusetts Turnpike to Exit 8 at Palmer. Follow signs to Rt. 181 and go north to Rt. 9. Go east (right) on Rt. 9 to entrance for Quabbin Reservation. Try the Enfield Lookout and the Winsor Dam.

· Mt. Wachusett, Princeton (Fall and Spring)
Directions: Take Rt. 2 to Rt. 140. Follow Rt. 140 south and go right onto Mile Hill Rd. (at Wachusett Mountain Ski Area sign). Continue past ski area to reservation entrance on right. Follow paved road to the summit. The Ledges (with a southern exposure) is the preferred spring lookout.

· Plum Island (PRNWR), Newburyport (Fall-Winter-Spring)*
Directions: From Rt. 95 take Rt. 113 (Exit 57, Storey Ave.) east to High St. Go right onto High St. and continue to Rolfe's Lane (3.6 miles from Exit 57). Go left onto Rolfe's Lane, right at the intersection with Water St., and straight to the Plum Island Turnpike. Take the first right after the bridge. See main-text account for directions to winter eagle sites. Mainly falcons in fall; spring migration highly variable.

· Provincelands (Cape Cod National Seashore), Provincetown (Spring)*
Directions: Take Rt. 6 (Mid-Cape Highway) to Provincetown. Race Point Rd. leads to the Provincelands Visitor Center and observation deck. Also, Beech Forest off Race Point Rd.: take trail next to restrooms, left at split-rail fence to high dunes. (Fort Hill in Eastham and Highland Light in Truro are productive spring and fall sites.)

RHODE ISLAND:

- Napatree Point, Watch Hill (Fall)*
  Directions: Take Rt. 1A from Westerly to Avondale and then Watch Hill Rd. to the boat harbor. Park here and walk to the high dunes west of the Beach Club (base of peninsula is better than tip of point).

- Sakonnet Point, Little Compton (Fall)
  Directions: Take Rt. 77 to Sakonnet. Park and walk back to the road leading toward Sakonnet Point. Walk the beach to Sakonnet Point. Sharp-shinned Hawks and kestrels often concentrate a short distance inland from the beach.

- Block Island (Fall)*
  Directions: Take the ferry from Galilee. Take Southeast Light Rd. to Southeast Lighthouse and Mohegan Bluffs.

CONNECTICUT:

- Quaker Ridge, Greenwich (Fall)
  Directions: Take Exit 28 (Round Hill Rd.) off the Merritt Turnpike and go north on Round Hill Rd. for 1.4 miles to John St. Turn left onto John St. and follow this 1.4 miles to the corner of Riversville Rd. Enter driveway for Audubon Center. Quaker Ridge is straight ahead.

- Chestnut Hill, Litchfield (Fall)*
  Directions: From Litchfield Center go south on Rt. 63 a little less than 1 mile. Turn left onto Camp Dutton Rd. and follow to intersection with Chestnut Hill Rd. at top of hill. Lookout is in large field at the intersection.

- Lighthouse Point Park, New Haven (Fall)*
  Directions: From New Haven take Exit 50 from Rt. 95 east. Proceed to second set of lights and go right on Townsend Ave. Follow this for 2.3 miles and go right on Lighthouse Rd. Park entrance is .6 mile ahead.

- Connecticut River, Essex (Winter)
  Directions: Take Rts. 91 and 9 south from Hartford. Take Exit 3 off Rt. 9 for Essex and proceed to the end of Main St. to look for wintering eagles.

Pelagic Birding in New England

by Wayne R. Petersen

Introduction

Of the many and diverse alternatives available to the bird finder in New England, pelagic birding can be especially rewarding, particularly for visitors from inland areas where pelagic opportunities are lacking. Birds such as shearwaters, storm-petrels, gannets, phalaropes, skuas, jaegers, Sabine's Gulls, kittiwakes, and alcids are among the pelagic birds that seasonally inhabit the offshore waters of New England. In addition, no fewer than 12 species of whales, dolphins, and porpoises occur with more or less regularity. Perhaps of greatest appeal to the bird finder, however, is the rel-

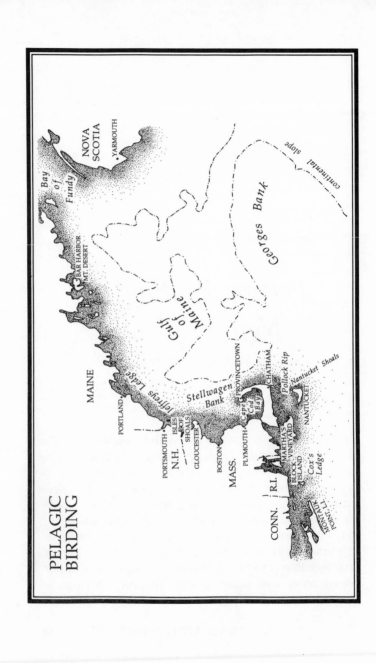

PELAGIC
BIRDING

ative ease with which many of these species may be observed, both from boats and occasionally from land.

Why such diversity? An oceanographic primer

To describe the marine environment, certain boundaries must be established. New England's coastal waters roughly include a large coastal indentation east of Maine and Massachusetts called the Gulf of Maine, the northern edge of which is bounded by the mouth of the Bay of Fundy and the southwestern end of Nova Scotia. The Gulf's southern edge lies approximately on a line running from Cape Cod, east about 100 miles to the northern edge of a major oceanographic feature called Georges Bank. The eastern edge of Georges Bank coincides quite closely with the outer boundary of the continental shelf of southern New England, which is defined by the 200-meter depth contour. South of Cape Cod and southeast of Nantucket Island, Georges Bank is bounded on the west (remember, the New England shoreline turns westward south of Massachusetts) by an area of shallow and turbulent seas called Nantucket Shoals. A final feature of importance to marine birds in New England is an area called Cox's Ledge, which lies about 25 miles east-southeast of Block Island, Rhode Island, and 40 miles east of Montauk Point, Long Island, New York. Within the boundaries here described, all approximately lying between 40° and 44° north latitude, there are a number of lesser oceanographic and bathymetric features which influence local concentrations of pelagic birds and marine mammals in New England waters.

Critical to an appreciation of the distribution of pelagic birds is an awareness of the mechanisms which concentrate the abundant food supplies upon which the birds depend while they are in the Gulf of Maine and Georges Banks waters. Without such oceanographic mechanisms, the waters of the region would be unable to sustain the tremendous predatory pressure which is exerted on prey populations by the combination of pelagic birds, marine mammals, and commercial fishermen. One of the principal factors contributing to the high productivity of prey populations in the Gulf of Maine and on Georges Bank is related to differing sea-bottom contours. On areas of the sea floor where submarine plateaus, ridges, or other similar configurations exist, significant differences in water depth may occur over the submerged banks, in marked contrast to the deeper water adjacent to them. In the shallower waters over these banks, sunlight is able to penetrate to the bottom, thus enhancing the development of photosynthetic phytoplanktonic organisms, which in turn provide food for zooplankton and larger fish predators. The total system derives nutrients in the form of dissolved nitrates and phosphates from the deeper water adjacent to the banks. Through a process called "upwelling," the variable interactions of tides and deepwater currents running against the walls of these submerged banks have the effect of bringing nutrients from the deep up to the surface. Where appropriate surface-water circulation patterns occur, these nutrients are drawn onto the fishing banks and are thereby made available to the phytoplankton in the shallower surface water. These planktonic organisms bloom in myriad abundance on a seasonal basis, thus providing a base for food chains which ultimately terminate with the various marine bird and mammal species. Not coincidentally, these same plankton support the commercial fish stocks which have made New England's fishing grounds famous the world over.

In addition to the high productivity of shallow seas and fishing banks, there are other oceanographic parameters which are important in concentrating pelagic birds. One of these features results when two water masses of differing temperature and salinity come together. Such convergences are called "fronts." A major front occurs where the waters of the continental shelf converge with the deeper and more saline waters of the continental slope (the deep-water region off the edge of the shelf). Such frontal areas often concentrate plankton and small fish, and thus pelagic birds frequently congregate in these areas to maximize their feeding efficiency.

Still another dimension influencing New England seabird distribution is the variability in surface-water temperature and salinity. Waters in the Gulf of Maine and Georges Bank are boreal in character and have a salinity of 31–35 parts per million and a surface temperature in August of 50–67° F. South of Georges Bank, in the deep waters along the continental-shelf edge, the waters come under the influence of the offshore flow of the Gulf Stream. Salinity there exceeds 35 parts per million, and August surface-water temperatures range from 67–74° F. In these southerly waters, an interesting characteristic of the Gulf Stream manifests itself. Periodically, large warm-core rings (Gulf Stream eddies) break away from the Gulf Stream and drift toward the slope waters of southern New England. These warm-core rings often entrain their own unique warm-water flora and fauna, sometimes including marine birds (e.g., Audubon's Shearwater, Band-rumped Storm-Petrel, and White-tailed Tropicbird) and mammals otherwise seldom seen in New England waters. This phenomenon is most pronounced in late summer when surface temperatures are at their highest.

Pelagic birding through the seasons

Along with the various factors which govern the concentration of pelagic birds and their food supplies, each pelagic species has its own season of greatest abundance. Because these seasonal abundance patterns largely coincide with local food availability, it stands to reason that in years of downward fluctuation in prey populations, most notably baitfish, pelagic-bird numbers in the Gulf of Maine characteristically exhibit similar fluctuations. This phenomenon is dramatically illustrated by the variability in shearwater, storm-petrel, jaeger, and humpback and fin whale populations on Stellwagen Bank. Here, fluctuations in schooling sand lance clearly regulate the numbers of these birds in summer, as well as inshore kittiwake concentrations throughout the winter season. Comparable fluctuations in summer copepod numbers can affect local concentrations of Red-necked Phalaropes and right whales in the Gulf of Maine in August. This element of unpredictability, however, is part of what makes pelagic birding so exciting.

SPRING (April–June). Pelagic birding possibilities in late winter and early spring are limited by the paucity of organized trips going out at that season. However, by mid-April, whale-watching groups from several Massachusetts ports begin to make half-day excursions into Cape Cod Bay and to Stellwagen Bank. These early trips afford some of the best chances for observing Northern Gannets and lingering Black-legged Kittiwakes, as well as for seeing the northward migration of the rare Atlantic right whale. The right whales often congregate in these waters for several weeks before they slowly make their way toward the Gulf of Maine, Bay of Fundy, and the coast of Nova Scotia for the summer. By early May, ready access to Stellwagen Bank and Jeffreys Ledge is made possible by increased numbers of public whale-watching trips. These early-May excursions occasionally give glimpses of northward-moving Leach's Storm-Petrels and small numbers of Red-necked Phalaropes. The migration route of both of these species, along with Red Phalarope, however, is primarily far offshore, along the continental shelf edge, and too far for most recreation boats to travel. Spring also heralds the arrival of humpback whales returning for the summer from calving grounds in the Caribbean, along with varying numbers of fin and minke whales.

By late May and early June, New England pelagic birding becomes increasingly rewarding. At this season, the Gulf of Maine sees the arrival of "winterers" from the southern hemisphere. In response to conditions of the austral winter in the South Atlantic and the Antarctic perimeter, species such as Greater and Sooty shearwaters, Wilson's Storm-Petrel, and South Polar Skua migrate northward to spend the northern summer season feeding on the bounty of the North Atlantic. Sooty Shearwaters reach peak numbers in June, then dissipate slowly during the summer. By contrast, Greater Shearwater and Wilson's Storm-Petrel numbers typically build up in July and remain at high levels through the end of August. As stated previously, however, the precise location of the greatest concentrations of these birds is always somewhat variable, depending upon seasonal fluctuations in bait and plankton numbers. The South Polar Skua's occurrence in the Gulf of Maine and on Georges Bank is difficult to define, principally because most of the birds are far offshore where access is difficult. Nonetheless, the occurrence of the species appears to coincide somewhat with that of the Greater Shearwater. Records would suggest that South Polar Skua is possible any time from June until sometime in

midfall on Georges Bank and also rarely at Cox's Ledge and Stellwagen Bank. Pomarine and Parasitic jaegers are considerably more dependable, the former being most common far offshore and at Cox's Ledge. Parasitic Jaegers are regular in small numbers in May throughout the Gulf of Maine and, unlike Pomarine, tend to be more frequent near shore.

Among other birds to be looked for on late-spring trips are small numbers of Northern Fulmars, most of which are probably nonbreeders from colonies in the Canadian Arctic. Likewise, migrating Common Loons are a frequent sight at this season, with many of the birds regularly crossing the Gulf of Maine on their way to the Canadian Maritime Provinces. Other migrants occasionally include Ruby-throated Hummingbirds, as well as a variety of passerines, most often following prolonged southwesterly winds.

SUMMER (July–August). During the warmest months of midsummer, bird finders going to any of the more accessible fishing banks (e.g., Jeffreys Ledge, Stellwagen Bank, Pollock Rip off Chatham, Massachusetts, and Cox's Ledge) can be more or less assured of encountering varying numbers of Greater and Sooty shearwaters and Wilson's Storm-Petrels. In the cooler surface waters north of Cape Cod and in the northern Gulf of Maine, the Manx Shearwater is a regularly occurring possibility, in most years being quite dependable, especially where concentrations of the larger shearwaters exist. By contrast, Cory's Shearwater avoids the cool waters of the Gulf of Maine. Instead, it is regularly encountered in the warmer waters south of Cape Cod and Martha's Vineyard. Cox's Ledge off Block Island affords one of the more dependable areas for seeing this large, eastern-Atlantic shearwater. It is often numerous all over the shelf waters of southern New England, however, perhaps most accessibly off the islands of Martha's Vineyard and Nantucket, where it can frequently be observed from headlands.

Cold-water marine mammals in summer typically include fin, humpback, and minke whales in many locations in the Gulf of Maine, as well as off Cape Cod's back side. The mouth of the Bay of Fundy can be especially productive for observers seeking views of Atlantic right whales. The spectacular white-sided dolphin regularly appears throughout the northern portions of the region at this season, while pelagic birders on the Maine coast can expect to get glimpses of the small harbor porpoise and the harbor seal, the latter most often hauled out on offshore ledges and small islands.

By late summer, the warm surface waters along the southern continental shelf of New England can provide both exciting and diverse pelagic-bird possibilities. Although difficult to get to other than by relatively expensive organized, overnight seabird and marine-mammal charter trips, the concentrations of birds can be worth the expense and effort. The waters in the vicinity of Hydrographer Canyon, a deep gash in the wall of the continental shelf, have consistently produced small numbers of Audubon's Shearwaters, and more rarely Band-rumped Storm-Petrels and the odd White-tailed Tropicbird—the latter two species invariably being associated with warm-water Gulf Stream eddies. Also in this area, White-faced Storm-Petrels have appeared with sufficient frequency to suggest that the species may be of regular occurrence in very limited numbers in late August and early September. By late August, these same deep waters 75 to 100 miles off Cape Cod see the passage of southward-migrating adult Leach's Storm-Petrels from breeding areas in the northern Gulf of Maine and eastern Canada. Earlier in the summer, this species is best viewed on crossings of the Bay of Fundy on the ferry from Bar Harbor, Maine, to Yarmouth, Nova Scotia.

Besides attracting pelagic birds, these warm, deep waters along the shelf edge provide habitat for some of the more spectacular cetacean species, such as sperm and sei whales, pilot whales, and bottlenose, striped, and common dolphins. In addition, such novelties as leatherback and loggerhead turtles, ocean sunfish, basking sharks, and flying fish are occasionally seen on cruises for pelagics birds.

Late August sees the arrival of bluefin tuna and numbers of bluefish in the waters around Cape Cod, especially in Cape Cod Bay and on Stellwagen Bank. These voracious predators wreak havoc with baitfish, and where large, feeding schools of these fish are located, quantities of bait are driven to the surface. These small fish attract large flocks of post-breeding terns and gulls, which further attract pelagic species, such as jaegers. In years of an abundance of bait, dozens of Parasitic Jaegers, along with lesser numbers of Pomarine Jaegers, can be seen in attendance on the feeding tern flocks. Considerably rarer, but nonetheless regular in small numbers among these gatherings, are Sabine's Gulls, although patience is required to find these striking birds. Besides the species just mentioned, large numbers of shearwaters, including Manx Shearwaters, and Wilson's Storm-Petrels, are often attracted by the chum that is used by the tuna fishermen.

FALL (September–November). Fall probably provides the best overall opportunities for seeing pelagic birds in New England. Nearly all of the species previously described can be found in varying numbers in the fall, with the addition of increased numbers of Northern Fulmars, Northern Gannets, phalaropes, jaegers, Black-legged Kittiwakes, and alcids. The best areas for observing these birds are much the same as during the summer, although expeditions to the continental shelf in September are more likely to increase the chances of encountering the ever-rare Long-tailed Jaeger and numbers of Red Phalaropes. Also during September, gradually increasing numbers of Northern Fulmars move into the Gulf of Maine and onto Georges Bank. By October, the migration of Northern Gannets and Black-legged Kittiwakes is in full swing. Observers able to get aboard the latest pelagic-bird trips off the Massachusetts coast (usually in late October or early November) also have a chance of seeing the vanguard of wintering Razorbills and more rarely, Dovekies and Atlantic Puffins. An alternative possibility for seeing some of the alcid species (e.g., Razorbill, Common Murre, and Atlantic Puffin) is by riding the ferry from Maine to Nova Scotia across the Bay of Fundy. This trip can also afford excellent comparative views of Red-necked and Red phalaropes, as well as the chance of seeing a skua.

A form of pelagic birding that can be especially productive in southern New England during the fall occurs with the passage of northeasterly storms. When these storms blow off the ocean for a day or more, they often drive pelagic birds shoreward. At favored coastal localities, large numbers of pelagics can be seen from the comfort of one's automobile. Some of the better coastal localities in Massachusetts include Andrews Point on Cape Ann, locations on Cape Cod such as Sandy Neck Beach in Sandwich, First Encounter Beach in Eastham, and Race Point in Provincetown. Point Judith, Rhode Island, is also a good spot. Any time between mid-September and late November can be especially productive; however, strong onshore winds at any season may produce exciting sea watching. The species most often affected in the fall include Greater and Manx shearwaters, Leach's Storm-Petrel (best at Sandy Neck), Northern Gannet, phalaropes, jaegers (Long-tailed Jaeger possible in September), Black-legged Kittiwake, Sabine's Gull, Razorbill, and Dovekie (occasionally in large numbers in November). The consistently best place to see many of these species is at First Encounter Beach in Eastham, particularly in the wake of a heavy northeasterly storm as the clearing winds back to the northwest. Optimum viewing is often during the first few hours after dawn following the passage of a storm at night.

WINTER (December–March). Pelagic birding in New England waters in winter can be difficult, at least from the deck of a boat. There are few organized trips at this season, and sea conditions and bitter temperatures can easily thwart the most stalwart bird finder. Nonetheless, research vessels have demonstrated that large numbers of Northern Fulmars, Black-legged Kittiwakes, and alcids regularly utilize the waters of Georges Bank and the Gulf of Maine in winter, and that Great Skuas occur in modest numbers, primarily on Georges Bank.

Land-based viewing from promontories and headlands is, at times, productive. Race Point at the tip of Cape Cod can often be counted upon to produce distant views of Razorbills (sometimes by the hundreds) and Black-legged Kittiwakes, as well as lesser numbers of species such as Northern Gannets, murres, and Black Guillemots. This location also provides a spot from which to look for fin, humpback, and occasionally right whales. Razorbills can also be encountered in modest numbers from the ferry to Nantucket, as well as at certain spots on the south side of Nantucket itself.

Pelagic trips in New England waters

Each year a plethora of whale-watching and pelagic-bird trips visit the coastal waters of New England. Most of the whale-watching trips take from five to eight hours, and the prices are moderate (usually $15–$20). Organized pelagic-bird trips, many of which are sponsored by state Audubon societies or the Brookline Bird Club in Massachusetts, usually cost slightly more, but ordinarily last about eight hours and specifically seek out concentrations of birds as well as marine mammals. The precise destination of all of these day trips varies, depending upon the starting point and where whales and pelagic birds are concentrated at the time. Fortunately, the two groups of organisms are often found together. Most of the Maine-based trips go to areas in the lower Bay of Fundy or to the waters off Mt. Desert Island. New Hampshire and northern Massachusetts whale-watching boats normally work the waters around the Isles of Shoals, Jeffreys Ledge, and the northern end of Stellwagen Bank. Public trips from Boston, Plymouth, and Cape Cod ordinarily go into Cape Cod Bay or to the southern end of Stellwagen Bank. Occasionally, extended whale-watching trips from Provincetown make day-long excursions to areas east of Chatham along the back side of Cape Cod. In general, the Stellwagen Bank area and the waters east of Chatham (Pollock Rip area) offer some of the most consistently good pelagic birding and marine-mammal watching. An alternative to taking a public whale-watching trip or an organized pelagic cruise is to join a party fishing boat that is bound for one of the inshore fishing banks (many go to Stellwagen Bank). Usually these are somewhat unsatisfactory because they tend not to move around. Cox's Ledge off Block Island, Rhode Island, however, is perhaps most easily visited in this manner, often with favorable results. Listed below are some of the more reliable, professionally operated whale-watching enterprises along the New England coast. Most of these groups run trips from April or May through August or mid-September.

Allied Whale
% College of the Atlantic
Bar Harbor, ME 04609
207-288-5015

Organizes periodic trips in spring and fall from ports in Maine, New Hampshire, and Massachusetts.

Butch Huntley
M/V Seafarer
9 High Street
Lubec, ME 04652
207-733-5584

Trips in Passamaquoddy Bay and lower Bay of Fundy. Can be superb for Red-necked Phalaropes. July through October.

Bob Bowman
Maine Whale Watch
Box 78
Northeast Harbor,
  ME 04662
207-244-7429

Full-day trips with experienced naturalist. Daily, June through September.

New England Whale-
  watch
55 Merrimac Street
Newbury Port, MA 01950
508-465-7165

Day trips, April through October. Accompanied by a naturalist. Usually go to Jeffreys Ledge or Stellwagen Bank.

Gloucester Whalewatch
(The Yankee Fleet)
75 Essex Avenue, Rt 133
Gloucester, MA 01930
508-283-6089

Half-day trips, twice daily, May through fall. Usually go to Stellwagen Bank; sometimes Jeffreys Ledge.

New England Aquarium
Central Wharf
Boston, MA 02110
617-742-8830

Day trips, spring through fall.

Web of Life Outdoor
Education Center
P. O. Box 530
Carver, MA 02330
508-866-5353

Half-day trips to Stellwagen Bank, April through September. Naturalist on board. Excellent boat for making observations and getting photographs.

Captain Al Avellar
The Dolphin Fleet
Macmillan Wharf
Provincetown, MA 02657
508-487-1900 (summer)
508-255-3857 (off season)

Four-hour trips, three times daily spring through fall. Usually go to Stellwagen Bank or Cape Cod Bay; occasionally to waters off Chatham. Naturalist on board.

F/V Super Squirrel II
Captain George Lockhart
45 Diane Drive
Kingston, RI 02881
401-783-8513

Three or four day trips per week, spring through fall, to area of Cox's Ledge. Occasional offshore, deepwater charters.

In addition to the sources listed above, bird finders can profitably ride the ferries between Maine and Yarmouth, Nova Scotia, any time between June and September. Both trips are lengthy, the Bar Harbor boat taking about 6 hours each way, and the Portland trip lasting 10.5 hours one way. Of the two, the Bar Harbor route aboard the *M/V Bluenose* tends to be most productive for birders, and a round trip can be accomplished in one day. The only drawback to these trips is the potential for heavy fog—a condition that can seriously impair birding success. For schedules and costs contact:

Canadian National   *M/V Bluenose*
  Marine
Eden Street
Bar Harbor, ME 04609
800-432-7344 (ME)
800-341-7981 (eastern U.S.)

Prince of Fundy Cruises   *M/V Scotia Prince*
International Terminal
Portland, ME 04101
207-775-5616

Of the groups most regularly scheduling pelagic-bird trips in New England, the Brookline Bird Club in Massachusetts is the organization with the most frequent offerings. The club annually sponsors eight-hour trips to Stellwagen Bank in late May or early June, late July, mid-August, September, late October, and occasionally in early November. From time to time the group also runs trips to Pollock Rip, east of Chatham on Cape Cod. All of the Brookline Bird Club trips are accompanied by competent and helpful leaders. For information and schedules, contact:

David J. Oliver, Field Trips Coordinator
Brookline Bird Club
60 Pleasant Street—Apt. 401
Arlington, Massachusetts 02174
617-641-4215

Another helpful source of information on the timing and scheduling of different organized pelagic trips in Massachusetts is available by contacting:

Information Services Department
Massachusetts Audubon Society
Lincoln, Massachusetts 01773
508-259-9500

For birders wishing to make extended trips to the outer continental shelf edge, the group most consistently offering trips to that area is Seafarers Expeditions in Maine. These trips are normally run in conjunction with other sponsoring organizations, such as the New England Whalewatch group. These three- to four-day trips in July, August, and September generally cost $350–$400 and normally depart from Portsmouth, New Hampshire, or Gloucester, Massachusetts. For more information, contact:

Seafarers Expeditions		New England Whalewatch
Box 102 HCR 70	or	55 Merrimac Street
Machias, ME 04654		Newbury Port, MA 01950
207-255-8810		508-465-7165

Helpful hints for pelagic birders

For anyone going to sea in search of pelagic birds, there are several basic considerations to keep in mind. One is to dress appropriately for the season. Normally, conditions at sea are considerably cooler than on shore, so outer clothing that will repel the wind and inner layers that will provide warmth are advisable. It is most important to dress in layers that can easily be removed or added as weather conditions dictate. If fog or showers are possible, rain gear, including rubber footwear, is essential. A hat that will not blow off, and gloves for holding on to chilly railings, are mandatory in cooler weather. Sunglasses and sun screen can be very useful in reducing eye strain from glare and in helping to avoid serious sunburn.

A second major consideration is the problem of seasickness. Prevention is the best remedy, and a number of commercial preparations are available to help reduce the likelihood of the mariner's getting sick. Over-the-counter medications include Dramamine and Bonine, both of which may cause drowsiness but work well for some people on a short-term basis. More expensive and longer lasting are two prophylactic medications called Phenergan and Transderm, the latter administered as a treated patch which fits behind the ear and is good for three days. As important as taking preventive medication is exercising caution in what one eats before going on board. Avoid greasy or fatty foods that are difficult to digest, and while at sea, eat mild foods and nibble on things like crackers and apples. It pays to be conservative in this department! Should one be stricken with mal de mer, try to remain on deck in the fresh air, watch the horizon, and keep close to the rail for the benefit of shipmates.

Birders taking cameras on pelagic trips should bring suitable protection (sealable plastic bags are one possibility) for their equipment. Keep cameras covered when they're not in use, and be sure to carefully and frequently remove salt spray from camera body and lenses. Photo hints are many, but the best general advice is to use fast film for slides (e.g., ASA 200 or 400) and to guard against exposure problems due to excessive light from the sky or glare off the water.

When searching for pelagic birds, concentration and persistence are very important. Many pelagic birds present themselves only briefly, and often under less than ideal viewing conditions. The casual bird finder can easily miss or overlook something of interest unless a constant vigil is maintained. Regularly scan the horizon for banking shearwaters, give close scrutiny to the wave troughs for hovering storm-petrels, make periodic checks of the sky for high-flying jaegers, examine ship-following gulls for uncommon species, and assume a forward location on deck to spot swimming alcids, many of which dive instead of flying upon the approach of a boat. By keeping all these considerations in mind, bird finders should be prepared to enjoy the thrills of pelagic birding at its best.

For more information

For further information and background on pelagic birding in New England, the reader is referred to the following sources:

Brown, R. G. B. 1986 *Revised Atlas of Eastern Canadian Seabirds: 1. Shipboard Surveys by R. G. B. Brown.* Dartmouth, Nova Scotia: Canadian Wildlife Service, Bedford Institute of Oceanography.

Harrison, Peter. 1983. *Seabirds: An Identification Guide*. Boston: Houghton Mifflin Company.

Katona, Steven K., Valerie Rough, and David T. Richardson. 1983. *A Field Guide to the Whales, Porpoises and Seals of the Gulf of Maine and Eastern Canada–Cape Cod to Newfoundland*. New York: Charles Scribner's Sons.

Parker, Henry S. 1985. *Exploring the Oceans: An Introduction for the Traveler and Amateur Naturalist*. Englewood Cliffs, New Jersey: Prentice–Hall, Inc.

Powers, Kevin D. 1983. *Pelagic Distributions of Marine Birds Off the Northeastern United States*. (NOAA Technical Memorandum NMFS-F/NEC-27). Woods Hole, Mass.: National Oceanic and Atmospheric Administration.

PART THREE

New England Specialties: Species Accounts

New England Specialties: Species Accounts

THIS ANNOTATED CHECK LIST INCLUDES BIRD species which are, for various reasons, of special note in New England. While some species are listed primarily because the northeast is the best locale in which to find them (e.g., Common Eider and Roseate Tern), others are included simply because they represent typically, but not exclusively, New England phenomena (e.g., Broad-wing Hawk flights and Canadian-zone warblers). Relative abundance and range information apply only to New England.

Northern Fulmar. Pelagic. Normally uncommon in spring and summer (May–August), increasingly common during fall and winter months (September–January) on Georges Bank, Stellwagen Bank, and in the Gulf of Maine.

Cory's Shearwater. Pelagic. Uncommon, most likely found in warmer, southerly offshore waters during summer and early-fall months (July–mid-October). Try a boat trip to Cox's Ledge. From land, try Point Judith (RI) with onshore winds.

Greater Shearwater. Pelagic. Common from June–October in waters from Georges Bank to the Gulf of Maine. Seen with some regularity from Andrews Point; Sandy Neck, Barnstable; First Encounter; and Provincetown (MA) during periods of onshore winds.

Sooty Shearwater. Pelagic. Fairly common late May–August; uncommon after August. Seen on 95 percent of *Bluenose* crossings in August. Occasionally seen from the mainland and from Monomoy Island (MA) in late spring.

Manx Shearwater. Pelagic. One nesting record exists for Massachusetts. Uncommon summer visitor to offshore waters between June and mid-October; seen on 60 percent of *Bluenose* crossings during this time period; recorded fairly regularly with onshore winds from Point Judith (RI) and Provincetown (MA) in the April-through-June period.

Wilson's Storm-Petrel. Pelagic. The common storm-petrel of offshore waters during the summer months (June–September). Seen in good numbers from Cox's Ledge to the Gulf of Maine during this period. From land try Point Judith (RI) and Provincetown and Cape Ann (MA).

Leach's Storm-Petrel. Pelagic. A rare summer resident in Massachusetts, more common in Maine. Uncommon offshore in more southerly locations to Cox's Ledge. Common in Gulf of Maine. Your best bet is the *Bluenose*, June–September. Fall storms may also push this species inshore to such sites as Sandy Neck, Barnstable (MA).

Northern Gannet. Pelagic. Common offshore migrant in spring and fall; variable numbers in offshore waters in winter; a few immatures in summer. Regularly seen from numerous east-facing coastal locales during migration, in numbers with onshore winds. Common to abundant in Cape Cod Bay in October and November.

Great Cormorant. Regular winter resident (October–May) along coast, concentrated in areas with rocky shores. Overlaps with Double-crested Cormorant in late summer and spring. Because of the increasing reports of wintering Double-crested Cormorants, check your bird carefully.

Mute Swan. Locally common, permanent resident from southern Massachusetts south. Found in coastal ponds and bays, reservoirs, and parks.

American Black Duck. Widespread but increasingly uncommon summer resident throughout region (May and June). At times a common migrant (March and April, July–November) found in a variety of inland and coastal wetlands. Winters (November–March) along coast in good numbers.

Common Eider. Permanent resident along the Maine coast, also found in winter (October–March) south to Long Island Sound with especially large concentrations off Cape Cod. Although it is a rare breeder in Massachusetts, a few nonbreeding, immature birds can usually be found south to Cape Cod in summer.

King Eider. An uncommon winter resident of coastal waters from Maine to Rhode Island, recorded only rarely in other seasons. Look for this species with Common Eider or scoters from November–March at locales such as Reid State Park and Prouts Neck (ME); Cape Ann, Marblehead Neck, and Cape Cod (MA); or Weekapaug (RI). Rare in Long Island Sound.

Harlequin Duck. Winter resident (late November–late April), usually in small numbers, along rocky sections of the coast from Rhode Island to Maine. Try **Sachuest Point** (RI), East Orleans (North Beach) and Magnolia Point (MA), and Prouts Neck (ME).

Barrow's Goldeneye. Uncommon winter (November–March) resident most often found in association with Common Goldeneye at coastal locales or open freshwater. Try Bluff Point State Park in Groton (CT); Point Judith (RI); Plymouth Harbor, Cape Ann, and the Merrimack River estuary (MA); and the Penobscot River near Bucksport (ME).

Black Scoter, Surf Scoter, White-winged Scoter. Each fall birders along the New England coast are treated to a major movement of seabirds. A significant component of the migration is the flight of scoters. The southbound flocks, which reach a peak in October, can be seen from numerous east-facing coastal locales including Schoodic Point, Mt. Desert Island, and East Point, Biddeford Pool (ME); Andrews Point, Cape Ann, Manomet Point, and Sandy Neck, Barnstable (MA); and Point Judith (RI). All three species of scoter winter along the New England coast in variable numbers.

Osprey. The 1980s have witnessed a regrowth in the New England Osprey population, due in large part to the stringent control of hard (DDT-type) pesticide use and active protection and nesting programs. Summer-resident Osprey are now fairly common along Connecticut's Long Island Sound and Atlantic coastal waters from Rhode Island to Maine. Nesting colonies can be found at Barn Island Wildlife Area, Stonington (CT); Great Swamp Management Area (RI); Westport–Dartmouth region and Martha's Vineyard (MA); and on numerous islands along the coast of Maine.

Broad-winged Hawk. New England hawk watchers counted over a quarter of a million migrating raptors in the fall of 1986. The majority of these birds were Broad-winged Hawks. The major push occurs in mid-September (10–20th). Good sites at which to see at least part of the action are Mt. Agamenticus (ME), Mt. Wachusett (MA), and Quaker Ridge (CT).

Peregrine Falcon. While the repopulation of peregrines in the northeast still has a way to go, there have been encouraging signs in the 1980s. The occurrence of migrants has shown a marked increase in the last five years. Birders wishing to see these magnificent birds will do well to head for Monhegan Island (ME), Nantucket and Monomoy (MA), or Block Island (RI) during late September and early October. Peregrines are also seen along coastal barrier beaches in the same season.

Spruce Grouse. Permanent resident of the three northern states; locally common in Maine, uncommon to rare in New Hampshire and Vermont. This elusive species is more often happened upon than found after a deliberate search. Locales with Spruce Grouse populations include Island Pond (VT), Connecticut Lakes (NH), and Baxter State Park and Quoddy Head State Park (ME).

Rough-legged Hawk. Winter resident (November–April) in variable number throughout the region in open fields and marshes. An excellent inland locale is the Dead Creek Wildlife Management Area (VT). Consistent coastal locales include Plum Island and Salisbury (MA) and the Scarborough estuary in southern Maine.

Piping Plover. Uncommon summer resident of coastal sand beaches. This species is an early migrant, arriving at nesting sites from Connecticut to southern Maine in late March and April. Piping Plover often nests in association with Least Terns. Because the northeastern population of Piping Plovers is threatened, most nesting colonies are closely monitored and off-limits during the breeding season.

Red Knot. A locally uncommon migrant at the coast during late May and early June, and a locally common migrant in late July and early August. Perhaps the best place to see this species is at Third Cliff, Scituate (MA), a traditional fall staging area for Red Knot. Other reliable sites are Milford Point (CT), Quonochontaug (RI), Plymouth Beach and Monomoy–Morris Island (MA), and Bar Island Bar at Bar Harbor (ME).

Purple Sandpiper. Winter resident along rocky sections of the coast. A few Purple Sandpipers are recorded at northerly locations such as Quoddy Head in late August. A more general arrival is to be expected in November, with some birds remaining into April. Try Milford Point (CT); Narragansett Pier (RI); Minot in North Scituate, and Cape Ann (MA); and Otter Point, Mt. Desert Island (ME).

Hudsonian Godwit. A rare spring and locally common fall migrant along the coast. The largest concentrations in New England occur on **Monomoy Island** (MA) in early August. Smaller groups are regularly recorded at the Scarborough estuary (ME) and Plum Island (MA). Farther south try Quonochontaug (RI) and Milford Point Sanctuary (CT).

Ruff. An Old World species seen rarely but with some regularity in spring (mid-April–May) and fall (early July–mid-September). Inland, the Ruff is found at various wetlands, coastally along tidal flats and estuaries. Areas with good track records for this species include the Guilford Sluice (CT) and Newburyport Harbor (MA).

Red-necked Phalarope. Pelagic. Abundant to uncommon

spring and fall migrant. Thousands of these birds can normally be found off Campobello Island and in the Deer Island thoroughfare from mid-July–September. Seen on 100 percent of *Bluenose* crossings in August and September. South of the Gulf of Maine your best bet is to take a pelagic trip in spring (late April–May) or fall (September and October).

Parasitic Jaeger. Pelagic. A fairly common summer visitor (nonbreeders) and migrant in offshore water from late June through September. A *Bluenose* crossing in late July, or a pelagic trip to Georges Bank or Cox's Ledge in September or early October should produce this species. Occasionally seen from land; try Provincetown (MA).

Little Gull. An uncommon migrant at shoreline locales in spring (mid-April–May) and fall (August–October). A few nonbreeding birds appear in summer, and a few linger through early winter. Try City Point in New Haven Harbor (CT); Newburyport Harbor (MA); and Back Cove, Portland Harbor (ME).

Common Black-headed Gull. An uncommon winter visitor at the coast. A few summer birds. This species is found at the same sites mentioned for Little Gull; other possibilities are Lighthouse Point Park (CT), **Watchemocket Cove** in East Providence (RI), and Boston Harbor (MA).

Bonaparte's Gull. An uncommon to abundant migrant and regular winter resident in variable numbers, primarily along coast. Spectacular concentrations can be seen in the Deer Island thoroughfare (ME) in late August and early September. Migratory flocks regularly move southward along the coast during the late summer and fall, passing numerous shoreline locales, including Otter Point, Mt. Desert Island and East Point, Biddeford (ME); Newburyport and Cape Ann (MA); Point Judith (RI); and New Haven Harbor (CT). Variable numbers of Bonaparte's Gulls overwinter, especially at the more southerly coastal sites.

Iceland Gull. A fairly common, but local, winter resident (mid-November–mid-April) at the coast. Consistent sites for this species are Milford Point and New Haven Harbor (CT); the fish pier in Galilee (RI); Eastern Point in Gloucester, and the Merrimack River estuary (MA); Hampton–Seabrook Harbor estuary (NH); Scarborough estuary, and Portland Harbor (ME).

Black-legged Kittiwake. Largely pelagic in our area. A common offshore winter resident along the northeast coast. The most consistent land-based observation point for this species is the Lubec (ME) vicinity, where it is present in numbers from September–March. Migrant Black-legged Kittiwakes are also regularly seen from shore during fall and winter storms at Andrews Point and Sandy Neck, Barnstable (MA), Point Judith lighthouse and Sakonnet (RI). Provincetown (MA) can be an excellent place to find this species in winter.

Roseate Tern. A locally common summer resident (May–early September). Consistent locales for this species include Milford Point (CT), Quonochontaug (RI), **Monomoy** (MA), and Biddeford Pool (ME). Because a majority of the entire North American Roseate Tern population breeds at a relatively few locales in Massachusetts, your best bet is to concentrate your efforts on and around Monomoy in early August.

Least Tern. A common migrant and summer resident along the coast (southern Maine south to Long Island) from mid-May–August. A majority of breeding birds in our region are found in scattered colonies along the Massachusetts coast. Consistent locales for this species include Milford Point Sanctuary (CT); Napatree Point

(RI); Monomoy, Nauset Beach, Plymouth Beach, and Plum Island (MA); and Wells Beach (ME).

Dovekie. Pelagic. Common to scarce migrant and winter resident of northern offshore waters from late October through March: Dovekie are occasionally driven inland during November and December northeasters. From shore try Andrews Point or Sandy Neck, Barnstable (MA) and Point Judith (RI). In recent years this has been a difficult species to find even under ideal (stormy) conditions.

Common Murre. Pelagic. A decidedly uncommon migrant and winter resident in northern offshore waters; a few nonbreeding birds summer on several of Maine's coastal islands. Your best bet for this species is a summer trip (June–July) to Machias Seal Island (off ME coast). Only rarely seen from shore.

Thick-billed Murre. Pelagic. A fairly common winter resident of offshore waters south to Massachusetts. November northeasters may produce this species at such sites as West Quoddy Head (ME), Cape Ann and Provincetown (MA), and Point Judith (RI).

Razorbill. Pelagic. A scarce to common migrant and winter resident in offshore waters, particularly on Georges Bank; a few nest on Maine coastal islands. A good place to see this bird in summer (June–July) is on Machias Seal Island (off ME coast). Between November and April, Razorbills are seen fairly regularly on pelagic trips out of Massachusetts. Also recorded from coastal sites from West Quoddy Head (ME) south to Point Judith (RI). Provincetown (MA) can be productive in January and early February.

Black Guillemot. Permanent resident along the coast of Maine; regularly winters south to Massachusetts, uncommonly to Rhode Island. This species can be found throughout the year at numerous Maine sites including West Quoddy Head and Otter Point, Mt. Desert Island. In winter, Black Guillemot is reliably found at Andrews Point and Provincetown (MA).

Atlantic Puffin. Pelagic. Locally common summer resident on several of Maine's coastal islands; uncommon to rare migrant and winter resident of northern offshore waters south to Massachusetts. At present, the best place to see Atlantic Puffin is on Machias Seal Island (off ME coast) in June and July. During August and September this species is seen fairly regularly in small numbers on *Bluenose* crossings. Pelagic trips to Stellwagen Bank and Jeffreys Ledge between October and May may also record Atlantic Puffin.

Snowy Owl. Irregular winter (late November–March) resident throughout the region; more common along the coast and in the northern portion of New England than inland or in southern New England. Try Back Cove, Portland, and the Scarborough Marshes (ME) or Salisbury and Plum Island (MA). The Boston Harbor islands and Logan Airport regularly have Snowy Owls during flight years.

Yellow-bellied Flycatcher. An uncommon migrant throughout the region from late May–mid-June and again from late August to mid-September; a summer resident of northern coniferous forests and boglands. Can be found in late June at Island Pond and on Mt. Equinox (VT); East Inlet Road, Connecticut Lakes (NH); and Seawall Bog, Mt. Desert Island, and Baxter State Park (ME).

Alder Flycatcher. A few migrants are noted during late May and early June in southern New England; summer residents are common in the three northern states, with additional nesting populations in the Berkshires and Taconics, thinning out eastward and southward. Try alder swamps and thickets in the southern Green Mountains and Island Pond (VT); Connecticut Lakes (NH); and Ship Harbor, Mt. Desert Island (ME).

Gray Jay. Uncommon permanent resident of spruce–fir forests of the three northern states; rarely a few birds move southward in winter. Look for this boreal species at Island Pond (VT), Connecticut Lakes (NH), and Baxter State Park and Quoddy Head State Park (ME).

Boreal Chickadee. Uncommon to locally common permanent resident of spruce–fir forests of the three northern states; occasionally, a relatively few birds migrate southward, with some overwintering. Look for this species at Island Pond (VT), Connecticut Lakes (NH), and Baxter State Park and Mt. Desert Island (ME).

Gray-cheeked Thrush. Uncommon migrant (late May and early June; mid-September and early October) and locally common summer resident at or near timberline in northern states. Nesting birds can be found on Mansfield and Killington mountains (VT); Hermit Lake, Mt. Washington and Lost River Gorge Reservation (NH); and Great Basin, Mt. Katahdin (ME).

Northern Shrike. Winter resident (November–March) in variable numbers throughout the region. Look for this species in semiopen habitat with suitable perches. Try Orleans County (VT) or open coastal habitat like Weskeag and Scarborough marshes (ME), Hampton–Seabrook Harbor estuary (NH), Plum Island (MA), and south-coastal agricultural lands in Rhode Island and Connecticut.

Philadelphia Vireo. Uncommon to rare migrant throughout region; uncommon summer resident of three northern states. While a few Philadelphia Vireos are reported each spring (latter half of May), more migrants are recorded in fall (late August–September) at coastal traps such as Marblehead Neck Wildlife Sanctuary and Morris Island (MA), and Block Island (RI). Nesting birds have been observed in cut-over deciduous habitats in the Cold Harbor Mountains south of Montgomery Center (VT), and birch and alder thickets such as those found at Lost Pond, Pinkham Notch (NH) and both Goodall Heath and Vose Pond at Moosehorn National Wildlife Refuge (ME).

The Wood-Warblers are a highlight of New England's summer-resident avifauna. Several species (asterisks, below) are largely restricted to boreal habitats in the northern portions of Vermont, New Hampshire, and Maine. Many of the other wood-warblers may be found there, as well as in more southerly locations. Productive areas for locating these breeding birds include Island Pond (VT); Connecticut Lakes (NH); and Baxter State Park, Mt. Desert Island, and Quoddy Head State Park (ME). Migrants can be found at various locales including White Memorial Foundation, Litchfield (also good for summer residents) and Hammonasset State Park, Madison (CT); Swan Point Cemetery, Providence, and Block Island (RI); Morris Island, Chatham, Mt. Auburn Cemetery in Cambridge, and Marblehead Neck Wildlife Sanctuary (MA); and East Point, Biddeford Pool (ME). See accounts for specifics of optimal times and places.

Golden-winged Warbler. Uncommon to rare summer resident of open, second-growth habitat in the early stages of succession; seldom seen on migration. Summer residents are normally on territory by mid-May. Look (listen!) for this bird in the latter part of the month in rural areas with proper habitat. Sites at which Golden-winged Warblers have nested in the past include Miles Audubon Sanctuary, Sharon (CT); Taconic Mountains region (VT); and Pikes Bridge Road, Newbury (MA). Because this species readily hybridizes with the Blue-winged Warbler and is often replaced by the latter species, nesting golden-wings may have a relatively short tenure at any one breeding locale.

Tennessee Warbler. Fairly common migrant throughout the region (latter half of May and early to late September). Rare to uncommon summer resident in clearings and boggy wetlands of boreal forest in northern portion of region.

Magnolia Warbler. Fairly common migrant throughout the region (latter half of May and September). Widely distributed and fairly common summer resident of northern states. Magnolia Warblers also nest south to western and central Massachusetts and northwestern Connecticut. Look for this species in mixed forest as well as in areas with young coniferous stands.

Cape May Warbler. Uncommon spring and common fall migrant throughout the region (latter half of May, and mid-August–September). Rare to uncommon summer resident of mature boreal forest northward.

Black-throated Blue Warbler. Fairly common migrant throughout the region (May and September). Widely distributed and fairly common resident of northern states, with smaller breeding populations in western and central Massachusetts and northwestern Connecticut. Look for this species in beech–maple-covered hillsides with undergrowth.

Black-throated Green Warbler. Fairly common migrant throughout the region (May and September). Widely distributed and fairly common resident of northern states with significant breeding populations in the three southern states, especially in western and central Massachusetts, northwestern Rhode Island, and northwestern Connecticut. Summer residents are found in mature hemlocks as well as in mixed coniferous and deciduous forests.

Blackburnian Warbler. Fairly common migrant throughout the region (May and September). Widely distributed and fairly common resident of northern states, with smaller breeding populations in the three southern states, especially in western and central Massachusetts, northwestern Rhode Island, and northwestern Connecticut. Nesting Blackburnian Warblers are normally associated with tall, mature coniferous woodlands.

*Palm Warbler. Uncommon to common migrant throughout the region (mid-April to mid-May and mid-September to mid-October). Rare to locally common summer resident of northern bogs in New Hampshire and Maine.

*Bay-breasted Warbler. Uncommon to fairly common migrant throughout the region (latter half of May and mid-August to mid-September). Rare to uncommon summer resident, limited to mature boreal conifers. Some nesting birds in Vermont, more in New Hampshire and Maine.

*Blackpoll Warbler. An uncommon to abundant migrant throughout the region (mid-May to early June and mid-September to early October). Rare to fairly common summer resident in spruce–fir forest in the northern portion of region and southward in the Green Mountains to northwestern Massachusetts in similar habitat.

Northern Waterthrush. A fairly common migrant in spring (late April–May) and uncommon fall migrant (late August–September) throughout the region. A fairly common and widespread summer resident of the three northern states, with smaller breeding populations in the three southern states, especially in western Massachusetts, northwestern Rhode Island, and northwestern Connecticut. Typical habitat is stagnant wetlands with heavy cover.

Mourning Warbler. An uncommon migrant throughout the region (late May to early June and late August to mid-September). An uncommon but widespread summer resident in Vermont, northern New Hampshire, and northern Maine, with a few birds nesting south to western Massachusetts. Look for this species in recently cut-over areas with shrubby second growth.

Canada Warbler. A fairly common migrant throughout the region (mid-May to early June and mid-August to mid-September). A fairly common and widespread summer resident of the three northern states, with smaller breeding populations in the three southern states, especially in western Massachusetts and northwestern Connecticut. Canada Warblers nest in the dense, moist undergrowth of mature coniferous and deciduous forests.

American Tree Sparrow. A common fall migrant (late October) and winter resident (mid-November to mid-March) throughout the region; uncommon spring migrant (mid-March to early April). Look for these sparrows in weed patches, brushy fields, and coastal thickets. Inland river valleys often have large numbers.

Rusty Blackbird. An uncommon migrant throughout the region (mid-March–April and mid-September to mid-October) and an uncommon summer resident of the boreal zone in the three northern states, with a few records for northwestern Massachusetts. Look for migrants along the edges of red maple swamps and other wetlands. Nesting birds are invariably found in association with bogs, swamps, ponds, or other wetlands of coniferous, boreal habitat. Try Island Pond (VT), Connecticut Lakes (NH), and Baxter State Park and Moosehorn National Wildlife Refuge (ME).

Winter Finches. A variety of finches add an interesting dimension to winter birding in New England. The annual anticipation of their arrival is often an exercise in hope, rather than one based upon clearly understood cycles; but when the flights do occur they are worth the wait. Species involved include Pine Grosbeak, Purple Finch, Red Crossbill, White-winged Crossbill, Common Redpoll, (rarely, Hoary Redpoll), Pine Siskin, and Evening Grosbeak. Actually, these species occur in New England each winter in variable numbers. Often, however, significant flocks are recorded only in the northern portion of the region. Southern New England typically has a number of lean years for one or more species before being "rewarded" with a good flight. Because of their erratic nature, it is impossible to say with certainty when or where to find the winter finches. In the northern states there are numerous suitable locales with conifers to attract the crossbills and siskins, as well as deciduous fruits and seeds for grosbeaks, redpolls, and other finches. In the south, areas that have been productive during flight years include Campbell Falls State Park, Norfolk and Devil's Hop Yard State Park, East Haddam (CT); Burlingame State Park (camping area), Charlestown (RI); Quabbin Reservoir, Belchertown, and Plum Island, Newburyport (MA).

Appendices
Bibliography
Index

Appendices

The following organizations have resources that may be useful to visiting bird watchers.

Maine Audubon Society, Gilsland Farm, 118 U.S. Route One, Falmouth, Maine 04105
Telephone: 207-781-2330

Audubon Society of New Hampshire, P.O. Box 528-B, Concord, New Hampshire 03301
Telephone: 603-224-9909

Vermont Institute of Natural Science, Woodstock, Vermont 05091
Telephone: 802-457-2779

Massachusetts Audubon Society, Lincoln, Massachusetts 01773
Telephone: 508-259-9500

Audubon Society of Rhode Island, 12 Sanderson Road, Smithfield, Rhode Island 02917
Telephone: 401-231-6444

Connecticut Audubon Society, 2325 Burr Street, Fairfield, Connecticut 06430
Telephone: 203-259-6305, 5606

Audubon Center in Greenwich, 613 Riversville Road, Greenwich, Connecticut 06831
Telephone: 203-869-5272

NEW ENGLAND BIRD ALERTS

The following numbers give updated tape-recorded information on birds of special interest for the various states. Unless otherwise indicated, the service is in operation 24 hours a day.

Maine : 207-781-2332
(Weekdays 5:00 P.M. to 8:00 A.M.; Weekends 24 hours.)

New Hampshire: 603-224-9900
(Weekdays 5:00 P.M. to 9:00 A.M.; Weekends 24 hours)

Vermont: 802-457-2779
(Monday through Saturday 5:00 P.M. to 8:00 A.M.; Sunday 24 hours)

Massachusetts: Western Massachusetts 413-569-6926
Eastern Massachusetts 617-259-8805

Rhode Island: 401-231-5728
(Thursday and Friday after 5:00 P.M.; Weekends 24 hours)

Connecticut: 203-254-3665

FLORAL AND FAUNAL REFERENCES

All standard English references to plants and animals in the text are consistent with the nomenclature used by the various authorities listed below.

Plants	· *The Flora of New England* (Second Edition). 1982. Frank Conkling Seymour. Plainfield, New Jersey: Moldenke and Moldenke.
Mammals	· *Wild Mammals of New England* (Field Guide Edition). 1981. Alfred J. Godin. Yarmouth, Maine: DeLorme Publishing Company.
Birds	· *Check-list of North American Birds* (6th Edition). 1983. American Ornithologists' Union. Lawrence, Kansas: Allen Press.
Fish	· *Fishes of the Gulf of Maine.* 1953. H. B. Bigelow and W. C. Schroeder. U.S. Fish and Wildlife Service, Fishery Bulletin 74.
Butterflies	· *The Audubon Society Field Guide to the Butterflies of North America.* 1981. Robert Michael Pyle. New York: Alfred A. Knopf.
Other Invertebrates	· *A Field Guide to the Atlantic Seashore.* 1978. Kenneth L. Gosner. Boston: Houghton Mifflin Company.

JOURNALS AND MAGAZINES

The following publications contain recent bird records for areas covered by this guide. In most cases these are presented in seasonal format and as such offer a relatively current view of bird life in New England.

Regional

American Birds. New England reports included in four seasonal summaries under "Northeastern Maritime Region" as well as annual Christmas Count data for all New England counts.

Contact: *American Birds*, 950 Third Avenue, New York, New York 10022.

State

Maine

The Guillemot. State field records, including birds, published bimonthly.

Contact: William Townsend, Editor, P.O. Box 373, Sorrento, Maine 04677.

Maine Bird Notes

Contact: Maine Audubon Society, 118 U.S. Route One, Falmouth, Maine 04105.

New Hampshire

New Hampshire Bird Records. Quarterly publication of field notes.

Contact: Audubon Society of New Hampshire, P.O. Box 528-B, Concord, New Hampshire 03301.

Vermont

Records of Vermont Birds. State records published quarterly.

Contact: Vermont Institute of Natural Science, Woodstock, Vermont 05091.

Massachusetts

Bird Observer of Eastern Massachusetts. Eastern Massachusetts records published bimonthly.

Contact: David E. Lange, 864 Massachusetts Avenue, No. 6E, Arlington, Massachusetts 02174.

Rhode Island

Field Notes of Rhode Island Birds. State records published monthly.
Contact: Audubon Society of Rhode Island, 12 Sanderson Road, Smithfield, Rhode Island 02917.

Connecticut

The Connecticut Warbler. Field-note summary published quarterly.
Contact: Connecticut Ornithological Society, 314 Unquowa Road, Fairfield, Connecticut 06430.

Mianus Field Notes. Monthly field records for the greater Greenwich and Stamford area.
Contact: Susan Bartels, 52 Druid Lane, Riverside, Connecticut 06878.

Bibliography

A.M.C. White Mountain Guide. 1966. Boston, Mass.: Appalachian Mountain Club.

Allen, Francis H. 1925. *Thoreau's Bird-Lore*. Boston and New York: Houghton Mifflin Company.

Audubon Society Field Guide to the Natural Places of the Northeast: Coastal. 1984. New York: Pantheon Books.

Audubon Society Field Guide to the Natural Places of the Northeast: Inland. 1984. New York: Pantheon Books.

Audubon Society Master Guide to Birding. 1983. Vols. 1–3. New York: Alfred A. Knopf, Inc.

Bailey, Wallace and Priscilla. 1980. Birding on Outer Cape Cod. *Where to Watch Birds in Massachusetts*. No. 18. Lincoln, Massachusetts: Massachusetts Audubon Society. Mimeographed.

———. 1955. *Birds in Massachusetts—When and Where to Find Them*. South Lancaster, Massachusetts: The College Press.

Bent, Arthur Cleveland. 1961. *Life Histories of North American Birds of Prey*. Part 1. New York: Dover Publications, Inc.

Bigelow, H. B. and W. C. Schroeder. 1953. *Fishes of the Gulf of Maine*. U.S. Fish and Wildlife Service, Fishery Bulletin 74.

Brewster, William. 1936. *October Farm*. Cambridge, Massachusetts: Harvard University Press.

Carson, Rachel. 1947. Parker River—A New England Conservation Project. *The Bulletin of the Massachusetts Audubon Society*. Vol. 31, No. 2.

Check-list of North American Birds (6th Edition). 1983. American Ornithologists' Union.

Conway, Robert A. 1979. *Field Checklist of Rhode Island Birds*. Bulletin No. 1. Rhode Island Ornithological Club.

Elkins, Kimball C. 1982. *A Checklist of the Birds of New Hampshire*. Concord, New Hampshire: The Audubon Society of New Hampshire.

Ellison, Walter G. 1981. *A Guide to Bird Finding in Vermont*. Woodstock, Vermont: Vermont Institute of Natural Science.

Finch, Davis W., William C. Russell, and Edward V. Thompson. 1978. Pelagic Birds in the Gulf of Maine. *American Birds*. Vol. 32, Nos. 2 and 3. pps. 140–155 and 281–294.

Finch, Robert. 1981. *Common Ground, A Naturalist's Cape Cod*. Boston: David R. Godine.

———. 1986. *Outlands, Journeys to the Outer Edges of Cape Cod*. Boston: David R. Godine.

Forbush, Edward Howe. 1912. *A History of the Game Birds, Wild-Fowl and Shore Birds of Massachusetts and Adjacent States*. Boston: Massachusetts State Board of Agriculture.

———. 1927, 1929. *Birds of Massachusetts and Other New England States*. Vols. I–III.

Forster, Richard A. 1981. Falmouth and Vicinity in Winter. *Where to Watch Birds in Massachusetts*. No. 19. Mimeographed. Lincoln, Massachusetts: Massachusetts Audubon Society.

———. 1981. Birding Newburyport Harbor and the Salisbury Beach State Reservation. *Bird Observer of Eastern Massachusetts* (BOEM). Vol. 9, No. 1, p. 5.

———. 1985. Birding Plum Island. *BOEM.* Vol. 13, No. 3, p. 116.

Fox, Robert P. 1980. Block Island. *BOEM.* Vol. 8, No. 4, p. 133.

———. 1985. October on Block Island. *Birding.* Vol. 17, No. 5, p. 216.

Garrey, Pat. 1973. Around Falmouth. *BOEM.* Vol. 1, No. 6, p. 132.

Godin, Alfred J. 1981. *Wild Mammals of New England* (Field Guide Edition). Yarmouth, Maine: DeLorme Publishing Company.

Gosner, Kenneth L. 1978. *A Field Guide to the Atlantic Seashore.* Boston: Houghton Mifflin Company.

Griscom, Ludlow. 1955. *Plum Island and Its Birdlife.* Lincoln, Massachusetts: Massachusetts Audubon Society. Pamphlet.

Guide Book of the Long Trail. 1985. Montpelier, Vermont: Green Mountain Club.

Halberg, Edith and Henry. *Guide to Summer Birding in the Connecticut Lakes Region.* (Unattributed copy of magazine article.)

Harrison, Peter. 1983. *Seabirds, an Identification Guide.* Boston: Houghton Mifflin Company.

Heintzelman, Donald S. 1979. *A Guide to Hawkwatching in North America.* University Park, Pennsylvania, and London: Pennsylvania State University Press.

History of Scarborough. 1973. Scarborough, Maine: Friends of the Scarborough Public Library.

Jorgensen, Neil. 1971. *A Guide to New England's Landscape.* Barre, Massachusetts: Barre Publishing Co., Inc.

Katona, Steven K., Valerie Rough, and David T. Richardson. 1983. *A Field Guide to the Whales, Porpoises, and Seals of the Gulf of Maine and Eastern Canada—Cape Cod to Newfoundland*. New York: Charles Scribner's Sons.

Laughlin, Sarah B. and Douglas P. Kibbe, eds. 1985. *The Atlas of Breeding Birds of Vermont*. Hanover, New Hampshire, and London: University Press of New England.

Leahy, Christopher W. 1973. Two North Shore Migrant Traps: Marblehead Neck and Nahant. *Where to Watch Birds in Massachusetts*. No. 5. Lincoln, Massachusetts: Massachusetts Audubon Society. Mimeographed.

———. 1983. Birding Cape Ann. *BOEM*. Vol. 11, No. 1, p. 5.

———. 1982. *The Birdwatcher's Companion: An Encyclopedic Handbook of North American Birdlife*. New York: Hill and Wang.

Marra, Peter and Milan Bull. 1986. The Norwalk Island Heron Colonies—A History. *The Connecticut Warbler* Vol. 6, No. 2, p. 23.

Massachusetts Bird List. 1983. Fauna of Massachusetts Series No. 1. Massachusetts Division of Fisheries and Wildlife.

Michelin Green Guide: New England. 1981. New Hyde Park, New York: Michelin Guides and Maps.

Newsletter of the Hawk Migration Association of America. 1985. Vol. 10, No. 2, p. 18.

Nikula, Blair. 1978. Birding in Provincetown. *BOEM*. Vol. 6, No. 2, p. 41.

———. 1981. Monomoy. *BOEM*. Vol. 9, No. 3, p. 97.

Palmer, E. Laurence. 1948. *Fieldbook of Natural History*. New York and Toronto: McGraw–Hill Company, Inc.

Pease, Robert F. 1974. Birding at Sandy Neck. *BOEM*. Vol. 2, No. 5, p. 141.

Petersen, Wayne R. 1976. Pelagic Birding for Landlubbers. *BOEM*. Vol. 4, No. 3, p. 64.

———. 1983. The Flight of the Sea Coot: A Look at Autumn Scoter Migration. *BOEM*. Vol. 11, No. 4, p. 193.

Pettingill, Jr., Olin Sewall. 1977. *A Guide to Bird Finding East of the Mississippi*. Boston: Houghton Mifflin Company.

Pierson, Elizabeth Cary and Jan Erik. 1981. *A Birder's Guide to the Coast of Maine*. Camden, Maine: Down East Books.

Proctor, Noble S. 1978. *25 Birding Areas in Connecticut*. Chester, Connecticut: Globe Pequot Press.

Pyle, Michael Robert. 1981. *The Audubon Society Field Guide to the Butterflies of North America*. New York: Alfred A. Knopf.

Richards, Tudor. 1965. In Northern New Hampshire. *The Bird Watcher's America*. Pettingill, O. S. Jr., ed., New York, Toronto, London: McGraw–Hill Book Company.

————. The Bird Life of Monadnock. 1970. *Monadnock Guide*. Henry Baldwin, ed. Society for the Protection of New Hampshire Forests.

Ridgely, Beverly S. 1987. *Birds of the Squam Lakes Region*. Plymouth, New Hampshire: Squam Lakes Association.

Roberts, Paul M. 1982. Hawkwatching In Massachusetts. *Where to Watch Birds in Massachusetts*. No. 20. Mimeographed. Lincoln, Massachusetts: Massachusetts Audubon Society.

————. *When and Where to Watch Hawks*. Eastern Massachusetts Hawk Watch. Mimeographed (available from Massachusetts Audubon Society, Lincoln, Massachusetts).

Ross' Gull Roundtable. 1975. *BOEM*. Vol. 3, No. 1, p. 12.

Rutledge, Lyman V. 1984. *Ten Miles Out*. Portsmouth, New Hampshire: Peter E. Randall, Publisher.

Sadlier, Heather and Hugh. 1985. *fifty hikes in Vermont*. Woodstock, Vermont: Backcountry Publishers, Inc.

Seymour, Frank Conkling. 1981. *The Flora of New England* (Second Edition). Plainfield, New Jersey: Moldenke and Moldenke.

Snow, John O. 1980. *Secrets of a Salt Marsh*. Portland, Maine: Guy Gannett Publishing Co.

Snyder, Dorothy E. 1978. Marblehead Neck Sanctuary. *BOEM* Vol. 6, No. 5, p. 157.

Steele, Frederic L. 1982. *At Timberline: A Nature Guide to the Mountains of the Northeast*. Boston: Appalachian Mountain Club.

Terres, John K. 1980. *The Audubon Society Encyclopedia of North American Birds*. New York: Alfred A. Knopf.

Thomson, Betty Flanders. 1958. *The Changing Face of New England*. New York: The Macmillan Company.

Trowbridge, C. C. 1895. Hawk Flights in Connecticut. *The Auk*. Vol. 12, No. 12, p. 259.

Vickery, Peter D. 1978. *Alcids of the Western North Atlantic*. Field Problem No. 19. Lincoln, Massachusetts: Massachusetts Audubon Society. Mimeographed.

Walton, Richard K. 1984. *Birds of the Sudbury River Valley: An Historical Perspective*. Lincoln, Massachusetts: Massachusetts Audubon Society.

Where to Find Birds In Eastern Massachusetts. 1978. Leif J. Robinson and Robert H. Stymeist, eds. Belmont, Massachusetts: Bird Observer of Eastern Massachusetts, Inc.

Williams, Dick. 1978. *The Historic Norwalk Islands*. Darien, Connecticut: Pictorial Associates.

Wood, Charles. 1981. *The Birds of Swan Point Cemetery*. Providence, Rhode Island: The Proprietors of Swan Point Cemetery.

Yaust, Rick. *Checklist of Birds: Vicinity of Mt. Monadnock*. Society For the Protection of New Hampshire Forests.

Acknowledgments

THE SINE QUA NON OF A REGIONAL BIRD GUIDE
is cooperation. This guide would not have become a
reality without the generous and constant support of
many individuals.

I would like to begin by thanking the birders from
the six New England states who read and commented
on portions of the text—Maine: Charles Duncan, William
Hancock, Jan Pierson, and Peter Vickery; New
Hampshire: Arthur Borror, Tudor Richards, Beverly
Ridgely, and Rick Youst; Vermont: Walter Ellison and
Whitney Nichols; Massachusetts: Richard Forster,
Christopher Leahy, Blair Nikula, and Peter Trimble;
Rhode Island: David Emerson, Robert Fox, and Douglas
Kraus; Connecticut: Milan Bull, Gordon Loery, Noble
Proctor, and Clay Taylor. I would also like to thank Neil
Jorgensen and John Kricher for commenting on the
chapter on regional geography and Paul Roberts for his
suggestions on the hawk-watching chapter.

Other individuals who helped in various ways are

Dorothy Arvidson, Dick Beyer, Rick Blatz, Jeff Bouton, Alden and Nancy Clayton, Neil Currie, Rick Enser, Davis Finch, Bernard Haubrich, Jr., Laura Hollowell, Don Hopkins, Seth Kellogg, Joe Kenneally, Sarah Laughlin, Dan Leary, Nancy Martin, Cindy Mathewson, Paul Miliotis, Simon Perkins, Fred Purnell, Carol Smith, Dawn Stavros, Tom Tyning, Barbara Vickery, and William H. Walker II.

A special note of thanks goes to Wayne Petersen for his chapter on pelagic birding as well as for his willingness to give counsel on other matters.

I would also like to express my appreciation to James Baird and the Massachusetts Audubon Society and to William B. Goodman and David R. Godine.

Last but not least my thanks go to Adelaide Walton for her map work, proofreading, and suggestions. More importantly, I want to thank Fid for her companionship during our travels throughout New England.

Index

Page numbers in **bold** type refer to descriptions in the "New England Specialties: Species Accounts."

Bird Finding in New England

was set in Palatino, a typeface designed by Hermann
Zapf. Named after Giovanbattista Palatino, a Renais-
sance writing master, Palatino was the first of Zapf's
typefaces to be introduced to America. The designs
were made in 1948, and the fonts for the complete face
were issued between 1950 and 1952.

Typeset by PennSet, Inc., Bloomsburg, Pennsylvania.
Printed and bound by Horowitz/Rae,
Fairfield, New Jersey. Designed by Dede Cummings.